A PATH APPEARS

A PATH APPEARS

Transforming Lives, Creating Opportunity

NICHOLAS D. KRISTOF
AND SHERYL WUDUNN

Alfred A. Knopf *New York 2014*

THIS IS A BORZOI BOOK
PUBLISHED BY ALFRED A. KNOPF

www.aaknopf.com

Knopf, Borzoi Books, and the colophon are registered trademarks of Random House LLC.

Library of Congress Cataloging-in-Publication Data
Kristof, Nicholas D., [date]
A path appears : transforming lives, creating opportunity /
Nicholas D. Kristof and Sheryl WuDunn.
pages cm
ISBN 978-0-385-34991-8 (hardcover)—ISBN 978-0-385-34992-5 (eBook) I. Charities.
2. Humanitarianism. 3. Fund-raising. 4. Social action. 5. Social service.
I. WuDunn, Sheryl, [date] II. Title.
HV48.K75 2014
361—dc23
2014006734

Front-and-spine-of-jacket photographs: (top) © Li Ding/Alamy; (bottom, left to right)
Samantha Paul, Audrey Hall, Lizzie Presser, Georgia Court, courtesy of
Vital Voices Global Partnership, Jeannie Hampton

Back-of-jacket photographs: (left to right) Nicholas D. Kristof,
Nicholas D. Kristof, Jonathan Sprague, Tsvangirayi Mukwazhi

Jacket design by Chip Kidd
Manufactured in the United States of America

First Edition

For our families, who raised and nurtured us with love,
and who sometimes drove us wild as we tried to nurture them.
That means you: David and Alice, and Sondra, Sirena, and Darrell
and Ladis and Jane
and Gregory, Geoffrey, and Caroline
And also to all of you around the world who have taught us that
witnessing the world's troubles isn't depressing but inspiring—
because crises bring out the innate helpfulness in people, and
because side by side with the worst of humanity, you see the best.

希望本无所谓有，无所谓无。这正如地上的路，其实地上本没有路，
走的人多了，也便成了路

*Hope is like a path in the countryside. Originally, there is nothing—
but as people walk this way again and again, a path appears.*

—LU XUN, CHINESE ESSAYIST, 1921

Contents

PART ONE

Giving Opportunity Wings

Introduction

A Meaningful Life

It is not enough to be industrious; so are the ants.
What are you industrious about?

— HENRY DAVID THOREAU

Rachel Beckwith wouldn't admit it, but her ninth birthday had been just a little disappointing. A girl living in the Seattle area, she had been shocked by a lecture in her church about people worldwide lacking clean water. So instead of birthday presents, Rachel had asked people to donate to an organization called charity:water that drills wells in impoverished villages around the world. Rachel aimed to raise $300 for her birthday, and she closely tracked the contributions that came in on her birthday page on the charity:water website.

All kinds of people, she saw, were celebrating occasions by raising money on the site to drill wells for needy people living half a world away. Liz and Kirk Ward married and used their well donation page as a wedding registry. Ezra Magaram raised $5,804, more than twice his goal, for his bar mitzvah. Frank and Megan Danna marked the birth of their daughter, Emma, by hosting a charity:water page that raised $735. Timmy Ho gave up alcohol for a year and raised $1,306. Erica Hanna turned a weight-loss struggle into a money-raising effort for a well. Rachel was excited to see all these people raising money so successfully, but her own birthday campaign felt a bit dispiriting. She raised only $220, much less than her goal.

Rachel, encouraged by her family, had early on shown a desire to give back. When she was five years old, she learned at school about an organization called Locks of Love, which uses hair donations to make wigs for children who have lost their own hair because of cancer or other diseases. Rachel asked to have her long hair shorn off and sent to Locks of Love. "It was her first haircut, so she had very long hair, but she said she wanted to help the cancer kids," recalls her mother, Samantha Paul. After the haircut, Rachel announced that she would grow her hair long again and donate it to Locks of Love after a few years. And that's what she did. Rachel found giving to be enormously satisfying, and that's what led her with great eagerness to set up a birthday fund-raiser through charity:water. It was just frustrating, though, that each time she went on the Internet, full of hope, to see her birthday page, the total would be unchanged and short of her target.

Then, less than six weeks after her ninth birthday, tragedy struck. Rachel was driving with her family on the highway when two trucks collided. One truck spilled logs onto the highway, causing a thirteen-car pileup. The Beckwith car was in the middle, and although other passengers in the vehicle weren't seriously hurt, Rachel was critically injured. In the next few days, as friends and church members comforted the family and prayed for Rachel's recovery, they also sought some more tangible way of showing solidarity. Remembering her birthday campaign for clean water, they began to donate to it on the charity:water website. Contributions climbed past her $300 goal, then past $1,000. As the little girl struggled for life in a hospital bed, and with everyone feeling helpless, donations surged past $5,000 and then $10,000. Family members gathered around Rachel's hospital bed were soon able to whisper to her—not knowing if she could hear them through her coma—that she had set a record by exceeding the $47,544 that Justin Bieber had raised for charity:water on his birthday. "I think she secretly had a crush on him, but she would never admit it," says Samantha Paul. "I think she would have been ecstatic."

It became evident that Rachel would never recover, and her family made the heartbreaking decision to remove her from life support. She died surrounded by a loving family and by a growing legend about a little girl's last fund-raiser. People all over the world, moved by Rachel's big heart, went to the website and donated, often in $9 increments. A five-year-old girl sent the entire contents of her piggy

SAMANTHA PAUL

For her ninth-birthday party, Rachel Beckwith aimed to raise
$300 to help build a well through charity:water.

bank, $2.27. Samantha Paul spoke eloquently about her daughter's dream, and that encouraged further ripples through social media, sending the total surging past $100,000, then past $500,000. In the end, Rachel's campaign raised $1,265,823 — enough to provide clean water for 37,000 people. Social networks managed to transform a tragedy into something triumphant as well, a celebration of Rachel's life and values that, halfway around the world, will save children's lives and improve their health. A year after Rachel's death, Samantha traveled to Africa and was stunned to see the impact that her young daughter had had on so many Ethiopian villages.

For a mother, there is of course no salve that can erase the pain of losing a nine-year-old daughter. But Samantha Paul was gladdened to see what her daughter had accomplished, and she was moved that the villagers were both giddy at getting clean water and profoundly sympathetic about her loss. Giving wells couldn't dissipate the grief but could turn it into something at least bittersweet, creating waves of meaning to commemorate a loss that otherwise felt infuriatingly random. "At times, it was a little overwhelming for me," Samantha remembers. "I talked to a woman who had children of her own, and she was in tears. She was genuinely touched and grateful about what Rachel had wanted. She was telling me that she's talking to her children about Rachel as a lesson in love and giving. These people have far less than what Rachel had, and knowing that they're also learning a lesson in giving and unconditional love from Rachel — that was really, really moving." As the vehicle drove away from that village, bouncing over rutted roads, Samantha Paul hunched over and cried.

Lester Strong had a very different childhood. When he was in the third grade, his teacher told his parents that their son was failing school and was basically not teachable; the school used the words "mentally retarded." His parents should not bother "wasting their time" trying to give little Lester a formal education, for he was suited just for manual labor and at best might learn to live independently. The teacher humiliated Lester by putting the boy's desk in the hallway and leaving him there on his own, stigmatizing him as an uneducable dunce. Lester was one of eight children in the Strong family, living just outside of Pittsburgh, and his parents—his father had only an eighth-grade education—were too overwhelmed to help much. He seemed to be one more African American boy who would never get a shot at a quality education.

Fortunately, Lester had three mentors: a barber, a minister, and the mother of a friend, and they all told him that he *could* learn after all. They checked his homework at night, looked over his report cards for signs of hope, and coached him on how to behave at school. Most important, they told him he could make it. These adult mentors transformed Lester's life. He ended up repeating third grade but then soared, becoming an honors student in the fourth grade and later graduating first in his high school class. He was chosen as a National

Lester Strong

Merit Scholar and attended Davidson College on a scholarship, then went on to Columbia Business School. He spent a career in television as a reporter and executive, rising through the ranks to become anchor of a nightly news program in Boston.

In his later years, he sought greater fulfillment. "I felt the pull to do something more meaningful, to give back," he recalls. "I wanted to stop children from being written off, as I almost was." So at sixty, Strong began a new career as chief executive of Experience Corps, an organization that uses volunteers over the age of fifty-five to mentor children as he was once mentored.

"I know the power of an older adult really giving loving and structured attention to a child who has not been accustomed to receiving it," Strong says.

Experience Corps now has 1,700 volunteers mentoring 30,000 students from kindergarten to third grade across the United States, typically in low-income schools. An Experience Corps volunteer tutors a small group of children for fifteen hours a week for the entire school year, helping kids use the library, pick books, and, above all, appreciate the thrill of reading.

D r. Gary Slutkin was back in Chicago, his hometown, feeling restless. He was a rumpled infectious diseases specialist who had spent most of his career in San Francisco and Africa, battling tuberculosis, AIDS, and cholera. But he had burned out in refugee camps, his marriage had fallen apart, and now it was time to be nearer to his elderly parents. He had no clue what to do for work.

As he explored options, Slutkin began hearing about gang violence in Chicago, about ten-year-olds shooting other kids; this was shocking, but it also sounded more like Somalia and other places he knew. Slutkin began to study inner-city violence and pored over graphs of homicides and shootings—and to an epidemiologist they all seemed oddly familiar.

"It hit me: this is an infectious disease," he said. The more Slutkin looked at urban violence, the more he felt that it had been misdiagnosed as solely a crime problem when in many ways it was a contagion analogous to cholera or leprosy. As with other contagions, an infection depends upon exposure among susceptible people who have low resistance or compromised immunity. Slutkin saw that "an

*Dr. Gary Slutkin applied his knowledge of infectious diseases
to tackle inner-city violence in American cities.*

epidemic of violence" is more than just a metaphor; in some ways murder actually spreads like a contagious disease.

"It is just as tuberculosis begets tuberculosis, or flu begets flu," Slutkin says, "that violence begets violence."

Once Slutkin had the insight that violence could be considered, in part, an infectious disease, he decided to tackle it as a public health problem and slow the epidemic. He started an organization called Cure Violence, and turned to ex-convicts and former gang members to act as health outreach workers and interrupt the contagion. When someone is shot, they go to the hospital room to counsel against a retaliatory hit. They gather intelligence on threats and negotiate peaceful solutions. More broadly, they try to change community norms so that those who use violence are scorned rather than respected. "Violence is learned behavior," says Gary Slutkin. "Violence can also be unlearned behavior."

In recent years, the Cure Violence model has spread to other cities in the United States and abroad—even to Iraq and Colombia—and results have been remarkable. Careful evaluations have found that Cure Violence can reduce serious violence by one-quarter or more, at a negligible cost. Gary Slutkin thinks that with some tweaking and enough resources, the model could reduce homicides by 70 percent.

Rachel Beckwith, Lester Strong, and Dr. Gary Slutkin reflect a yearning to express our humanity by finding innovative and effective ways to give back. We crave meaning and purpose in life, and one way to find it is to connect to a cause larger than ourselves. This book is about innovators who are using research, evidence-based strategies, and brilliant ideas of their own to prevent violence, improve health, boost education, and spread opportunity at home and around the world—and to suggest to the rest of us specific ways in which we too can make a difference in the world. Some of these people we highlight raise or contribute the money, such as Rachel and her family and admirers who made something inspiring out of a tragedy. Some are organizers, such as Slutkin and Strong. Many more are foot soldiers. Together, they are all part of a revolution in tackling social problems, employing new savvy, discipline, and experience to chip away at poverty and injustice. On many issues ranging from failing schools in America to intestinal parasites in Africa, there are fascinating new approaches to making a difference; in some cases, the progress is startling.

So many social problems in the twenty-first century seem intractable and insoluble. We explore Mars and embed telephones in wristwatches, but we can't keep families safe in the inner cities. We can map subatomic particles such as gluons, and we can design robots that drive cars, respond to speech, and defeat grandmasters in chess, but we grudgingly accept failure in our struggles to keep kids in school, off drugs, and out of gangs. Many of us know that it's wrong and unfair that boys growing up in certain zip codes are more likely to end up in prison than in college, but we throw up our hands and surrender to the exigencies of ghetto life. Violence and poverty, whether in Congo or Chicago, remain towering realities.

We started our married life together as foreign correspondents for *The New York Times*, and we have wondered for years how we can do a better job addressing the needs around us. Not everyone can help fight crime in a city's worst neighborhoods or volunteer in schools, so most of us are left to engage in piecemeal efforts such as a donation here or there. Like many Americans, we have day jobs we need to keep, and we have been busy raising our children; that has left us looking for great causes and people to support in modest ways. We aren't regular churchgoers who focus our giving on a particular religious establishment, and although we wanted to lend a hand, we never knew how to choose among the appeals from nonprofits that inundated us. Basically, we were mystified about how best to assist at home as well as abroad. So we investigated how one can do a better job of making a difference, how one can help institute effective change. This book is the fruit of our labors.

A mericans are among the most generous of people, though perhaps not the most generous. The World Giving Index, which tries to measure generosity across countries, varies in its annual results, but over five years Australia came out at the top, Ireland second, and the United States third. Almost three-quarters of the $335 billion that Americans donate to charity each year comes from individuals. Philanthropy cuts across social class, and poor and middle-income Americans are particularly generous. Strikingly, those in the bottom 20 percent of incomes give away a higher percentage of their money (3.2 percent) than those in the top 20 percent (1.3 percent). About two-thirds of Americans donate to charity each year, an average of about $1,000 per man, woman, or child.

Helping people is harder than it looks, however, and good intentions aren't enough. People rarely give money away as intelligently as they make it, and frankly, much charitable giving isn't very effective. We decided that our focus should be on expanding opportunity worldwide, because *talent is universal, but opportunity is not.* We have seen great talent residing in a trailer park in Kentucky, under a tree in Darfur, and in a remote hillside shack in Burma. One obstacle to expanding opportunity is the repression of women and girls in much of the world, and we described those searing challenges in our book *Half the Sky.* Now we are broadening the lens to examine other obstacles to opportunity and how they might be overcome.

Obviously there are good causes and solutions that do not involve opportunity: funding hospice care for dying cancer patients, protecting abused animals, bolstering the arts, supporting one's church or temple, or, in the spirit of the Make a Wish Foundation, making a dream come true for a pediatric cancer patient. Those are commendable efforts and we endorse them. But we also face the transcendent challenge of spreading opportunity so that a person's prospects depend less on the lottery of birth. Almost half the kids born worldwide this year will have strikes against them—they're girls in societies where that is a handicap, they lack access to decent schools, they're born in violent vortexes such as Somalia or gang-ridden neighborhoods of Baltimore—making it extra hard for them to live up to their potential. They are the losers, but so is the world, for it is robbed of their contributions. Spread opportunity around, and these people can flourish and grow. We spend trillions of dollars treating the symptoms of poverty (the United States alone has spent $20 trillion on means-tested social programs since 1965), and much of that is essential. But the more important challenge is to address underlying causes, and it seems that those of us who have won the lottery of birth have some responsibility to use our good fortune to help address these fundamental inequities.

The good news is that experts are gaining a much better understanding of how to make an impact. Researchers are developing new evidence-based approaches, and more charities are starting to measure and track their results, so there is an emerging science of how best to make a difference. Anyone can harness this science and be reasonably confident that donations are having an impact, through interventions that until recently were unavailable or uncertain. Evidence Action, an aid group based on the pioneering work of development economists Michael Kremer of Harvard, Esther Duflo of MIT, and Dean Karlan of Yale, allows a donor to deworm a child in Africa or Asia for 50 cents a year. Indeed, recent research has found that this is a cost-effective way of making a child healthier and more likely to attend school. The improved health and education from deworming will allow that child to earn 20 percent more as an adult—all for a penny a week today. Or, for a donation of $1.98, Evidence Action can provide a chlorine dispenser so that an impoverished family gets clean drinking water for a year. That has been shown to reduce diarrhea, a major factor in child deaths, by 40 percent.

If you prefer to help American children, a $25 program can reach a pregnant American woman who smokes and explain how doing so puts her child at risk, leading 14 percent of those pregnant women to quit smoking. Smoking during pregnancy increases testosterone in the uterus, with long-term effects on the behavior of male offspring in particular. Men whose mothers smoked when they were in utero are significantly more likely to be imprisoned as adults. We'll see how such initiatives to reduce substance abuse during pregnancy, or to help teenagers avoid pregnancy, can have far-reaching benefits for society as a whole.

For $20 a year, you can pay for an impoverished child in America to get a "prescription for reading" from a doctor during pediatric visits, along with children's books. This program, Reach Out and Read, carried out by a network of doctors and medical providers, gives books to young children and advice to parents on reading to their kids to promote brain development. The program substantially increases the vocabulary of the children, as well as the proportion of parents who read regularly to their kids. These aren't magic wands that make problems disappear overnight, but they are simple, rigorously tested ways of chipping away at challenges around us. To put it another way, these are paths to opportunity.

It's also much more feasible today, through the Internet, to see the impact of your contribution, for a wave of social entrepreneurs have built organizations that act as bridges between donors and beneficiaries. One young American, Conor Bohan, spent time after college as a ski bum in Europe and then, "looking for something different," found a job in 1996 as a high school English teacher in Haiti. The most outstanding girl in his school was Isemonde Joseph, and Conor was bewildered to hear that she planned to attend a secretarial course after graduation. He asked her why she didn't aim higher. She explained that her dream was to become a doctor but that her parents, who had never finished primary school, could not afford university tuition. Conor lent her $30 so that she could apply to medical school (in Haiti, students enter medical school as undergraduates), and when she was accepted, he used his savings to pay the $3,000 annual cost of Isemonde's medical education. Isemonde did her part, too, studying by candlelight and sometimes walking five miles each way to school to save on the 12-cent bus fare. To help more students like Isemonde, Conor set up the Haitian Education and Leadership Program, or HELP, which offers university scholarships to the most outstanding straight-A high school graduates from across Haiti. To make the program sustainable, the scholarship recipients commit to contributing 15 percent of their salaries back to HELP for their first nine years of employment. More than 150 students are in university on these scholarships—and Isemonde is now a doctor.

The benefits of outreach flow in both directions. It's not only the Isemondes who gain, but also those who help. A growing number of American students are learning about the world and about public service because their schools support schools in poorer countries, sometimes even building them. Through a group called World Assistance for Cambodia, it is possible to build a three-room school in Cambodia for $45,000. Other Americans find their own entry point. At a guesthouse in Haiti, Seth Donnelly, a teacher at Los Altos High School in California, ran into a local principal named Réa Dol. That chance encounter has led to an ongoing relationship, with Los Altos High School raising $200,000 for Dol's new school for impoverished Haitian students. "We could never do this without the Los Altos students," Dol told us as she showed off the new school. Every summer a group of Los Altos students visits Haiti to meet their counterparts and help them with English. It would be too glib to say that the Los Altos students have gained as much as the Haitians, but there's no doubt that the exchange has given the California students a perspective on the world that they never would have garnered in the classroom.

Aid projects are also run better—and often more transparently—these days because increasingly there are local, home-grown project leaders such as Dol who know the terrain and operate much less expensively than foreign aid workers. Whether in the Bronx or a Haitian slum, it's invaluable to have solutions bubbling up through local leaders, who can get buy-in from the community for new projects.

We have written before about Tererai Trent, a Zimbabwean villager who received only a year of elementary school education, and she's now creating something new. Tererai was married at age eleven to a man who beat her, and she was an uneducated cattle herder when a meeting with Jo Luck, then the head of Heifer International, led Tererai to write down her goals. It seemed absurd, but Tererai wrote of her ambition to study in the United States, to earn a college degree, an M.A., and even a Ph.D. Then she wrapped the paper with these goals in plastic, placed it in a tin can, and buried it under a rock in the field where she herded cattle. She began taking correspondence classes, did brilliantly, and eventually was admitted to the University of Oklahoma on a scholarship. After earning her B.A., she returned to Zimbabwe, dug up the tin can and piece of paper, and checked off the first goal. She flew back to America for her master's, earned that degree, and returned to dig up the paper and check off the second goal. Finally, at Western Michigan University, in 2009, Trent earned her doctorate—and went back to the cattle field in Zimbabwe, dug up the can, and checked off her very last goal.

Now Dr. Tererai Trent is working with Save the Children and building schools so that other children can achieve their dreams as

Tererai Trent visits students in front of the
school she helped build in Zimbabwe.

well. She started a foundation named Tinogona—the name, which in the Shona language means "it is achievable," is her personal credo—and in 2014 opened her first school, in her home village. When Tererai talks to Zimbabwean parents and children about the importance of educating girls, when she plans new schools in remote villages, she has far more credibility than any outsider ever could.

Successful people often scorn those who are poor or homeless. A Princeton University scholar, Susan Fiske, has used scans to show that the brains of high-achieving people see images of poor people and process them as if they were not humans but things. Those who have made it sometimes see poverty as a moral failure and perceive in themselves the triumph of a simple narrative: you study hard, work assiduously, sacrifice for the future, obey the law, and create your own good fortune. Yet that pathway is much less accessible if you are conceived by a teenage mom who drinks during pregnancy and so you are born with fetal alcohol effects. Likewise, if you're born in a high-poverty neighborhood to a stressed-out single mom who scolds you more than she hugs you, in a home with no children's books, you face a huge handicap. As we'll see, a University of Minnesota study found that the kind of parenting a child receives in the first three and a half years is a better predictor of high school graduation than IQ.

The upshot is that for now, one of the strongest determinants of who ends up poor is who is born poor. As Warren Buffett puts it, our life outcomes often depend on the "ovarian lottery." For all our talk of the American dream, it has emigrated, and there's now greater economic mobility in Europe than in the United States. An American boy in the bottom 20 percent in earnings has only a one-in-twelve chance of making it to the top 20 percent over a lifetime, compared to a one-in-eight chance in class-conscious Britain. We'll dig deep into the cycles of poverty and deficits of education that are so damaging in the United States and other countries, and into strategies that have shown success in snapping the cycles. As we'll see, early interventions—beginning in pregnancy and infancy, and continuing through preschool—seem particularly cost effective in breaking the cycle of poverty. Our past efforts have often failed in part because they come too late.

John Rawls, the brilliant twentieth-century philosopher, argued compellingly for judging a society's fairness by considering it from behind a "veil of ignorance"—meaning we don't know whether we'll be born in that society to an investment banker or a teenage mom, in a leafy suburb or a gang-ridden inner city, healthy or disabled, smart or struggling, privileged or disadvantaged. That's a shrewd analytical tool—and who among us would argue against funding nursery schools if we thought we might be that deprived child trying to get in? Let's remember that the difference between being surrounded by a loving family or being homeless on the street is determined not just by our own level of virtue or self-discipline but also by an inextricable mix of luck, brain chemistry, child rearing, genetics, and outside help. Let's recognize that success in life is a reflection not only of enterprise and willpower but also of chance and early upbringing, and that compassion isn't a sign of weakness but a mark of civilization.

The challenge is to nurture a culture of altruism and empathy, seeking to imbue an instinct for social engagement. That is to say, it's not *you* or *me,* but *we.* That is already beginning to happen, and the progress in expanding empathy over the past 250 years is stunning. The first large social movement on behalf of others—rather than demanding more for oneself—was the British antislavery movement that began in the 1780s, and the first international relief effort in response to global poverty came during the Irish potato famine of the 1840s. (The sympathy was limited: Queen Victoria asked the sultan of the Ottoman Empire not to donate £10,000 to save the Irish because that would have outshone her own gift of £2,000.) Today, almost any university bulletin board will have a poster appealing on behalf of some faraway group, but in historical terms that is a recent phenomenon. There's probably more regard for chickens and cows today than existed a few centuries ago for slaves or foreigners. Princeton University professor Peter Singer is the philosopher of this growing humanitarianism, Harvard psychologist Steven Pinker its chronicler, the singer Bono its muse, and it has a vast and growing army of ordinary donors and volunteers.

This is an area that is sometimes perceived as discouraging, but that's a false rap. Some of the greatest successes the world has experienced have come from movements to address inequities or injustices, from slavery to hunger. Just in the last generation, Mothers Against Drunk Driving helped change norms about drinking and driving, saving thousands of lives every year. Environmentalists managed to ban leaded gasoline, reducing infants' developing brains' exposure to lead and adding several points to the average child's IQ in the United States and abroad. Improved access to contraceptives has reduced the teen birth rate by more than 50 percent in the United States since 1991. The child mortality revolution has used vaccines, treatments for diarrhea, micronutrients, and improved nutrition to reduce the number of child deaths worldwide each year from 20 million in 1960 to 6.6 million today—even as the number of children has risen. The World Bank now aims in effect to eliminate extreme poverty, which was the condition of the great majority of humanity for most of our existence as a species, by 2030. Huge challenges and injustices remain, including in the United States and other wealthy countries, but the progress is a reminder of what is possible if we forge ahead. We don't have perfect tools or endless resources, as individuals or as nations, but we can do better if we put our hearts and minds to it.

We wrote this book mostly to encourage others—rich and poor alike—to join in this push to improve the world. We'll first try to address the basic skepticism that so many people have about whether giving or volunteering really can make a difference. We will also explore how some social change leaders and executives are rethinking how best to help, in some cases endorsing new approaches such as the use of for-profit companies that generate cash to make them sustainable.

There's a good deal of cynicism about charities, some of it deserved, but the pitfalls needn't deter anyone from seeking to have a substantial impact on other people's lives. In a postscript to each chapter, we will spotlight a person or organization to demonstrate how change can happen.

Talk about helping others can easily sink into soggy sentimentality, even sanctimony. But the most important counterpoint is that reaching out to try to help, especially when we do it as a social activity, isn't a Gandhi-style sacrifice. It's a source of fulfillment, even joy. Over the past couple of decades, a growing stack of evidence has shown that social behavior — including helping others — improves our mental and physical health and extends life expectancy. One study on mortality following 7,000 people found that the risk of death among men and women with the fewest social ties was more than twice as high as the risk for adults with the most social ties, independent of physical health. Maybe this deep-rooted social element in all of us explains our yearning for a life of meaning. We wonder about our purpose; we care about our legacy.

Certainly the practical evidence is mounting. Among adults with coronary artery disease, those people who are socially isolated are 2.4 times more likely to die of heart attacks. Social isolation of female rats accelerates their aging, increases their incidence of mammary tumors, and shortens their lives, although it's impossible to know if the effects on humans are similar. Recent research indicates that one biological pathway for this impact of social isolation is that it increases chronic inflammation, particularly for men, and that this inflammation in turn causes ill health and death. Of course, there are many ways to become social without giving: one can simply join a country club. Yet the evidence suggests that social activities that involve helping others are particularly healthful and fulfilling. Altruism is a powerful force for health and happiness alike, and it seems to be deeply embedded in human neurochemistry.

In experiments, toddlers not yet able to speak attempt altruistic behavior, offering comfort (even offering to share a teddy bear) to an adult who appears to have injured a finger. If you scan the brain of a person who is injured and also that of a witness to the injury, the areas activated are similar; at a neurological level, we are pained by other people's suffering. The "pleasure centers" in the brain that light up in brain scans when we receive gifts, eat fine food, flirt, or have sex also light up when we help others. We underwent brain scans ourselves so that our pleasure centers could be monitored as we made charitable donations. Ah, but we're getting ahead of our story. For now, let's just emphasize that to help others isn't a heroic burden but a transcendent source of fulfillment in our busy, often materialistic lives. There are few more selfish pleasures than altruism.

So think of giving back not as a dreary means to a tax deduction but as a chance to inject meaning, wonder, and fun into life. Social organizations have emerged to help others through hosting dinners (Dining for Women) or partying at a bar (Beers for Books). There are countless other such initiatives, for elementary school children, grandmothers, and everyone in between.

A generation ago, we didn't have much more than hunches to guide us in trying to make a difference and build a life of greater meaning and satisfaction. "Giving back" was then what we did in December, hunched over a checkbook and relying on guesswork. In recent years, as we said, advances in neuroscience and economics—and a flowering of carefully monitored experiments—have given us much greater insight into what works to create opportunity worldwide, and much greater prospects for personal satisfaction from giving. That's partly why we chose our title from an essay by the great Chinese writer Lu Xun. A path is now appearing to show us how to have a positive impact on the world around us. This is a path of hopefulness, but also a path of fulfillment: typically, we start off by trying to empower others and end up empowering ourselves, too.

CHAPTER TWO

A Drop in the Bucket

One person can make a difference, and everyone should try.

— JOHN F. KENNEDY

Rashida Yayé, a girl in the West African country of Niger, was born with one of the most common birth defects in the world: clubfoot. About one baby in a thousand is born with this deformity, with one or both feet pointing in the wrong direction. In fact, Nick's mother, Jane Kristof, was born with a clubfoot. But in the United States or Europe, a doctor places the baby's foot in a series of corrective casts for about a month, and—presto!—the foot is healed. Because there is such effective treatment and no lasting disfigurement, we in the West almost never see clubfoot and are therefore unaware of how common it is. We didn't even know until we were writing this book that Jane Kristof had had a clubfoot. We never would have guessed it because she is an exceptionally vigorous walker even in her eighties.

That's common in the West. Kristi Yamaguchi, the Olympic gold-medal-winning figure skater who symbolized grace and beauty, was also born with a clubfoot. So was Mia Hamm, who scored more international soccer goals than any other player in the history of the sport. Ditto for Charles Woodson, who won the Heisman Trophy as the best collegiate football player in America and, as a member of the Green Bay Packers, shared in the Super Bowl XLV victory. Indeed, there are so many professional athletes in America who started out with this condition that the San Francisco Giants claims to be the team with the most athletes born with clubfoot!

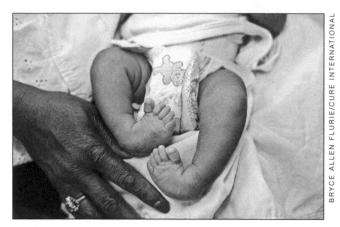

*When children with clubfoot can't get treatment,
they may never walk or work as adults.*

Yet in poor countries, children such as Rashida often don't get corrective treatment. They have trouble walking or even standing, and they are stigmatized as disabled or even cursed. Children with a clubfoot are usually not sent to school and have little chance to marry or get a job. They commonly survive as beggars, objects of shame and ridicule—all for want of a simple medical intervention that costs about $250.

We all get deluged with mail exhorting us to donate $50, $75, or even $250. We want to help out, but the problems today, from gang violence in America's inner cities to disease in India, seem so overwhelming and unrelenting that we often turn away. What possible good could one measly donation do?

The truth is that in recent years it has become clear that modest sums can help overcome disease and ease malnutrition and that innovations allow organizations to become more effective in saving lives and attacking the cycle of poverty. A policeman who rescues a citizen from a crazed gunman will rightly be honored. But there are plenty of other ways to save lives. A study in Kenya using randomized controlled trials, the most rigorous standard of evidence, found that antimalarial bed nets delivered through a group called TAMTAM Africa saved one child's life for every $284 donated. Such an outcome for so modest a sum may be difficult to replicate, but many interventions—such as giving children vitamin A, zinc, or other micronutrients, distributing bed nets, or immunizing children—save a life for a couple of thousand dollars or less. Bill Gates says that his foundation's investments save lives at a cost of $2,000 each. Susan E. Horton, an economist at the University of Waterloo in Canada who is an expert on these calculations, notes that even a higher sum is a bargain. "If you can save a life for $5,000, that's still pretty incredible," she says.

These programs don't just save lives; they also create healthier children. For example, $5,000 worth of bed nets will prevent scores of children from becoming sick and stunted. Sums invested in distributing vitamin A can prevent blindness. There are few greater bargains than investing in children's health—such as the surgery that transformed the life of Rashida Yayé.

When Shoshana Kline, in Venice, California, received a mailing about clubfoot from an American aid group called FirstStep, she was intrigued. Her mailbox was filled with appeals to address other needs in the world, but the photos on the leaflet caught her eye, because Kline herself had been born with a severe clubfoot. It was family lore that her first pediatrician had told her parents that she would never be able to walk. "My parents really freaked out," Kline

Shoshana Kline, who had clubfoot as a child in California,
decided to pay to repair a child's clubfoot overseas.

says. Although she has no memories of those early days, "there are 20,000 pictures of me like that—all my baby pictures have me with these disgusting casts on my feet!"

Those casts solved Kline's clubfoot, and in high school and college she excelled at sports. "Not only do I have normal legs, but I was a skilled athlete," she says. "The idea that there are people in other countries who don't get it treated and corrected, that really means something to me." The letter from FirstStep was written by Brian Mullaney, the former head of an aid group called Smile Train whose work fighting cleft palates Kline had heard of and respected, so she sent in a check for $250.

"This is something that affected my life, that I care about and that I want to contribute to," she explained to us. FirstStep forwarded the money to CURE, a Pennsylvania charity that in 2010 had opened a hospital in Niamey, the capital of Niger, to repair clubfoot. Niger is one of the world's poorest countries, and most children born with clubfoot there never get help. "If you go out on the streets, you will see many children with clubfoot who are begging," Moutari Malam Saddi, a hospital administrator, told us when we visited the hospital in Niamey. "They never go to school, they just become a kind of curse on the family, and little by little they accept their status. They think they are useless and have to beg."

That seemed likely to be the fate of Rashida, for she was born with clubfoot on both feet (which is not unusual) in the remote farming village of Torodi, in the far west of Niger near the border with Burkina Faso. Torodi is a collection of thatched-roof mud huts, a few wells, a mud-walled mosque, and surrounding fields of millet. Not many farmers there are literate, and none of them have electricity or plumbing. Over the years, other children in Torodi have been born with clubfoot, and none ever received medical help. Rashida, especially as a girl in a country with a strong preference for sons, seemed destined to become one more disabled person unable to walk, work, or go to school.

"I thought it was impossible for my daughter to be healed," her father, Yayé Hamma, a farmer and tea seller, told us. Initially he accepted Rashida's condition as fate. But Yayé has only three children, fewer than most villagers, and he grew particularly fond of Rashida's bubbly and affectionate nature. His heart broke as he imagined her being mocked or forced to become a beggar. So he took her to a local doctor, who could do nothing himself to help but did mention he had heard that in Niamey a new foreign hospital had just opened that could treat clubfoot. It was a long shot, but Yayé was determined to find this hospital and get help for Rashida, now two years old. He asked friends for help with transportation money, but they scoffed.

"People told me that I was wasting my money," Yayé said. "Nobody helped." But he loved Rashida too much to give up, so he left his other children behind in the village with his wife and boarded a bus to Niamey. After walking about the city for miles and making endless inquiries, he found the CURE hospital. When he walked in, he saw dozens of children just like Rashida; others were already mostly cured. Yayé began to dare to hope.

The $250 cost of the repair would have been prohibitive for the family, but Shoshana Kline's donation covered all the expenses. Doctors placed Rashida's feet in a plaster cast that straightened them just a bit. After a couple of weeks, another cast straightened her feet further. After six of these successive foot casts were employed over seven weeks, Rashida was brought in for a simple procedure called a tendonotomy, in which an incision is made under local anesthetic to release the Achilles tendon so that the foot will open up more. Dr. Chris Carter, a Canadian orthopedic surgeon who has spent much of

Rashida and her father shortly after
surgery in Niger. Rashida will grow up
normally and be able to go to school.

his career as a missionary doctor in Africa, performed the brief procedure on each of Rashida's feet as his wife, Danielle, a surgical nurse, held Rashida's hand to comfort her. In twenty minutes, Rashida's legs were swathed in two final casts, which would be removed in a few days—and then her treatment would be over. Soon she was sitting in her dad's lap in the hospital courtyard as the sun set over Niamey. Both were beaming contentedly.

"I believe that she will heal completely," Yayé said. "I love my daughter very, very much, and that is why I am here."

So that's how a California woman, by donating $250, underwrote the transformation of a life halfway around the world. In Torodi, Rashida was soon walking and running normally and going to school, the first child in the area to be cured of clubfoot. She is the pathbreaker, and other parents and children will follow. Villagers previously doomed will grow up to become teachers, nurses, village leaders. Kline's donation will ripple through the community. To us, it is positively inspiring that $250 can accomplish so much. That's not a sacrifice but an opportunity.

N ot every donation has the impact of Shoshana Kline's, and we don't want to gloss over the difficulties of making charity work effectively. Plenty goes wrong in the humanitarian aid world. Skeptics such as Angus Deaton and William Easterly, distinguished economists at Princeton University and New York University, respectively, raise valid concerns about the effectiveness of aid in generating self-sustaining economic growth. The charity "industry" has shortcomings, one of which is that most charitable giving isn't targeted at the needy. The biggest recipients of charity are churches, followed by universities and other educational institutions. That's fine of course. But we're still troubled that when Indiana University's Center on Philanthropy tried to determine what share of religious donations go to benevolences to help the poor or how much of university giving supports scholarships for them—as opposed to other recipients—it estimated that a bit less than one-third of overall charitable giving ends up helping the truly needy.

Charities across the United States employ 13 million people and take in $1.5 trillion in revenues each year, not just from donations but also from government grants for running programs for the homeless or low-income schoolchildren. That means that the charity industry accounts for 10 percent of the economy—twice the share of national defense. Yet there is negligible scrutiny or accountability, and among the 1.4 million charities in the United States, including churches, there are some that do little more than benefit their founders.

The lesson is to be careful about writing checks, and to take the kind of care in donating to charities that you would in making a large purchase. If you're buying a large-screen television, you'll probably conduct a bit of research to make sure you get your money's worth. Do the same with your donations. Be wary of organizations with names similar to those of famous nonprofits or that are vague about their background and how the money will be used, and consult the Federal Trade Commission's website on avoiding charity scams, www .ftc.gov/charityfraud. Later we'll offer a few more specific tips for charitable giving. But remember that while there is the risk of a scam, there is also potential for enormous impact with the right group.

The remedies don't just involve writing checks. Giving back can also mean donating blood or taking a minute to register as an organ donor. One of the most important avenues is volunteering, which is particularly satisfying because it involves meeting the people benefiting from your efforts. Often, volunteering among the young starts from cynical or selfish motives, as high school students think they will improve their chances of getting into college if they show an enthusiasm for "service." But when wealthy suburban kids actually encounter others who are less fortunate and try to help, they sometimes find it deeply satisfying in a way that they had not anticipated. Volunteering is also a way to address poverty and inequity here in the United States. A wonderful smorgasbord of searchable volunteering opportunities, in America and around the world, can be found at www .idealist.org and also at www.omprakash.org.

Many volunteers help a few hours a week at an after-school program called Citizen Schools to coach low-income youngsters toward a path that will lead to university and a professional career. Some older adults have turned to volunteer opportunities at Experience Corps; young people have tried DoSomething.org. Others have taught art in a prison, or read books to at-risk children in a doctor's waiting room through Reach Out and Read. Mentoring is a huge need for troubled kids in low-income communities who don't have enough role models or adult support, and Big Brother and Big Sister programs are a way to have an impact that money can't buy. One new initiative to make it easier to volunteer is iMentor, which matches college graduates with low-income high school students so that they can work together for several years. The mentor and student meet in person and online, and also exchange emails. The idea is to help the high school student think about college and navigate the application process. Since 1999, iMentor has connected more than 11,000 students to mentors, providing the kind of support and encouragement that is routine in middle-class households.

Aside from donations and volunteering, the third major way of making a difference is advocacy, and it is just as crucial. There are myriad opportunities to lend our voices to others through advocacy. We need innovative, evidence-based programs on a wide scale, whether run by government or by other organizations, and that means smarter lobbying to achieve them. Advocacy groups such as ONE offer shrewd guidance about contacting your member of Congress and taking other actions to create a more equitable world around us.

We once asked one of the world's leading experts on global health where he would direct $1 million if he were running a foundation. Would it go to providing micronutrients to aid in child nutrition? To vaccination? Bed nets? "I would take that money and spend it on a big public advertising campaign and a lobbying campaign to raise more money," he said. "People don't understand the needs, and I bet with $1 million I could raise $100 million for the cause." There's something to that. Why does the United States spend more than $20 billion a year on farm programs but less than $4 billion a year on education and early care for children in the critical first two years of life? Are corn and soybeans really a higher priority for America's future than our children? The explanation, of course, is that there's a vigorous agribusiness lobby, and much less of a lobby for vulnerable children. So America needs volunteers not just to deliver bowls of soup to the homeless but also to demand—through organizations such as ONE—that the president, members of Congress, cabinet members, governors, legislators, and mayors make kids a higher priority.

A little-known group called RESULTS is another effective advocacy organization. It was founded in 1980 by Sam Daley-Harris, a musician who was distressed by global hunger and by the lack of any political pressure to address it. Daley-Harris believed that many Americans were in principle concerned about global suffering but didn't know how to translate that concern into change, so he built RESULTS and its sister organization, RESULTS Educational Fund, as platforms for citizen advocacy. That means recruiting volunteer citizen lobbyists and helping them educate themselves about global and domestic poverty and other issues, teaching them how to write letters to the editor, meet newspaper editorial boards to suggest editorials, call and write congressional offices, and meet members of Congress to make their case in a professional way.

One of the first big campaigns by RESULTS volunteers was to create grassroots support for UNICEF's "child survival revolution," which used vaccinations and oral rehydration therapy to save children's lives. The 1,000 well-informed RESULTS volunteers who met with newspaper editorial boards generated 100 editorials in one year alone, and in part because of these efforts United States financial support for child survival around the world has increased from $25 million a year in the early 1980s to $600 million today. Cumulative American spending on child survival since the 1980s is on the order of $5 billion, and one result is that the number of children under the age of five who die each day has dropped from 41,000 to 18,000—nearly 8.4 million lives saved per year around the world. Clearly, the RESULTS campaign wasn't the only reason for the increase. But it made a difference. The writer David Bornstein, one of the best chroniclers of change agents around the world, notes that RESULTS has been transformational in getting Congress to pay attention to the global scourge of tuberculosis, a huge killer worldwide.

"I got involved in tuberculosis work because a bunch of RESULTS volunteers came to me in Oberlin and Medina, Ohio," says Sen. Sherrod Brown of Ohio. "They were convincing, well informed, and they were persistent." The upshot is that federal support for tuberculosis has gone from $1 million a year in 1997 to nearly $250 million annually. While RESULTS can't take full credit, government officials and congressional representatives say RESULTS has been a key player in securing more funding. So far, the United States has given a cumulative total of $1.8 billion to fight this once-neglected disease—once again saving millions of lives.

Expanding preschool across America is another challenge RESULTS has taken on, helping pressure Congress to include the largest allocation ever for Head Start and Early Head Start in 2009 in the post-recession economic stimulus package. Since then RESULTS has lobbied for further increases to sustain enrollment. RESULTS has volunteer chapters in 100 cities around the United States, covering half of all congressional districts, as well as affiliates abroad in Great Britain, Canada, Australia, Mexico, and Japan.

A dvocacy may sound anemic, the recourse of armchair dilettantes who pale in comparison to heroic aid workers in the field. But speaking up for the voiceless can be every bit as lifesaving as delivering AIDS medications. Insisting on human rights helps individuals imprisoned for their dissent but more broadly creates accountability in dictatorships and makes it harder to steamroll minorities. It's true that your letter to a politician is unlikely to change policy, and you probably can't "solve" a global problem. But don't discount the value of mitigating a problem as opposed to eliminating it, or the value of human rights advocacy that helps an individual here or there. Just because we can't help everyone doesn't mean that we should help no one.

That's a lesson from the story of a Polish Armenian refugee in Romania whose life was altered forever by a single brief note on his behalf. The man's name was Wladyslaw Krzysztofowicz. In the aftermath of World War II, a time when Europe was awash with refugees and troubles, Krzysztofowicz tried to escape the Communist bloc by swimming across the Danube River to Yugoslavia with an inner tube — which developed a leak halfway across. He was arrested, gasping for air, on the Yugoslav side of the river and sent to a prison labor camp at an asbestos mine. Then he was transferred to a prison labor camp in the mountains, where he felled timber while the authorities tried to figure out what to do with him and other escapees from Eastern Europe. After a couple of years, Yugoslavia decided to release some of these refugees to Italy to win favor in the West. It shot others, to affirm to Joseph Stalin that it was still politically reliable.

Krzysztofowicz was brought from the mountain labor camp with other prisoners and stuffed into a railroad cattle car. The prisoners along the walls peered through the cracks to see the name of the next station and shout it out to the others. If they were headed west, they were probably bound for Italy and freedom. If to the east, they faced execution.

As it happened, Krzysztofowicz had managed to inform the French embassy in Belgrade in his polished French that he was detained and had relatives in France. And so a French diplomat sent a note to Yugoslavia's government mentioning Krzysztofowicz's name and asking about his case. It was a brief note, no more than an inquiry, but it was enough to save a life. The cattle car Krzysztofowicz was on headed west. A week later, those prisoners arrived in Italy, and Krzysztofowicz credited his survival in part to that brief note from the French diplomat—who never knew the role he played.

Krzysztofowicz made his way to France. He found a job as a janitor but soon yearned for greater opportunity and saw America as a place to get it. As it happened, Krzysztofowicz cleaned the rooms of Marge Cameron, a young woman from Portland, Oregon, who was working in Paris for the Marshall Plan. They grew friendly and she urged her parents to sponsor this war refugee's application for immigration. Although Krzysztofowicz spoke no English, the Camerons took a chance and sponsored this man whom they had never met to move to Oregon. Portland's First Presbyterian Church helped with the sponsorship, even though Krzysztofowicz was Catholic, and a church member found him a job in a logging camp in Valsetz, Oregon. In 1951, he traveled by ship and train to Oregon.

Neither the French diplomat's note nor the Cameron family's kindness solved the global refugee problem, but they had a transformative impact on Krzysztofowicz's life—and on ours. After arriving in Portland, Wladyslaw Krzysztofowicz decided that his name was unworkable in America, and so he changed it to the more pronounceable Ladis Kristof. He was Nick's father.

So take it from us: don't disparage the impact of a letter, or scorn a "drop in the bucket." That's how buckets get filled, that's how lives are changed, and that's how opportunity is created.

Changing Lives, Bead by Bead

Torkin Wakefield, a former Peace Corps volunteer and longtime aid worker, was strolling through the Ugandan capital of Kampala one day with her grown daughter, Devin Hibbard, and her friend Ginny Jordan. They idly paused to watch a Ugandan woman, Millie Akena, make beaded jewelry out of trash paper. Each bead was made by carefully balling up and pasting together a colorful bit of magazine. The beads weren't painted and were the color of the paper—sometimes the writing was still faintly visible—and they looked quite lovely. The three women talked to Akena, whose "shop" was a spot of ground outside her mud-walled home, and bought a few of these colorful necklaces for about 75 cents each. In the next few days, they were struck by how many compliments they received on the necklaces—especially when they explained that the beads were made in a slum, jewelry from garbage!

An idea began to form. Torkin, Devin, and Ginny returned to Akena's home and bought up more than 225 beaded necklaces to take back to the United States and sell to friends. Americans loved the beads, so the three women took a leap and formed Bead for Life as a nonprofit to support Ugandan women by selling their jewelry in America. To avoid customs duties, they asked friends traveling back to the United States to smuggle bags of necklaces in their suitcases. (They later realized that this was unnecessary; the necklaces were duty-free under American law.) Then they began selling the jewelry in the United States through "bead parties"—a bit like Tupperware parties. One woman invites all her friends over, and then the women sit down to admire necklaces, bracelets, and earrings and buy them for $5 to $30 each. There are now thousands of these parties each year, attended by more than 100,000 people annually, and each bead party raises enough money to send one Ugandan girl to boarding school for a

CHARLES STEINBERG

*Torkin Wakefield and her daughter, Devin Hibbard, founders of
Bead for Life, wearing jewelry made from scrap paper*

year. "It's not a handout; we're totally opposed to that," says Hibbard, now based in Uganda. "This is a symbol for us of women really working hard."

There has been a flowering of organizations like Bead for Life that bridge the gulf between those who want to help and those who need help. These include online sites such as GlobalGiving, Kiva, and Givology, all of which let you find a particular beneficiary to support with a gift or loan. If your passion is education, you can support needy American students through DonorsChoose.org or sponsor an impoverished Haitian student through the SOPUDEP school for needy students in Port-au-Prince, on the site of a former torture chamber. Such groups make only the most modest demands of people, while offering a way to learn more about problems at home and abroad. Simply writing a check may seem uncertain or sterile, but groups such as Bead for Life offer a way for people to engage in a more intimate manner.

In Uganda, the Bead for Life program starts with impoverished women who are earning less than $1 a day and who seem particularly hardworking and entrepreneurial. The recruited women get meticulous training to make high-quality beads, starting with finding the right raw materials. Magazine ads and aid group brochures are always prized for their rich colors, and Wakefield winces as she recalls the women delightedly making beads from brochures about AIDS prevention. "I just hope that someone had looked at them before they were cut up," she says. These bead makers now earn about $200 per month, part of which is deposited into new savings accounts controlled by the women. The fact that the women now have protected financial assets may also win them more respect from their husbands, for a man cannot simply raid a wife's bank account the way he can a jar of cash under the bed.

Bead for Life also gives women access to health-related products such as antimalarial bed nets, condoms, deworming medicine, and family planning supplies. A crucial element of the eighteen-month bead-making course for these women is training them to start other small businesses. The women get coaching in business management, and some learn local trades such as making jam or raising chickens. Then they get help starting a small business, and it's time for them to move on to a new trade. The aim is not to create lifelong jewelry manufacturers but to turn women into bustling entrepreneurs. Bead for Life now sells more than $2.6 million worth of jewelry-from-garbage annually, and it has used these jewelry parties in the United States to teach Americans about global poverty. The program also takes groups of Americans to visit the jewelry makers and learn a bit about Africa. "At first, we thought Bead for Life was just for Ugandans," Wakefield says. "Then we realized that a lot of this was about helping Americans get involved."

CHAPTER THREE

From Anecdote to Evidence

We only have what we give.

— ISABEL ALLENDE

O ne of the trendiest ways in recent years to help the poor—
especially women—has been to provide "clean cookstoves"
that burn less fuel and produce less smoke. That's because nearly half
the world's population now uses inefficient, smoky, old-fashioned
stoves or open fires to burn wood, coal, or animal dung for cooking or
for heat. These use vast amounts of wood or other fuel, which usually
means that women in the family spend a great deal of time looking
for firewood, and girls are sometimes pulled out of school to help
with the task. The search for fuel leads to deforestation and then soil
erosion, and these traditional cooking fires are so rickety that pots of
boiling water routinely topple off stoves, scalding toddlers who have
bumped into them. We've seen far too many of these children with
horrific burns.

Another huge drawback of traditional cooking fires is that they
produce dense smoke that is a health hazard. In 2012, a major study
concluded that household air pollution was the biggest single health
risk factor in India, and the second-biggest in Africa. This smoke
caused the premature deaths of 4 million people annually, due to
respiratory illness or heart and lung diseases, the study found. It also
causes blindness through cataracts. This study suggested that old-
fashioned cooking fires were responsible for more deaths annually
than AIDS, malaria, and tuberculosis combined.

Engineers have designed simple, inexpensive clean cookstoves that seem, on their face, to solve the problems. Clean cookstoves are usually enclosed—like an old-fashioned woodstove in the United States—so they burn fuel much more efficiently than open fires, and they use chimneys to channel smoke out of the hut. Aid groups worldwide have been vigorously promoting these clean cookstoves.

In a village in southern Malawi, a farmer named William Mahamba led us into his hut and showed off his clean, two-burner cookstove, built with the help of an aid group. It was made of mud, with smoke theoretically funneled out through a hole in the back wall. (In fact the room was so smoky it was almost impossible for us to take notes, but Mahamba kept insisting that in the old days it had been even worse.)

Enthusiasm built quickly. Hillary Rodham Clinton, always a passionate advocate of development involving women, launched the Global Alliance for Clean Cookstoves, a public-private partnership that grew to more than 600 partners, including thirty-eight governments around the world. "Clean cookstoves?" Clinton said about the concept. "What does that have to do with world peace and prosperity and human rights and democracy and freedom? Well, everything actually." Her point was that initiatives that empower women and bring them out of the margins are good for all society, and there were plans to invest $70 million in promoting clean cookstoves in East Africa alone. The aim was to have 100 million clean cookstoves in place by 2020.

Esther Duflo, a development economist at MIT, believed in clean cookstoves, and she decided to measure their impact precisely using a randomized controlled trial. Duflo worked with the aid group Gram Vikas, in the Indian state of Orissa, to measure the improvement from clean cookstoves on farmers' health and productivity. Children in the area were ingesting cooking smoke equivalent to seven cigarettes a day, so Duflo wanted to see how many fewer respiratory infections would result after clean cookstoves were introduced, and how much more land villagers would be able to farm as a result. "We went into stoves absolutely convinced that they would make a difference," Duflo remembers. "We tested them in the lab and they worked fine."

Yet the study found that clean cookstoves were an utter failure, at least in that experiment. While development experts in America loved the stoves, Indian villagers were unimpressed—and so didn't rely on them much. In real-world conditions, stoves broke, developed cracks, or didn't work well, and families used them less and less. Sometimes the chimney clogged and wasn't cleared out. Other times a woman would cook over one burner and neglect to cover the other burner, so smoke would pour out of it. The upshot was that for most members of the household, there was no difference in exposure to smoke. The study also showed no difference in amounts of wood consumed.

Most important, Duflo and her colleagues found that, based on spirometry measures of lung capacity and carbon monoxide testing of exhaled breath, "there were no improvements in measured health outcomes, such as respiratory functioning, blood pressure, infant mortality and child body mass index. Moreover, there were no changes in self-reported health outcomes, such as coughs and colds."

Once that study was reported, a dam seemed to break and more problems with clean cookstoves were reported from the field. Other researchers found that a year after clean cookstoves were introduced in Ghana, only half were still in use. In Senegal, a study found that the introduction of solar cookstoves—which technophiles have been excited about as a way to reduce the burning of wood—seemed to have little impact on villages, with only a 1 percent decline in the amount of wood collected.

The episode is a reminder that even the most brilliant ideas don't always work as intended, and that it's important to conduct careful experiments to know where to invest in creating a better world. Historically, we've mostly relied on intuition and anecdotes rather than solid evidence in determining strategies to fight poverty. Every aid group in the history of the world has claimed that its interventions are cost effective, but the evaluations are usually approximately as rigorous as those of grandparents evaluating their grandchildren.

That is beginning to change, though, in part because of the work of Professor Duflo. She's a modest, unimposing woman who will flinch as she reads this and then immediately protest that she's merely part of a large team whose other members deserve just as much credit. At forty-one, Esther is thin and slight, with a soft voice and mid-length brown-blond hair framing a serious face. She is the kind of person you might hurry past on the street and never remember. Yet she is helping to revolutionize poverty economics by developing tools to measure impact and cost effectiveness.

Duflo, born and raised in Paris, has spent almost half her life in the United States, but she wears her French accent proudly. The daughter

DOMINIC LEGGETT

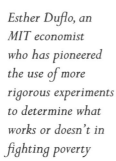

Esther Duflo, an
MIT economist
who has pioneered
the use of more
rigorous experiments
to determine what
works or doesn't in
fighting poverty

of a pediatrician mother and a mathematician father, she grew up exposed regularly to global poverty concerns. Her uncle cofounded Doctors of the World (a spin-off of Doctors Without Borders), and her mother regularly treated children in conflict-torn countries such as El Salvador. Duflo's own concern for the developing world began in part when she read a comic book at age six about Kolkata, India, and was flabbergasted to learn that each inhabitant had only about a square meter of living space. Her mathematical mind conjured a vast grid, a checkerboard in which each person was assigned a small square. Ever since then Duflo has been trying to demystify global poverty. She studied history at the superb École Normale Supérieure in Paris, but time spent in Russia and Madagascar convinced her that economics could be a better tool than history to make a difference in the world. She earned a master's in economics in Paris and then applied to MIT to work on a Ph.D. The MIT economics faculty almost rejected her, but a French professor in the department lobbied for her and she squeaked in.

Duflo stayed on at MIT as an assistant professor, and a few years later she found herself the target of a bidding war among rival universities. She deftly used this leverage to become, at age twenty-nine, one of the youngest tenured faculty members in MIT history and to help create, with the financing of a Middle Eastern tycoon, the Abdul Latif Jameel Poverty Action Lab. The lab linked a network of development economists who use randomized controlled trials to determine what is most cost effective in fighting poverty. These are like the clinical trials of a pharmaceutical: people are assigned randomly either to an experimental group or to a control group, and then both groups are carefully measured for change. The aim is to bring science, metrics, and precision to the global war on poverty.

This experimental approach has rocketed Duflo to the top of her field. She won a MacArthur "genius" grant and the John Bates Clark Medal for the best economist under forty. The Poverty Action Lab has been involved in more than 350 randomized controlled trials and has inspired similar initiatives in other areas including crime and domestic poverty.

One experiment found surprising benefits from deworming children. We in the West don't think of intestinal worms as a barrier to education, partially because our kids don't have such parasites. Yet worms leave children weak and anemic—especially high school girls, who because of menstruation are more prone to anemia. In the early 1900s, many American children (especially in the South) had worms, and the Rockefeller Foundation dewormed children in the United States as one of its first initiatives. Schoolchildren in those areas suddenly began to do far better in school.

The majority of children in many developing countries have parasites in their gut. All that's needed to kill the worms is one or two albendazole pills, which cost 2 cents each when purchased in bulk on international markets. The whole operation including distribution can cost less than 50 cents per child per year. African schools tend to have high absenteeism, partly because kids are frequently sick, and deworming reduced rates of absenteeism by a quarter. Professor Michael Kremer of Harvard University and a colleague, Edward Miguel, tested deworming by examining an area in Kenya where some schools were randomly assigned to have all students undergo deworming. Kremer and Miguel found that the cost of getting one more child into the school system for a year by deworming was $3.50. (For roughly every seven children who are dewormed, school attendance increases by one.) The next cheapest way was paying for school uniforms, which cost about $100 per extra child brought into the school system. Building schools costs several hundred dollars per additional child educated.

Not every study has found such impressive results from deworming, but some follow-up randomized trials in Kenya highlighted the long-term benefits. Children who don't get dewormed are 13 percent more likely to remain illiterate as adults. What's more, deworming seems to benefit even those who aren't treated—presumably because it confers "herd immunity" by reducing parasites in the area.

If these conclusions were just before-and-after comparisons, we would be suspicious. After all, maybe the entire area has been improving for other reasons. But given the nature of a randomized trial, it's easier to be confident that deworming is the factor making the difference.

The importance of rigorous trials is also evident in Duflo's work with Abhijit Banerjee on microfinance, which for years was hailed as something close to a magic bullet for fighting global poverty. Muhammad Yunus, one of our heroes, won the Nobel Peace Prize for his work in Bangladesh championing financing for the world's poor. The website Kiva became a huge success by allowing Americans to lend modest sums to entrepreneurs around the world. Yet when Duflo carefully measured the impact of microlending, she found that it was no magic bullet. She examined the expansion of an Indian microfinance institution, Spandana, in Hyderabad. Out of 104 neighborhoods, Spandana began lending in half that had been randomly chosen, while the other half were a control group for comparison. Duflo found that Spandana's small loans helped some people start small businesses—7 percent—but that was only slightly higher than the 5 percent who started businesses in the control areas. People in areas getting the loans were no more likely to invest in children's education, and women didn't seem to be empowered. All in all, microloans offered a modest impact, not the breakthrough that many in the field had expected.

"We were quite pleased with these results," Duflo and Banerjee wrote in their book *Poor Economics*. "The main objective of microfinance seemed to have been achieved. It was not miraculous, but it was working." Nearly everybody else felt a huge letdown. Microfinance institutions themselves responded by trying to cast doubt on the study—which became more difficult when other randomized trials in Ethiopia, Mongolia, Mexico, Bosnia, Morocco, and the Philippines came to the same conclusion.

On the other hand, randomized trials found a surprisingly positive effect from microsavings programs, which help the poor save small amounts of money. One-third of the world's population has no access to bank accounts and must resort to hiding cash somewhere, such as in a shack that has no lock. Moreover, impoverished farmers often receive money in large sums just once or twice a year, after a harvest, and then they are deluged with loan requests. The result is pressure to spend money rather than save it, and the cash often goes for alcohol, tobacco, or prostitution. Then there is usury—not just on loans but also on deposits. In West Africa, villagers can deposit money with *susu* money traders, but they must pay 40 percent annual interest on their deposits! Someone who deposits $100 now is protected from theft and loan requests but gets back only $60 a year later.

Microsavings initiatives address these problems by allowing people to hold money securely and build up a nest egg. In a 2013 study conceived by Pascaline Dupas of Stanford University, savings accounts were provided to women who were market vendors in rural Kenya. These savings accounts paid no interest and charged a fee for withdrawals, but 87 percent of the women signed up. After less than six months, the market women in the program were investing 50 percent more in their businesses each day than those in a control group.

One of the most common models for microsavings is the village savings and loan. It is very simple and has spread around the world since being launched by CARE in Niger in 1991. The model has been backed by the Bill and Melinda Gates Foundation, and organizations including Opportunity International, Oxfam, and Catholic Relief Services have embraced it. Typically, the aid group provides a simple cash lockbox with three padlocks, all of which must be unlocked to access the contents. Then a group of about twenty village women (and occasionally men) meets perhaps once a week, each member bringing five cents or a similar small amount to be placed in the lockbox. The three keys are distributed to different members, and the box is kept at the home of a fourth woman who doesn't have a key. Hugh Aprile, a Catholic Relief Services aid worker who showed us how the program worked in rural Nicaragua, noted that these village savings and loans are very cheap to start because villagers supply their own capital. "It's people using their own money," he said, "to build far more than they ever thought they could." It costs $25 per participant to start a microsavings group through CARE, and it strikes us as a particularly cost-effective way to help people help themselves. Contributions to CARE can be earmarked for the village savings and loan program.

Microsaving is so powerful that it functions even without outside aid organizations promoting it. Between 1999 and 2001 a women's empowerment program called WORTH organized 35,000 Nepalese women into savings groups. Then the Maoist insurgency there forced the sponsors to pull out and abandon the project. As the insurgency subsided, aid workers returned and discovered that the savings groups had continued on their own and in some cases spread. A follow-up study found that two-thirds of these groups were still operating in 2007, six years after outside support had been cut off, and villagers themselves had created 425 new savings groups with no outside assistance.

R andomized controlled trials, of course, also have limitations. Such trials are expensive and often impractical, and a trial in Kenya doesn't necessarily show what will work in Ethiopia. There are thousands of possible permutations that can affect an outcome, and they can't all be tested—or extended long enough to reveal slow changes. While these trials work well in testing one particular approach, they're less useful in other areas, including the evaluation of complex programs with several elements. A broader complaint is that randomized trials address only small questions rather than big, basic ones, such as whether foreign aid works. Sanjay Reddy, an economist at the New School for Social Research in New York, has denounced trials for leading "not so much to increasing rigor as to rigor mortis, by severely limiting the questions that can be asked."

We don't entirely buy that critique, because we feel it is helpful to get guidance on as many essential questions as possible—such as whether to invest tens of millions of dollars in the present technology of clean cookstoves. Duflo's randomized trial on stoves understandably frustrated advocates who had spent years spreading the gospel of clean cookstoves. They are, after all, working on a promising technical solution to the premature deaths of 4 million people annually, and they say that they have already developed much better stoves than those Duflo tested. Should this entire endeavor be abandoned because of Duflo's trials in one location with an early generation of stoves? Our own view is that we will probably see continued experimentation with the stoves, but at a low level until they are a proven success. Our bet is that one day a new technology of stoves will win approval from Indian villagers and make a huge difference, but that this is still some way off.

Rigorous evaluation is essential, whether we're talking about poverty in India or in America. The stakes are too great to fight the global war on poverty based on hunches and intuition. Just as the investment world has become increasingly rigorous, the nonprofit world should as well. If it's important for businesses to be meticulous in planning a new business line, it's even more critical for an aid organization or donor to rely on careful evidence to plan the best way to fight malaria or educate children. Throughout this book, we'll often talk about randomized trials and other robust evidence as a way to avoid tired old arguments about what is the best way to create opportunity.

Duflo's students and colleagues, including Professor Dean Karlan of Yale, have gone a step beyond research and scholarship to create an organization called Evidence Action, which invests in the programs whose effectiveness has been proven in randomized controlled trials, often by the Poverty Action Lab. As we noted earlier, Evidence Action includes a deworming initiative—which has already treated 37 million children in twenty-seven countries—as well as a program to use chlorine dispensers to provide safe water for just $1.98 per family per year.

In the domestic sphere, a nonprofit research organization in New York City called MDRC conducts randomized trials on how best to address social issues in the United States. The Coalition for Evidence-Based Policy provides an outstanding website listing programs that have the most rigorous backing, usually from randomized trials, in fields such as prenatal care, mental health, and homelessness. These resources mean that an ordinary donor trying to ease poverty, whether in Los Angeles or South Sudan, need no longer rely on hunches about what might work but can employ rigor once available only to giants of philanthropy such as the Rockefeller Foundation or Ford Foundation. The information revolution has come to giving.

Doughnuts with CARE

Biti Rose Nasoni, a farmer in the southern African nation of Malawi, is a thirty-nine-year-old woman who covers her short hair with a stocking cap. She has a receding chin and a mouthful of crooked and missing teeth that are overshadowed by the warmth of her smile. She didn't used to laugh much, though, for Biti Rose and her husband, Alfred Nasoni, were desperately poor. They often farmed only part of their two and a half acres of land because they lacked money for seeds. They live in the village of Masumba, a collection of mud-walled huts with grass roofs not far from the capital, Lilongwe. Biti Rose never went to school and is completely illiterate, while Alfred dropped out of school in the fifth grade. They had seven children—there was no family planning available—but two of the children died without ever seeing a doctor. Malnutrition was likely a factor in their deaths.

Biti Rose Nasoni runs a business selling doughnuts thanks to a CARE microsavings program in her village in Malawi.

"I couldn't take them to the hospital, both because of the distance and because we didn't have the money," Biti Rose recalls. Speaking of the older child, she adds with a catch in her throat: "We kept him in the house while he was critically ill for four days, and then he died."

To make ends meet, Biti Rose worked as a day laborer for other farmers. Sometimes she was paid with a plate of beans, most of which she distributed among her children to keep them alive; other times she was paid in corn husks, which typically are used to feed animals but in desperate times are eaten by humans. She would dry the husks in the sun and then pound them into flour. When there was nothing else, Biti Rose would boil wild leaves to feed her family. The poverty seemed likely to be transmitted to the next generation: Alfred and Biti Rose pulled their eldest son out of school in the fourth grade because they couldn't afford a $5 school uniform. They then sent the boy off to another village to work as an animal herder, because the livestock owner agreed to feed him.

Alfred told us that even as his children were starving, he spent an average of $2 a week on local moonshine, and 50 cents on cigarettes. He added that he also often spent $2 or more a week buying sex from local girls, even though AIDS is widespread. All this left Biti Rose furious and humiliated, feeling that Alfred was lazy as well as wasteful and hurtful. "Our marriage nearly broke apart," she says, and she acknowledges that she was a constant scold. "I couldn't allow him to chat with his friends when in the house we had no food. Most of the time we were quarreling because I was accusing him of not caring for us. . . . We spent sleepless nights fighting."

Then, in 2005, Biti Rose heard about a village savings and loan being started in her village by CARE. "As a married woman, I had to seek my husband's permission, and with his approval, I joined," she recalls. She and nineteen other women in her group began meeting every Tuesday, each bringing the equivalent of 10 cents to a meeting. Typically these funds are lent to a member who wants to start or expand a small business. Biti Rose, with coaching from CARE, borrowed $2 and started making a local version of doughnuts, which she sold for 2 cents each.

"People really liked my doughnuts," she says proudly, and soon she was selling 100 each day. She eventually raised her price to 4 cents per doughnut, scaling up to 250 doughnuts a day. At that point she earned a profit of more than $2 daily—a huge improvement over earning corn husks. Biti Rose gave Alfred $7 to buy tomatoes in the villages and haul them to the town market to sell, and on his first day of trading he cleared more than $3. He began to grow and sell vegetables, and showed promise as a businessman.

Biti Rose had been depositing her savings in the village savings and loan, and now she withdrew $100 to try something new with Alfred. They purchased fertilizer for their patch of peanuts, allowing them to increase their yield from the customary one or two bags of peanuts to seven bags. "It was our first time to have such a bumper harvest," she notes. They worked steadily harder and began to farm all their land, and then to lease two additional acres from others.

"At peak harvest times, I have to hire seven to ten people" to pick the crops, Biti Rose says proudly. When we visited them, they had just harvested a record sixty-four bags of peanuts.

Alfred joined his own microsavings group, made up of twenty men. It wasn't as successful as the women's group, partly because the men often missed the meetings and because men who took loans sometimes disappeared. Still, the group gave Alfred a place to put money rather than drink it away in bars. Moreover, seeing steady improvements in the family's living standards and sensing his stature rising, Alfred dropped the girlfriends and stopped smoking and drinking. This meant more money for the children's education, and Alfred and Biti Rose are hoping to send their youngest child to university. They are also now a real couple.

"We aren't quarreling now, and when we make decisions we make them as a household," Biti Rose says. "Alfred is closer to me, and he won't make a decision without consulting me. He has seen that I'm someone who is helping the household generate an income. He has seen that without me, we would not be in this position. You can see yourself—this is one of the best houses in the village."

It was true. Alfred and Biti Rose had replaced their leaky grass roof with a tin one and had added a nice wooden door. They built a solid storage hut that keeps mice out, which means that they don't have to sell grain in October when they harvest the fields. Instead, they can store crops and sell them in February for a price that is 60 percent higher. Biti Rose's success isn't typical, of course. She's especially entrepreneurial and shrewd, and now she's thinking of investing in an oxcart, partly to carry her own produce to market and partly to rent out to other villagers. She's also planning to buy a television powered by a solar panel. It would be the first television in the village, and Biti Rose has figured out how to monetize it.

"I'm a businesswoman," she says. "I can't give anything away. If there's a soccer match or something, anybody who comes in my house to watch will have to pay."

CHAPTER FOUR

The Land of Opportunity—If You Catch Them Early

The child is father of the man.

— WILLIAM WORDSWORTH

As our kids were growing up, one of their playmates was a girl named Jessica. She lived near the family farm Nick grew up on in Oregon, and every summer we would go back to the farm for a long visit with Nick's parents. Our kids would disappear into the forest with Jessica and her brother, Nathan, to make forts, work on their treehouse, and share their dreams. We were always a little concerned about this, because—there's no polite way to say this—Jessica was a mess.

Her mother was involved in the methamphetamine trade, in and out of prison, and Jessica had never known her father. Even as a young girl, she seemed headed for jail or pregnancy, and she was a reminder to us that poverty in the United States can be as obdurate as in Bangladesh. It's true that the greatest levels of absolute deprivation are in countries such as the Central African Republic or Chad, but we also have enormous challenges in the industrialized world. Impoverished Americans may own cars and watch television, but in the twenty-first century poverty remains a fundamental part of life in the United States and some other Western nations.

We're going to confront here the question of poverty in the United States and other wealthy countries—and the surprising evidence of what works to overcome it. First we'll look at the earliest interventions, including those that start before birth, and then turn to preschool and efforts to promote reading. There are some remarkable programs that help build character and offer teenagers a last exit ramp before a life of crime or unemployment. Finally, we'll look at promising turnaround programs for some of our nation's vulnerable adults.

This is an area of social policy that we tend to leave in the hands of government, so it may seem odd to encounter it in a book about how we can make a difference. But while it's true that none of us have the resources to underwrite a national program, insights about what is most effective can still guide our priorities. After all, we may not be able to fund an entire university, but that doesn't prevent us from contributing to higher education. In the same way, we can pitch in to help support some of the early childhood programs we'll introduce, which often get higher economic returns than tertiary education. We can also volunteer and give voice to the importance of interventions to give needy children a fairer chance at life. Whether a child ends up in university or prison should not depend to a significant extent on birth circumstances; we can do better than that. If a smarter social policy is needed to create opportunity, then let's help build it. If we fail to do so, society will continue to pay an enormous price.

For us, the problems in the developed world were personified by Jessica, whom we had known since birth. Jessica's mom was sixteen when she had her first baby, Nathan. Her father warned her that if she became pregnant again, he would kill both her and the baby. Yet within a year, she was expecting again—and Jessica soon arrived, born in the bathroom of a family friend's house, with no doctor present. When Jessica's mother was imprisoned for meth-related offenses, it fell to the grandparents—our Oregon neighbors—to look after the children. They tried hard to do the right thing, especially the grandmother, who was also working full-time and caring for her terminally ill husband. Nathan somehow emerged from this cauldron mild, earnest, and endlessly good-natured. Jessica, who had a different father, was unusually smart but also rebellious and impossible to control. In a small farm town, everybody knows each other, and so schoolkids would bully Nathan and Jessica or tease them about their parentage. When you're in second grade and the class is making Mother's Day cards, it's wrenching that everyone knows your mother is in prison. It's worse on Father's Day, when you have no idea who your father is.

Jessica got in trouble at school for defiance, fighting, and every possible sin. Her mind worked very quickly, and she used this intelligence to become a fluent, prodigious liar. One neighbor banned his daughter from playing with her, and we wondered if we should do the same. Then Jessica was expelled in the sixth grade for bringing alcohol into school. She was also caught setting fires, and her grandmother felt she could no longer cope. Jessica moved with Nathan to a nearby town with her mother, newly released from prison. The house was full of drug users and had no electricity or running water. When the kids asked for food, the adults would offer them drugs. Jessica mostly got along with Nathan, but on one occasion she grew enraged at him and chased him around the kitchen table with a knife. He felt lucky to have escaped with his life.

Nick's family had lived on a farm alongside Jessica's family for decades, trading stories about well water, vegetable gardens, and elk hunting. As our children played with Jessica and Nathan, it was clear that they came from different worlds. Nick's father was a university professor who had gradually turned the farm outbuildings into libraries, eventually accumulating 30,000 volumes in eight languages. Nathan and Jessica didn't seem to have access to books other than the ones we gave them for birthday presents, and they didn't evince much interest in those. We were stymied.

W e had been gallivanting around the world, trying to help people in Zimbabwe and Cambodia, and now we found ourselves up against a wall at home. Many others share this frustration that poverty in the rich world feels so intractable. A Florida teacher, Penny Malkin-Becker de Silva, told us about her time as a teacher in rural Nepal. "I grew to love the hour-plus climb to my school six days a week and the rhythms of village life," she wrote. "What our crowded school lacked in basic facilities, equipment and materials, it made up for with a sense of shared mission." Then she returned to the United States and began to teach in a high-poverty district in rural Florida. She concluded: "Teaching in a village school in Nepal was a freaking piece of cake compared to teaching in my native land."

We began to broaden our interest in poverty to include the quagmires of crime, broken families, and substance abuse in America and other advanced countries. One window into the challenge is the county with the lowest per capita income in America: Shannon

County, South Dakota, inside the Pine Ridge Indian Reservation. The reservation is a vast expanse, the size of Connecticut, consisting of arid plains and rolling hills that stretch out to the horizon, bisected by ribbons of highways devoid of traffic. Pine Ridge, one of America's largest Indian reservations, is home to the Oglala Lakota Sioux, who used to be great warriors. On that reservation today are men such as Ben Mesteth, forty-one years old and jobless, struggling endlessly for traction.

"What's a man or woman to do?" said Mesteth as we chatted outside his dilapidated home. He's a big man, very overweight and struggling with diabetes, and he was blunt about the challenges that residents of Pine Ridge reservation face. He said he started drinking at age twelve, about the same age as other reservation children. "I felt helpless, I felt worthless, and I wanted a drink to get rid of my pain," he explained. "But then you get more pain." By his late teens, Mesteth said, he was an alcoholic who sometimes added marijuana and cocaine to his daily routine. With no legal way to make money, he turned to crime and violence to fund his habits. "I did a lot of things to get money to drink," he said apologetically. These included beating people up as a debt collector and driving girls to beer stores where they exchanged sex for alcohol.

Six years ago, Mesteth quit alcohol. He still sees no hope of getting a paid job—unemployment on the reservation hovers at about 70 percent—and he now survives on disability payments while volunteering as a social worker to help the elderly. He has sent his family to live off the reservation, for he sees little future on Pine Ridge. He blames white society for racism, and he blames tribal leaders for corruption and incompetence.

People like Mesteth are born here in the United States with the same rights and talents and dreams as anybody else, but they don't begin to have the same opportunities. They never get to the starting line. Pine Ridge has been a whirlpool from which it is very difficult to escape, except by suicide. Half the population over the age of forty on the reservation has diabetes, and tuberculosis runs at eight times the national rate. The tribe estimates that two-thirds of adults may be alcoholics and that one-quarter of children on the reservation are born with fetal alcohol effects.

"Every person on this reservation has personally seen the negative effects of alcohol, with loved ones or themselves," says John Yellow Bird Steele, the tribe's president.

Partly because of the alcoholism, life expectancy is more like that of a developing country than of an advanced industrial country. The police say that 90 percent of arrests on the reservation are alcohol related. We spoke to one family that lost the father to cirrhosis of the liver and a son to a knife fight with his own cousin over a bottle of beer; then despair and depression drove a daughter to suicide at the age of sixteen. All that was within a few weeks. Poverty here isn't just about lack of money; it's also about a lack of jobs, a lack of hope, a lack of family and social structures — a toxic brew of pathologies that become self-replicating generation after generation.

There are some bright spots on the reservation. The Red Cloud Indian School, a private Catholic school on Pine Ridge, is led by Robert Brave Heart. He works to address Pine Ridge's problems by providing an excellent education that outfits young people to go to college and return as leaders, and also by nurturing self-discipline, self-confidence, and hope. Five of Red Cloud Indian School's graduates have earned Ph.D.'s, and fifty-seven have been chosen as Gates Millennium Scholars, funded by the Bill and Melinda Gates Foundation. A partnership between the Jesuits and Sioux leaders since 1888, the Red Cloud Indian School is an example of a charity that is treating not just symptoms but also underlying causes. It is supported by

ANGEL WHITE EYES

Robert Brave Heart leads the Red Cloud Indian School
on the Pine Ridge reservation in South Dakota.

private donations, by volunteers who come from around the country to work at the school for a year or two, and by people who shop at the school's online store, purchasing Indian jewelry and other items.

Pine Ridge Indian Reservation is an extreme but useful place to glimpse the challenges of poverty in America. It's pretty obvious here that past efforts haven't worked brilliantly and that something new is needed. One reason decades of efforts have not achieved as much against poverty as we would like may be that, in general, our well-meant interventions come too late. If there's one overarching lesson from the past few decades of research about how to break the cycles of poverty in the United States, it's the importance of intervening early, ideally in the first year or two of life or even before the child is born. That's often where our assistance will be most effective and efficient.

Within four weeks of conception, a human embryo has formed a neural tube, which then begins to produce brain cells. As the brain is forming, it is shaped by the uterine environment in ways that will affect the child for the rest of his or her life. A mother who drinks alcohol may leave her child with fetal alcohol syndrome or, less serious, fetal alcohol effects. People born with fetal alcohol syndrome can be recognized by facial abnormalities, and they disproportionately engage in substance abuse themselves. They often have trouble with memory, with thinking, with impulse control—and with the criminal justice system. A study by Ann Streissguth at the University of Washington found that by age fourteen, 60 percent of children born with fetal alcohol syndrome or effects have been suspended from school or expelled. Almost half have displayed inappropriate sexual behavior such as public masturbation. One estimate puts the total associated costs over a lifetime for a child born with fetal alcohol syndrome at $800,000. Obviously, the most cost-effective—and humane—way of dealing with the problem is to prevent it from occurring in the first place, by discouraging mothers from drinking while pregnant.

And from smoking while pregnant. Children with fetal alcohol effects account for 1 percent of births; 20 percent of births in America are to mothers who smoked during pregnancy. These children are more likely to face problems many years later because of the impact those cigarettes have on the biochemistry of the fetal brain. These babies have smaller head circumferences on average, and because nicotine increases the testosterone in the woman's uterus, some theorize that this may lead to a greater penchant for aggressiveness, particularly among sons. Patricia A. Brennan of Emory University found that when a mother smoked a pack a day during pregnancy, the offspring were more than twice as likely to be violent criminals as adults. Indeed, even smoking just one or two cigarettes a day during pregnancy increased the risk, much more modestly, of producing criminal offspring.

There's a simple intervention to help pregnant women stop smoking called the Smoking Cessation and Reduction in Pregnancy Treatment (SCRIPT). It consists of a video and a twenty-minute one-on-one session at a prenatal clinic or at home, and each woman receives a simple pamphlet about quitting. The cost is $25. In randomized trials at low-income public health clinics, 14 percent of the women assigned to the program quit smoking, compared to 8 percent in the control group. Considering that it's so cheap and so simple, it sounds like a bargain.

Nutrition is another area in which we can see the lifelong importance of what happens in utero. Researchers have found that when a fetus is undernourished, there are consequences for his or her health decades later as an adult. For example, one study examined Muslims in Uganda and Iraq who were conceived during Ramadan, when their mothers were in many cases fasting during the daytime. This was far from a famine, since the custom is to compensate by eating a great deal at night, and the period of fasting lasted only a month—often, perhaps, before the mother was even aware that she was pregnant. Yet the study found that those individuals whose early fetal experience overlapped with Ramadan were 20 percent more likely to be disabled as adults, with especially high rates of mental and learning disabilities.

Likewise, when a pregnant woman is exposed to lead from old paint or from air pollution, her fetus absorbs it in ways that impair the development of the brain. Some research suggests that the rise of crime in the mid-twentieth century may have been caused in part by the increasing presence of lead in the environment, and that one factor in the decline in crime from the 1990s on was the phaseout of lead from gasoline (and thus from air pollution) beginning two decades earlier. Many scholars believe that the removal of lead from gasoline was one of the great public health successes of modern times, adding billions of IQ points to humanity while reducing crime. Yet even today, about 5 percent of children in the United States—mostly in low-income neighborhoods—have excessive lead in their blood, primarily from paint and dust.

The lifelong impact of what happens early in life was reinforced by a series of studies on laboratory rats by Michael Meaney of McGill University in Canada. Professor Meaney noticed that some rat mothers are always licking and grooming their pups (baby rats are called pups), while others are much less attentive. He decided to test the long-term impact of this licking. So he waited for the pups to grow up; then he put them through a battery of social and intelligence tests and compared their performance with the parenting style of their mothers. Adult rats who had been licked and cuddled as pups were far more self-confident, curious, and intelligent. They were also better at mazes, healthier, and longer-lived.

Meaney mixed up the rat pups, taking biological offspring of the licking mothers and giving them at birth to the moms who licked less. Then he took pups born to the laissez-faire mothers and gave them to be raised by those committed to licking and grooming. When the pups grew up, he ran them through the same battery of tests. What mattered, it turned out, wasn't biological parentage but whether a rat pup was licked and groomed attentively. Genes mattered less than being lovingly nurtured as an infant.

The licking and grooming seemed to affect the development of brain structures that regulate stress. A rat's early life in a lab is highly stressful (especially when scientists are picking up the pups and handling them), leading to the release of stress hormones such as cortisol. In the rats with less attentive mothers, the cortisol shaped their brains to prepare for a life of danger and stress. But the attentive mothers used their maternal licking and grooming to soothe their pups immediately, dispersing the cortisol and leaving their brains unaffected by the stress.

In the past couple of decades a series of studies have found similar patterns in humans. Scientists can measure cortisol in an infant's saliva, and babies turn out to be easily stressed. Anything from loud noises to hunger to a soiled diaper floods the child's brain with cortisol. But when Mom or Dad hugs the child, the stress and cortisol almost disappear. If a baby is in a bassinet and gets a shot, its cortisol level soars; if the mom is holding the baby, the cortisol level rises, but much more modestly. And a baby's cortisol level doesn't spike in response to noises and threats if it is emotionally attached to its mother and she is near.*

Dr. Jack P. Shonkoff, founder of the Center on the Developing Child at Harvard University, has been a pioneer in this research. He argues that the constant bath of cortisol in a high-stress infancy prepares the child for a high-risk environment. The cortisol affects brain structures so that those individuals are on a fight-or-flight hair trigger throughout life, an adaptation that might have been useful in prehistory. But in today's world, the result is schoolchildren who are so alert to danger that they cannot concentrate. They are also so suspicious of others that they are prone to preemptive aggression.

Shonkoff calls this "toxic stress" and describes it as one way that poverty regenerates. Moms in poverty often live in stressful homes while juggling a thousand challenges, and they are disproportionately likely to be teenagers themselves, without a partner to help out. A baby in such an environment is more likely to grow up with a brain bathed in cortisol. Shonkoff argues passionately that the time to intervene is at the beginning of life, as the brain is forming, and that waiting until the child reaches school age is a costly delay. In 2012 the American Academy of Pediatrics endorsed these findings by calling on "the entire pediatric community" to seek fundamental changes in early childhood policy so as to reduce toxic stress and the lifelong harm it causes.

It's important to note that child poverty has anatomical consequences that can be seen in brain scans. When researchers scanned the brains of five-year-olds as they performed a battery of cognitive and linguistic tests, they found that children's brains function differently depending on the socioeconomic status of their parents. Kids from poor families had less brain specialization, particularly in areas important for language development. "Environmental effects may

---

* These findings, that simply holding a baby reduces stress and cortisol levels, may partially explain why two innovations in neonatal care worldwide are really just rediscoveries of ancient practices. One is promotion of six months of exclusive breast-feeding, which *The Lancet* estimates could save 800,000 children's lives each year, and which offers emotional as well as nutritional advantages. The other is "kangaroo mother care," which is a fancy way of saying that newborns should have skin-to-skin contact with Mom as much as possible. Medical researchers advocated breast-feeding and kangaroo mother care because of practical evidence that they lead to better health outcomes for children, and one pathway may be in part the reduction of cortisol and improved maternal attachment.

NICHOLAS D. KRISTOF

Three-year-old Johnny Weethee and his
mother, Truffles, in West Virginia

manifest themselves in the brain anatomically as well as function-
ally," as the peer-reviewed journal *NeuroImage* put it. Neuroscientist
Martha Farah is more blunt: "Growing up poor is bad for your brain."

We saw the importance of intervening early when we met a tow-
headed boy named Johnny Weethee in a trailer home in a rural part of
the Appalachian Mountains of West Virginia. Now age three, Johnny
is a friendly, curious boy prone to giving people hugs, but he is devel-
opmentally delayed and still can't speak. As Johnny runs around the
room, his mom, Truffles, explains that he had a preventable hearing impairment that left him deaf until it was detected at the age of
eighteen months. At that point, tubes were put in his ears. While he
eventually recovered all the hearing in one ear and much of the hearing in the other, the result still was that for a crucial period of brain
development, he wasn't hearing any sounds. It's unclear whether he
will ever be able to speak normally and overcome the setback that he
experienced at the beginning of life.

It seems like such a simple thing—screen all babies for hearing—
and yet children like Johnny fall through the cracks. West Virginia
requires hearing screening for all infants at birth, but the problem
either wasn't detected or developed later. One possibility is that it
was related to formula feeding, since only about one-third of low-

income moms in the area breast-feed their babies. Many more would like to, partly because of the financial savings, but there is no free help available for moms like Truffles who run into problems of one kind or another. So most moms bottle-feed their babies, and bottle-feeding is linked to 70 percent more ear infections in infants. Those ear infections are a special concern for children like Johnny who are on Medicaid and have only haphazard access to reliable health care, because the infections can lead to complications and deafness. Truffles noticed that something was wrong with Johnny's hearing and asked his pediatrician about it. But the pediatrician didn't see a problem, she says. Truffles was dealing with simultaneous stresses ranging from a broken car to job-hunting to frozen pipes, and with the reassurances of the doctor, Johnny's deafness wasn't addressed until the aid group Save the Children arranged a screening.

This is where everything depends on your birth circumstances. A middle-class child with an attentive pediatrician will have a hearing problem addressed at once; a disadvantaged child like Johnny, perhaps not until it is too late for the developing brain. "Poor kids are already at a disadvantage," says Dr. Irwin Redlener, a Columbia University professor who is president of the Children's Health Fund. "Add chronic, untreated ear infections and you have extreme risk of insufficient language development—inevitably leading to increased rates of learning challenges and school failure." Dr. Redlener says that to prevent such tragedies, all young children should have a primary care physician who screens them for eight barriers to learning: vision problems, hearing deficits, undertreated asthma, anemia, dental pain, hunger, lead exposure, and behavioral problems.

One prism for considering the long-term impact of childhood is "adverse childhood experiences," or ACEs. These are traumas such as physical, sexual, or verbal abuse; living with an alcoholic or drug abuser; or losing a biological parent through death or divorce. A ten-question survey determines how many ACEs a person has experienced. Most people have at least one, and 12 percent have four or more. The first big ACEs study, published in 1998, found that the more ACEs a person experiences in childhood, the greater the risk of adult physical and mental disabilities, from diabetes to lung disease. With four or more ACEs, the risk of hepatitis or jaundice increases 230 percent, depression 460 percent, and suicide 1,220 percent. Since then, there have been dozens of studies confirming that the more

ACEs, the more health problems decades later. Those with four or more ACEs are also far more likely to become pregnant as teenagers or, as adults, to become alcoholics, to face financial problems, or to have increased absenteeism at work. To improve an adult population's physical and mental health, in other words, it is essential to reduce trauma in children.

Adrian Raine, a criminologist and neuroscientist, has scanned the brains of many murderers and other criminals and found visible differences arising from early childhood development. Many murderers have much less activity in the prefrontal cortex than is normal. That's crucial because the prefrontal cortex is involved in impulse control and in "executive function"—controlling overall thinking and decision-making processes. Many studies in the United States and Mexico have shown that children in poor families are more likely to have reduced executive function, apparently because of chronic exposure to stress, and that this is linked to poor school performance, to risky adolescent behavior, and in adults to smoking, excessive drinking, and trouble with self-control.

The hippocampus, which influences memory and navigation, seems to be at risk when children grow up in poverty and neglect. Those who were exposed to great stress as small children have a smaller hippocampus decades later as adults. Conversely, children with nurturing mothers average a hippocampus 10 percent larger than those with less attentive mothers. Stress is also associated with structural changes in the amygdala, next to the hippocampus, which processes emotions such as anger and anxiety. As Charles A. Nelson III and Margaret A. Sheridan of Boston Children's Hospital write: "Traumatic and chronic stress during childhood has a lasting effect on amygdala and hippocampal volume and function, leading to decreased emotion regulation and increased risk for mental illness, particularly anxiety and depression."

Early development is not crudely deterministic, of course, and we're still in the early stages of understanding the brain. But the importance of very early interventions emerges from the tragedy of Romanian orphans who were discovered living in wretched conditions in Bucharest and other cities after the collapse of the Communist regime at the end of 1989. Thousands of infants growing up in those orphanages received food and water but negligible human contact. When they cried no one picked them up, and no one hugged them. After the demise of the regime, sixty-eight of those orphans were randomly selected to be placed in good foster homes, while sixty-eight others were, heart-rendingly, randomly assigned to stay behind in the orphanages. The result is a randomized controlled trial called the Bucharest Early Intervention Project. The researchers found that what mattered for these children to recover ground was removal from the orphanage before the age of two. Orphans who were taken out and placed in good foster care before then managed to recover and adjust to a considerable degree. In contrast, those removed after the age of two showed less recovery, and their IQs remained stuck in the 70s. Brain scans show the difference: those children left behind in the orphanages after age two have brains with much less activity, much less gray matter, and some brain structures shrunken.

One implication is that children's brains lose their plasticity after about the age of two, and it then becomes more difficult to recover lost ground. Another implication is that foster parents or family-style situations are usually better for children than institutions such as orphanages, no matter how well meant. In impoverished post-genocide Rwanda, survivor children did better even in child-headed households than in institutions. Worldwide, UNICEF says, there are up to 8 million children still raised in institutions.

The majority of human mothers seem to achieve a real emotional attachment to their babies.* But a significant minority of moms are less attentive, too young and immature, too overwhelmed by substance abuse, or too stressed or depressed themselves to relieve a child's stress. It was once thought that children could surmount a tough beginning, or even that coddling infants would create shy and timid crybabies. Then a pioneering scholar named Mary Ainsworth,

---

* Experts think fathers can have the same effects as mothers in creating attachment and reducing stress and cortisol levels, though most of the research on humans and laboratory animals was conducted on mothers. Psychologists suggest that what matters most is the parent's touch, talk, and interaction, not gender. Likewise, studies on children raised by same-sex parents have been accumulating in the past few years, and there's no indication that these children face setbacks; on the contrary, several studies show that those children do better by some measures than children of straight couples. That may be because same-sex couples have to really want a child to raise one, while some heterosexual couples negligently care for a child that they didn't much want. The largest study of children of same-sex couples, the Australian Study of Child Health in Same-Sex Families, examined 500 children up to age seventeen and found no difference compared to children of straight couples in most areas and higher measures for family cohesion, an assessment of how family members get along.

whose work at Johns Hopkins University led to our modern under-standing of attachment, found that babies with the most attentive moms, those who picked them up and cooed to them at the first wail, actually cried less at a year of age. Ainsworth argued that maternal attachment creates more self-confident children who then feel secure enough to venture out and try new things—an echo of what Professor Meaney had found with rats that had been licked as pups.

A University of Minnesota research team backed Ainsworth's work with a pathbreaking study of the long-term impact of early attachment. The researchers monitored 180 members of low-income families for three decades, beginning when they were still bumps in their mothers' bellies. Early parenting turned out to be critical, start-ing with whether the mothers were attentive, immediately picking up a distressed child and anticipating its needs. Those infants who had been carefully attended by their moms, just like the rat pups who had been licked by their mothers, became better adjusted, were more confident, and did better in school. Astonishingly, observations of parenting skills in the first forty-two months of life could predict with 77 percent accuracy whether the child would graduate from high school. "Thus, by age three and a half years, dropping out was sub-stantially predictable," the researchers write in their book, *The Devel-opment of the Person*. These psychosocial assessments were a better predictor of whether a child would graduate from high school than his or her IQ.

What seems to happen is that infants with attentive parents learn that they can influence their environment—they cry and Mom comes running. Instead of becoming spoiled or manipulative, they become empowered. Conversely, those who don't get a response conclude that they are helpless, and in some cases they succumb to a passivity that gnaws at initiative, grit, and self-discipline. This can be passed down generationally. Serena, one of the children in the study, was born to a single teenage mother with few resources, who nonetheless married soon after Serena was born. Serena's grandparents helped out finan-cially, and Serena's mom and dad were devoted to their daughter and fully nurturing. The authors describe Serena and, later, her own son:

> Serena, age two, works hard on the lever problem, following her
> mother's leads until, finally, she gets the candy out of the box by

weighting down the board. Her mother, Jessica, smiles and says in an animated voice: "There, now you've got the candy out! You got it!" Two decades later, Serena watches Dustin, her own two-year-old, as he works hard to solve the same problem. At last he solves the problem and smiles brightly. "There you go. Good job!" she says, and smiles warmly at him.

A boy named Ellis doesn't get the same support from his mom, and once again the results echo a generation later:

When Ellis seeks help from his mother as he struggles with the problem, she rolls her eyes at the ceiling and laughs. When he finally does manage to solve the problem, his mother says: "Now see how stubborn you were." Two decades later, as Ellis watches his son Carl struggle with the same problem, he leans away from the child, laughing and shaking his head. Later, he taunts the child by pretending to raise the candy out of the box, then dropping it as the child rushes to try to get it. In the end he has to solve the problem for Carl and says, "You didn't do that, I did. You're not as smart as me."

Obviously, we need to help high-risk parents produce more children like Serena; we need to help troubled parents nurture their children with love and hugs. One reason many people feel poverty is a hopeless cause is that they think some parents are inevitably going to do a wretched job and that there is no way for outsiders or governments to make a difference. Happily, a scholar named David Olds has shown that they are wrong.

Olds grew up in the small railroad town of Conneaut, Ohio, in the 1950s and 1960s, in what started out as a contented small-town American family. Then his life was shaken as his father, who had had a rough upbringing himself, increasingly turned to drinking and carousing. When David was eleven years old his parents divorced; his dad moved to Florida and largely disappeared from the family's life. David's mother, who worked in an electronics factory, raised him and his sister on her own. At the time, in small-town America of the 1950s, divorce was intensely painful and embarrassing. Out of that crucible, Olds resolved that he wanted to do something that would help people. "All I knew as a teenager was that I had this romantic desire to do something good with my life," he remembers. "This led me to international relations. I had the vision that I was going to go to Africa or India and save poor children."

Olds accepted a scholarship to study international relations at Johns Hopkins University in Baltimore. As a freshman, however, he found the courses were mostly about superpower frictions and nuclear doctrines, and he began to worry that his foreign focus was misplaced. He took classes in psychology and studied under Mary Ainsworth. Nurturing self-assured children seemed more urgent and relevant to helping people than global security studies, so Olds switched his focus to developmental psychology.

After graduating in 1970, Olds put his idealism into practice by taking a job supervising four-year-olds at a day care center in a run down neighborhood in west Baltimore. The Union Square Day Care Center, which served impoverished children ages three to five, was jammed into three rooms in a church basement. Bursting with enthusiasm, Olds tried to turn these young lives around. He invited parents to come in during nap time to discuss parenting. He introduced an especially stimulating curriculum to improve the children's cognitive skills. Yet progress turned out to be far more elusive than he had expected. The parents who came in for discussion were the ones whose kids were doing fine, while he never saw the parents of the children who most needed help. These were the kids he was trying to champion. Many of these children had been abused and came from broken homes; their parents were often struggling with alcohol and narcotics addictions. Some children were suffering from problems of such magnitude that they couldn't take advantage of what was offered. One sweet four-year-old boy could communicate only with barks and grunts, because his mother was a drug addict who had abused alcohol and narcotics during pregnancy. Another boy, Bobbie, a four-year-old with thick glasses, was restless at nap time and avoided sleeping. When Olds asked Bobbie what was wrong, the boy cursed him furiously. Later Olds found out that Bobbie was a bed wetter, and his mother whipped him each time he wet the bed, so the boy was afraid to fall asleep. Then there was a girl who was withdrawn, with behavior that led Olds to worry she was being sexually abused.

Olds felt that instead of healing children, he was applying Band-Aids. Staff at the center would talk about the importance of healthy diets, but there were no supermarkets with fresh vegetables for several miles around. Jobs were scarce, and parents were constantly stressed, short-tempered, and dealing with one crisis or another. Meanwhile, the entire neighborhood suffered from high crime rates that left everyone jittery. Childhood experts have long noted that poor and working-class families have a more authoritarian child-rearing style than middle-class families, with more spanking and peremptory orders. This authoritarian style can impair the child's emotional development, but Olds saw that it was in part an outgrowth of living in a dangerous place. "Unless your children adhere to the rules, they're at risk for getting killed," he said.

It was impossibly frustrating to see children desperately in need of help, and yet to feel as if he wasn't making enough of a difference in their lives. It felt like glorified babysitting. Even at the age of four, these children were hard to reach. Olds concluded that even waiting until preschool to help at-risk children was an unconscionable delay. He returned to school to earn a Ph.D. at Cornell University in psychology. While earning his degree, Olds took a job evaluating a children's program in nearby Elmira, New York, a blue-collar city suffering from a crumbling manufacturing economy. The director of the program, which screened at-risk children and tried to get them extra help, asked Olds his opinion of the initiative. Olds was blunt: *I don't think this program makes a difference, and we won't know with available data. But I think we can design an intervention that will make a difference and that can be evaluated so we'll know whether it works.*

The director, fortunately, was tolerant of insubordination. He invited Olds to put together a proposal. Olds outlined a randomized controlled trial to coach moms and dads on parenting skills. The idea was to hire nurses to meet regularly with high-risk, first-time moms living in poverty, with the sessions to begin in pregnancy and continue until the child turned two years old. The nurse would go to the woman's home, because Olds had seen in Baltimore that home was where the action was and that it was difficult to get at-risk moms to go to a designated location. During pregnancy, the nurse would counsel the mother on avoiding alcohol, narcotics, and tobacco, and win trust by offering advice on what to expect. After birth, the nurse would continue the visits and offer advice on physical risks—*watch out for marbles that your baby might swallow; look out for lead paint chips!* The nurse could also encourage breast-feeding, offer a shoulder to cry on, and gently encourage maternal attachment (and paternal attachment, if the father was in the picture). The federal government awarded Olds a grant to implement the program, later backed by crucial support from the Robert Wood Johnson Foundation. The Elmira project began enrolling women in the program in 1978, with half randomly assigned nurse visits and the other half given screenings and referrals to social agencies—the program Olds was originally supposed to evaluate.

Most of the women enrolled in Olds's Elmira initiative were stressed-out, unmarried, pregnant teenagers. The nurses were under instructions to be patient and warm so as to build trust. They were not to dictate, but to guide and encourage. One nurse, Stacy, found herself visiting Bonnie, a pregnant seventeen-year-old who lived in a dirt-floor basement in a house infested with cockroaches. Bonnie smoked, drank, got into fistfights, and regularly collided with the law. When Stacy suggested that Bonnie stop smoking while pregnant, Bonnie threatened to slap her. "This baby's taken everything else away from me," Bonnie raged. "It's not going to take away my cigarettes."

Stacy backed off and continued trying to nurture trust. It turned out that Bonnie had been physically tortured as a child, and as a babysitter, she had abused other children. During one of Stacy's weekly visits, Bonnie broke down crying and said, "I'm afraid I'm going to do that to my own baby—especially if it's a crier." Stacy gently suggested some coping strategies and asked whom Bonnie could call for help if the baby started wailing. Bonnie had no idea. Stacy prodded, and Bonnie finally suggested an older woman living nearby. At Stacy's suggestion, Bonnie wrote down the older woman's name and phone number on a piece of paper and taped it to the wall, ready for a crisis. With Stacy's encouragement, that older woman did help Bonnie, and Bonnie's boyfriend began to show an interest in parenting as well. Against all odds, Bonnie and the boyfriend took good care of the infant—and that may be why, many years later, that child ended up graduating from high school.

In Elmira, almost from the beginning, the results of Olds's intervention were impressive. In the first two years of life, the children of mothers at greatest risk (poor, unmarried teens) visited by nurses were only one-fifth as likely as those in the control group to be subjected to state-verified abuse or neglect. During the second year of life, a traditional danger period when toddlers totter around and eat things they shouldn't, children visited by nurses were 56 percent less likely to be taken to the emergency room.

Children and mothers from both groups continued to be assessed after the nurse visits ended when the children turned two. The differences remained stark, especially for the families of the mothers who had been low-income, single mothers when they entered the program. Women in that category who had been visited by nurses had 69 percent fewer arrests by the time of the fifteen-year follow-up than the similar women randomly assigned to the control group. Those visited by the nurses had 79 percent fewer cases of verified child abuse or neglect. Partly because the nurses provided counseling on contraception, these mothers had 32 percent fewer subsequent births at the fifteen-year follow-up, and had been on welfare for thirty fewer months, than similar moms in the control group. As for the children, they had fewer than half as many arrests by age fifteen.

The David Olds experiment has become the Nurse-Family Partnership, still run very much as it was in Elmira, and it is exhibit A in the case for early interventions to create opportunity. The program costs $4,500 per mother enrolled per year, or a bit more than $10,000 per mom in the two years and several months that the woman is in the program. The Rand Corporation crunched the numbers and found a huge payoff: with low-income unmarried mothers, each $1 invested in nurse visits produced $5.70 in benefits. Tracy Palandjian, who monitors nonprofits as head of an organization that raises social impact bonds to finance their work, describes the Nurse-Family Partnership as "peerless among nonprofits" in terms of its evidence basis and management.

Elmira has a largely white, semirural population. Would the Nurse-Family Partnership succeed in inner cities or with minority groups? Olds ran the randomized controlled trial again beginning in 1988 with an overwhelmingly black, urban population in Memphis, Tennessee. The results were very similar. Then, in 1994, Olds began the same kind of trial in Denver with a population that was heavily Hispanic. Again the results were very encouraging.

Local governments became interested in the Nurse-Family Partnership as a way to fight poverty and save on welfare costs. Oklahoma introduced the program and found that infant mortality dropped in half for families visited by nurses. The Nurse-Family Partnership has now grown to have a presence in more than forty states and is spreading to other countries, including Britain, Netherlands, Canada, and Australia. Yet, because of limited financing, it still serves only 2 to

*Professor David Olds, founder of the Nurse-Family
Partnership, a highly regarded program to help
small children have better futures*

3 percent of the need in the United States. That's a stark example of mistaken priorities. Here we have one of the most rigorously backed antipoverty programs in America, one that pays for itself several times over in reduced costs later on, and yet it has funds to serve only 2 to 3 percent of eligible families. That's infuriating.

There are a couple of lessons we can learn from the Nurse-Family Partnership and other programs that have shown clear evidence of success. First, it is critical to intervene early in life, in the crucial window when the brain is developing and the foundations for adult life are being laid. That means helping women avert pregnancies they don't want and, if they become pregnant, helping them deflect dangers such as drug use, alcohol, and tobacco. Pregnancy and infancy barely register in public policy debates about how to fight poverty, but new research from neuroscience and economics suggests that that's where the highest return may be. James Heckman, a Nobel Prize–winning economist at the University of Chicago, says that our society would be better off taking sums we invest in high school and university and redeploying them to help struggling kids in the first five years of life. We certainly would prefer not to cut education budgets of any kind, but if pressed, we would have to agree that $1 billion spent on home visitation for at-risk young mothers would achieve much more in breaking the poverty cycle than the same sum spent on indirect subsidies collected by for-profit universities. Resources now go in inverse relation to their best use, with universities getting by far the most and early childhood the least.

Second, children's programs are most successful when they leverage the most important—and difficult—job in the world, parenting. Give parents the tools to nurture their child in infancy and the result will be a more self-confident and resilient individual for decades to come. It's far less expensive to coach parents to support children than to maintain prisons years later.

What does that mean for all of us? If we want to nurture university graduates, maybe the most cost-effective way is to donate not to a college but to a nursery school or parent visitation program. We wish more donors would endow not just professorships but also the jobs of nurses who visit at-risk parents; we wish tycoons would seek naming opportunities not only at concert halls and museum wings but also in nursery schools. Many churches, synagogues, and mosques have opened their spaces productively to nursery and pre-kindergarten programs already. If a church or civic group wants to take a step further and invest in its community for the long run, it can hardly do better than by helping struggling moms take more loving care of their children. Yet it's also true that early childhood neglect can't be solved by private donations, any more than the federal highway system could be built by individual sponsors. We need advocates to push federal, state, and local governments to invest in the first couple of years of life, to underwrite home visitation programs, and to support parents during pregnancy and a child's earliest years. If we miss that opportunity at the front end, it can be far more difficult and costly to try to undo the damage later.

Save the Children, in the USA

As a young girl, Britny Hurley aspired to become a pediatrician, and in a middle-class home she probably would have achieved that dream. Although she speaks in a strong Appalachian accent that is sometimes difficult to understand, her mind is razor sharp. But life was stacked against her, partly because she grew up in a family plagued by addictions in Breathitt County, Kentucky, a land of jutting hills and verdant hollows. The county had a rough past (it was called "Bloody Breathitt" because of its penchant for feuds), and it is struggling today.

Just about every family in the county has been seared by meth, alcoholism, prescription painkillers, and other addictions. The local economy, once dependent on timber and coal, has been devastated, and there are few jobs. The per capita income in the county is $15,500, and its population has fallen by almost half since 1940. Many of the homes are dilapidated trailers with junk strewn outside. Inside the trailers are, too often, dysfunctional families. When Britny was twelve, she says, a family member raped her. When she sought comfort and help, other family members introduced her to prescription painkillers and other narcotics to dull the hurt, and so at the age of twelve she became an addict.

In material terms, Breathitt County has improved over the past couple of generations: most homes now have electricity and plumbing, which many lacked in the 1960s. One study found that 80 percent of American homes below the poverty line (disproportionately in the South) now have at least one air conditioner, and nearly all have microwave ovens. A majority have a washer and dryer. Yet while America's poor enjoy such material possessions, what they lack is hope. Breathitt County is 99 percent white, but it exudes the same sense of surrender and hopelessness as Pine Ridge Indian Reservation in South Dakota, or slums in Lagos or Mumbai. You see the despair in the substance abuse, in the broken families, in the high school dropouts, in the teenage girls standing each evening by the bridge over the north fork of the Kentucky River, waiting for drivers to come by so that they can trade sex for prescription drugs.

We tend to think of Save the Children as an aid group that helps starving kids in places such as Somalia. It does that, but it also operates in America with a program similar to the Nurse-Family Partnership. For $28 a month you can sponsor a child in America, with a focus on getting the child early assistance while the brain is forming. We tagged along with Save the Children in Breathitt County to see how the program works, and spent time with Britny Hurley.

Britny, who has dark brown hair, striking blue eyes, and an impulsive, warm smile, had a reputation in school as a bright student but a troublemaker. In her sophomore year of high school she dropped out and ended up in a drug rehabilitation program called The Ridge, in Lexington, Kentucky. That was where she became sober again and found mentors and life coaches who encouraged her to think through what she wanted in life. She emerged from The Ridge with new goals: to stay clean and get a job and an education. She moved in with her grandmother, a former alcoholic now seems the most stable member of the family. Britny brought her younger sister with her, to spare the girl the rapes that she had endured. Britny also found romance with Stanley, twenty-six, a mechanic at the local garage.

Britny Hurley and her son, Landon, enrolled in a
Save the Children program in Kentucky.

Stanley had dropped out of junior high school and didn't inspire confidence when we met him. Dark-haired, lean, and taciturn, he initially described himself as a former alcoholic who had quit drinking; a few minutes later it turned out that he still drinks, but "not too often." On the bright side, he seems to care deeply for Britny and has married her. He also has settled down and has a solid job, which represents a good find in Breathitt County. They had a baby together, Landon, when Britny was seventeen. We visited Britny, now nineteen, in the trailer that she shares with Stanley and Landon in a small trailer park. We watched as she and twenty-month-old Landon received a home visit from a local Save the Children outreach worker, Courtney Trent. Blond and soft-spoken, Trent is twenty-two and seemingly a distant relative of just about everyone we met locally. Because she grew up here, Trent always knows the backstory—who is using meth, who really wants to find a job, who is abusing disability, who is an alcoholic. Trent herself is clean and working toward a college degree, and thus a local role model.

Britny and Courtney played with Landon on the floor for a little bit and caught up on gossip. Then Courtney asked Britny about any issues she was having. It turned out that one of Britny's family members had recently been arrested for running a meth lab and had called her from jail, asking for help with bail. "I told him to go to hell," Britny said. "And then I hung up." She is working full-time at a Wendy's and is determined to give Landon the kind of caring start that she didn't have. She chatted about her plan to move out of the area, partly to find better job prospects and partly to escape the miasma of despair and drugs. Britny and Courtney talked about how Landon was doing and cooed together over how smart he is.

Very few of the homes in Breathitt County seem to have children's books, but Trent is a walking library. On every visit to a home, she drops off a half-dozen picture books and picks up the ones she left on the previous visit. Then she and the moms go over the books with the children. "If a mom can't read, or can't read very well, then I just tell her to look at the pictures and make up a story," Trent says. "The baby isn't going to know the difference. And the important thing is just to talk to the baby and play with it." Britny doesn't seem to need any prodding, for she reads well and enjoys telling stories to Landon. While playing with Landon on the floor, Britny and Courtney exchanged a bit of girl talk, and Britny confided her hope of going to college and becoming a nurse. Courtney encouraged her and told her that this was possible. They smiled warmly and dreamily as Landon careened around the living room, babbling happily.

"He says really big words that a twenty-month-old shouldn't be able to say," Hurley declared joyfully. "I'm really proud of him."

While there is broad agreement among experts that home visitation programs are enormously effective, there are plenty of disputes about the optimal strategy to employ. The Nurse-Family Partnership has data showing that nurses have far more impact than others because of the authority they bring. Rival research suggests that even outreach workers or home visitors without a college-level or graduate education can have a significant impact on parenting styles, child abuse, child health, and maybe cognitive development. Save the Children argues that nurses are relatively expensive, so it's more cost effective, particularly in rural areas, to use local people like Courtney Trent who can build trust with other community members. It has started a tracking and evaluation process, and preliminary results are promising.

The Coalition for Evidence-Based Policy examined eight home visitation programs and found the strongest empirical backing for the Nurse-Family Partnership, with lesser evidence for the success of two other programs, the Early Intervention Program and the Family Check-Up. Proof of impact of other home visitation initiatives was weaker. Deborah Daro of the University of Chicago argues that there are effective elements of a number of the organizations in this space. Some say it's important to continue home visits with second and third children, when a mom may be under particular stress. Two major organizations that operate this way with home visitation and parent coaching are Healthy Families America and Child First. All these groups are trying to undertake some of the nation's most critical work, creating opportunity and equality while also saving money in the long run. There are myriad ways to support them, and their websites suggest options—including sponsoring an infant or toddler like Landon. Advocacy can also make a difference by encouraging states and cities to introduce home visitation programs.

One woman we met in Kentucky with Save the Children, along with Britny Hurley, is Anastasia McCormick, a young working mother living in a trailer home. She has a six-year-old daughter and a nine-month-old daughter, and she's expecting twins. McCormick survives by working two or three days a week at a pizza parlor. When we visited, her car had just broken down and she had to walk two miles each way to her job. As her pregnancy progresses, she acknowledged, at some point she would have to quit the job. She's living from bill to bill, crisis to crisis. She is behind in payments on her washer and dryer, so she expects that they'll be taken back, and she faces similar problems with the utilities. "I got a discontinue notice on the electric," she says, "but you get a month to pay up." Her boyfriend, a ninth-grade dropout, isn't very employable and survives on disability for a leg injury.

Efforts to get Anastasia and her partner out of poverty will be a challenge. That is reality. But there is time to transform the fortunes of the two boys she's carrying. With some help they can break this cycle of poverty. Helping them and millions like them do so should be a national priority. They're too small to fail.

CHAPTER FIVE

A Thirty-Million-Word Gap

He who opens a school door closes a prison.

— VICTOR HUGO

Two pioneering scholars, Betty Hart and Todd R. Risley, spent more than two years observing forty-two families. Hart and Risley taped the parents' interactions with young children, transcribed the tapes, and then counted the words. They found that the age at which babies began to speak didn't correlate to family income, but the number of words they heard depended hugely on socioeconomic status. A child on welfare heard about 3 million words spoken a year, a working-class child about 6 million words a year, and a child of professionals about 11 million words annually.

By the age of four, a child of professionals would have heard 32 million more words than a child on welfare. This "thirty-million-word gap" appears to have a huge impact in the child's development. "With few exceptions, the more parents talked to their children, the faster the children's vocabularies were growing and the higher the children's IQ test scores at age three and later," Hart and Risley wrote. They continued to follow the children until they were nine years old and found that the number of words young children heard seemed to have a substantial impact on their brain development, IQ, and school performance. Later research has confirmed their findings, as well as their conclusion that by school age poor children are often so far behind that it is difficult for them to catch up. Moreover, many of the words low-income children heard were stern ones of scolding, while professional parents praised their children at every oppor-tunity. Children on welfare heard two words of discouragement for every encouraging one, while children of professionals received six encouraging words for every discouraging one.

As David Olds and many other researchers have found, it's not that poor families are averse to talking to their babies or to prais-ing them. Nobody aspires to be a bad mom or dad. By and large, parents of every background love their kids, want them to succeed, and are happy to help them thrive. The problem is that struggling single moms living in poverty are stressed and busy, don't realize that talking to a baby is critical, and often are accustomed to a parenting style that is authoritarian. Some mothers think that putting a child in front of a television set is a substitute for conversation. Hart and Ris-ley discovered in their data that what mattered was an actual human being speaking to a child: television had no impact on vocabulary and cognitive development. I-LABS, a Seattle brain laboratory, exam-ined babies' brains in a $4 million magnetoencephalography scan ning room—the only one in the world set up for infants—and found the same thing. When a baby listens to a real person, it treats this as a social interaction and processes the information. When the baby is in front of a television screen, the child's brain treats the words as random noise.

We've already discussed some of the earliest interventions that improve long-term outcomes and help chip away at the cycle of pov-erty. Research also points to effective ways to help children continue through pre-kindergarten to build literacy and verbal skills. Children who are readers help themselves, and nothing gets kids more ready for school than giving them the joy of reading. Oklahoma, Georgia, West Virginia, and other states have shown what works in creating broader opportunity through early childhood programs. Some of those programs offer ways that each of us can play a role in advanc ing these goals.

Rosa Llaurador, a nineteen-year-old single mom who lives in Bos-ton with her sixteen-month-old boy, Calvin, is an energetic, talk-ative young woman who grew up eating in soup kitchens and living in shelters for the homeless, and then became pregnant in high school, giving birth on the day of graduation. She has struggled since to make ends meet and doesn't have money for children's books, but she has received them, along with coaching on how to read to a child, from Reach Out and Read, an innovative charity that seeks to remedy gaps in verbal skills. Reach Out and Read was founded at Boston Medical Center in 1989 by a group of pediatricians and educators who were troubled because they saw doctors spending almost all their time on children's colds and coughs while ignoring their mental development. So the group established a system for pediatricians around the country to hand out children's books to low-income parents as part of routine exams and wellness visits, and then use those books to promote the importance of reading to children.

Rosa brings Calvin regularly to a pediatrician, Gabriella Muscolo, who for nearly seventeen years has been handing out children's books in her practice through Reach Out and Read. Dr. Muscolo figures she has introduced several thousand new moms to reading aloud to their infants, and she incorporates the books into the physical exam. Seeing how the baby holds the book can be a way of assessing motor skills, and also fuels a discussion with the parent about engaging the child in reading and conversation. She says that at first many parents think it's ridiculous to focus so much on books and reading when they have other basic problems. "There's a lot of 'Why is she talking to me about reading when I don't have my evening meal, or I'm struggling with abuse,'" said Dr. Muscolo. She tells them that babies have many needs, and that to break out of the poverty cycle it is essential to give

Rosa Llaurador, age nineteen, right, plays with her son, Calvin, and a Reach Out and Read volunteer at Massachusetts General Hospital's Chelsea Health Care Center.

JUDITH FORMAN

the baby a strong brain architecture. "And how do you do that?" she asks. "Well, in order to be successful in school, you need to learn how to read." In effect, doctors in Reach Out and Read prescribe reading almost as if it were a medication.

Many low-income parents weren't read to themselves and have no idea of the importance of reading until a pediatrician emphasizes it, says Perri Klass, the medical director of Reach Out and Read. "It's hard for you as a parent to know to do something that wasn't done for you when you were a child," says Dr. Klass. "For many parents, reading to a six-month-old before she can even speak seems alien. And in many homes, the only book is a Bible on a high shelf, and you wash your hands before taking it down, and you certainly don't hand it to a toddler."

Getting a doctor to hand out books and prescribe reading aloud is an absurdly simple and cheap intervention, yet it has an astonishing impact. One randomized controlled trial in Rhode Island started with 205 babies from low-income families, half of whom were assigned to participate in Reach Out and Read. Those enrolled received *Babies, Goodnight Moon, Moo, Baa, La, La, La!, Bedtime for Bunnies,* and *Three Little Chicks.* The parent also received a one-page handout (written very simply, at third-grade level) about the benefits of reading to a child, suggesting a bedtime story as part of a nightly routine. At eighteen months of age, after an average of 3.4 well-child visits, the impact was stark. Parents assigned to the program were much more likely to list books as one of their child's favorite activities, and 78 percent read to the child three or more times a week, compared to 46 percent in the control group. A follow-up of both groups when the children were about two years old found that those in Reach Out and Read had significantly greater vocabularies than those not enrolled. As the journal *Pediatrics* reported, "This simple and inexpensive intervention, delivered as part of well-child care, changed parent attitudes toward the importance of reading with their infants and toddlers."

Another rigorous trial focused on low-income Hispanic children. Those randomly assigned to Reach Out and Read received bilingual books and handouts. At the start, 64 percent of the families reported that they didn't have a single children's book in the home. Fewer than one-quarter in each group read to the child three or more days a week. Ten months later, in the control group, it was still true that fewer than one-quarter were reading to the child. But among families enrolled in Reach Out and Read, two-thirds were now reading to the child three or more times a week. Parents in the Reach Out and Read group were also three times as likely to say that reading was one of their favorite things to do with their child.

Partly because physicians are not paid to participate and Scholastic has donated millions of books to the program, Reach Out and Read costs only $20 per year per child. It is an excellent example of a cost-effective, evidence-based program that helps kids in a crucial window of development. More than 28,000 doctors have undergone Reach Out and Read training, and one-third of poor children in America are enrolled. Given the minimal cost, it's unconscionable that the percentage isn't higher. "The constraint is funding," says Dr. Klass. "We could reach many, many more kids if we had the funding. We need books and money—we spend a lot of time begging." Reach Out and Read is looking not only for checks but also for donations of books, bookcases, and storybook "reading rugs" that can be placed in doctors' waiting rooms. The organization's website also invites volunteers, who typically read aloud to low-income children in the doctor's office as they wait for their appointments.

While poverty in America has a strong racial dynamic, the achievement gap in America is not just about race; the race gap is actually narrowing. Instead, it is the rich-poor achievement gap that is widening, and not just because of differences in talent. Sean Reardon of Stanford University has found that the achievement gap between the richest 10 percent and the poorest 10 percent is nearly twice the size of the black-white achievement gap. A half century ago, the black-white gap was twice as great as the income gap. Reardon says that the rich-poor achievement gap for children born in 2001 is about a third larger than for children born in 1970. To be born poor in America today is to have a much smaller chance statistically of entering the middle class than was true a generation ago.

One reason for these widening gaps is the changing patterns in how parents invest in their children. Rich and poor parents alike were once fairly hands-off. One study found that for the first half of the twentieth century, articles with parenting advice in popular magazines mostly addressed medical issues. Since the 1960s the focus of such articles has shifted to advice on how to promote a child's brainpower. The amount of time that richer parents spend with their children has increased, and the proportion of children attending top-notch preschools has surged among the wealthy. Poor parents often remain hands-off, while wealthy moms and dads drag their sons and daughters from violin practice to chess tutors to soccer, and in between the child is supposed to play mind-stretching games on the iPad. In the early 1970s, the richest 20 percent of families already spent four times as much on childhood enrichment as the poorest 20 percent of families; now they spend almost seven times as much. Likewise, in recent decades college attendance has increased more among the well-off than among the poor.

All this means that while preschool does offer benefits to the middle-class child who is already getting stimulation, it's a particular lifeline to those at the bottom of the economic ladder. One of the most-studied antipoverty interventions was the Perry Preschool Project, a randomized controlled trial beginning in 1962 for three- and four-year-old African American children living in poverty in Ypsilanti, Michigan. Those children who received preschool and home visits through the local school district eventually had a 65 percent high school graduation rate, compared to 45 percent in the control group. The Perry girls were only half as likely to become pregnant as teenagers, and participants were 46 percent less likely to have served time in jail. At age forty, those former Perry students were earning 42 percent more money and were three times as likely to own their own homes. They were also 26 percent less likely to have received welfare or other government assistance. Investing in those preschool children saved the government money.

It should be acknowledged, though, that Perry was a tiny pilot program with technical problems in the way randomization was carried out, and when initiatives like these are scaled up outcomes often aren't as good. Moreover, the alternative to Perry in 1962 was no social safety net at all, while today there tends to be a patchwork of alternatives, so the gains would probably be less. Critics of early interventions sometimes point to the Infant Health and Development Program, which assisted families of low-birth-weight babies with home visits and preschool, as an example of failure—but that's not quite right. It's true that this initiative had no long-term impact at all for the tiniest babies, weighing less than 4.4 pounds at birth, perhaps because of medical complications. But for those born weighing a bit more at birth, 4.4 pounds to 5.5 pounds, the children did enjoy clear and lasting benefits; at age eighteen they were less likely to engage in risky behaviors and were more successful in math and verbal tests.

Head Start, the biggest early childhood program of all, clearly hasn't been as successful as Perry, partly because the quality of child care has often been low. Critics have noted that within a few years, Head Start students seem to be doing no better in school than those who weren't in the program. A randomized trial called the Head Start Impact Study released in 2012 found that by third grade, gains made by students randomly assigned to Head Start had faded, and the result is a widespread view that Head Start is simply a failure. The Heritage Foundation summarized the report: "Government Preschool Fails Completely." Joe Klein put it this way in *Time* magazine: "Head Start simply does not work. . . . This is criminal, every bit as outrageous as tax breaks for oil companies—perhaps even more outrageous, since we are talking about the lives of children."

Critics such as Klein are right that the educational fade-out is genuinely disappointing. But the Head Start Impact Study had a couple of fundamental flaws. First, most of the children who didn't attend Head Start attended other preschool programs—and some later participated in Head Start itself as four-year-olds as well. So the study mostly measures the difference between Head Start and other early

*Reading time in a pre-kindergarten class for
disadvantaged children in Tulsa, Oklahoma*

childhood programs. Second, the study ended at third grade, and there is growing evidence that although Head Start doesn't produce lasting cognitive or educational gains, it does produce what is even more important—long-term improvements in life outcomes.

David Deming of Harvard University conducted a rigorous large-scale study of former Head Start students and found that they were significantly more likely to graduate from high school and attend college. They were less likely, many years later, to be out of school and out of a job. All in all, Deming found that Head Start had about 80 percent of the impact on these life outcomes as Perry Preschool. What is the pathway if educational gains fade by third grade? Researchers surmise that students may pick up habits of self-discipline, persistence, and cooperation that last longer than the "book learning." In addition, Alexander Gelber of the University of Pennsylvania pored over the Head Start Impact Study data and found something interesting: parents of children who had been randomly assigned to Head Start were significantly more likely to read to them, even years later. The parents were more likely to take them to museums or historic sites. Fathers not living with their children spent one day more a month with children who had been to Head Start than with those who hadn't. It may be that Head Start fosters parent engagement and builds good parental habits, and that this is a pathway by which children have better life outcomes.

Oklahoma and Utah have been leaders in early education. They see it not as a welfare entitlement but as a cost-effective initiative to create equal opportunity and curb the need for social spending later. In a Tulsa pre-kindergarten, we watched as a teacher named Kara Lowry rode herd over ten four-year-olds who were variously drawing, playing with letter blocks, and racing toy cars. "We're not skill-drilling them, we're not doing flash cards," Lowry explained. "We focus mainly on social skills." The aim is to encourage student curiosity about letters and numbers, build children's vocabulary and verbal skills, and above all teach children to cooperate and self-regulate. Lowry helps the kids to express their wants and needs and to feel more secure in the classroom. All this will benefit them in kindergarten and prevent disruptions that make it difficult for other children to learn.

This kind of program can be of enormous assistance for low-income children who endure challenges that middle-class families can barely fathom. Pre-kindergarten teachers have told us of children who are hungry in the last few days each month before food stamps are distributed. "Kids can't focus on studying when their stomachs are grumbling," says Kisha Hill, another Tulsa teacher. She says that water and electricity have been turned off in some homes for non-payment of bills, so children can't easily bathe or read in the evening even if they want to. And boys, she says, have a particular challenge because so many don't have dads in their lives or any other male role model. "Moms can't teach boys to be men, so with boys it's really hard," she says.

Oklahoma began a pilot pre-K program in 1980, and the state legislature expanded it in 1998. Now more than three-quarters of four-year-olds in Oklahoma attend pre-K, and the state has pioneered even earlier interventions for disadvantaged children age three and younger. It is a leader in Educare, a model for high-quality (expensive) nursery schools beginning in the first year of life, and it also makes good use of the Nurse-Family Partnership, other home visitation programs, and Reach Out and Read. We accompanied an Educare social worker, Tracy Goodlow, as she made a home visit to Whitney Pingleton, a single mother of three small children. They chatted amiably and talked about job anxieties and nutrition, and then Pingleton read to her youngest child. In the most pleasant and supportive way, Goodlow urged Pingleton to read more to her children and to speak to them constantly.

"When you're driving along, you can point to a McDonald's and say, 'There's an M,'" Goodlow said. "Or when you get to a stop sign, you can point it out: 'S-T-O-P spells stop.'" Pingleton gets children's books through the home visits, and she seemed to welcome the encouragement—maybe it even bucked up her own self-discipline. We delicately asked about family planning. She grinned and said that she had settled on a surefire method of contraception. "It's abstinence," she said, adding that she just wanted to focus on her children until the right, dependable man came along.

William T. Gormley Jr. at Georgetown University has carefully evaluated the Oklahoma programs over the years and found a significant impact. Children who go through pre-K start far ahead of their peers, and Gormley projected that as a result, the lifetime earnings of these low-income children will be about 10 percent higher. Benefits outweigh costs by a ratio of more than 3 to 1, he found.

Yet it's also true that the early education programs in Oklahoma haven't been a magic wand. The National Assessment of Educational Progress reading and math tests given to all fourth graders in the United States show Oklahoma children making at best average progress in reading and math since pre-K broadened. Frankly, that's disappointing. Still, Oklahoma spends less than almost every other American state on education, and its teacher pay is just about the lowest in the nation, so it may be that without pre-K Oklahoma would be at the bottom rather than the middle. It may also be the case that, as with Head Start, greater gains will be seen in lifetime outcomes than in educational and cognitive improvements.

"I see a huge difference with those children who have had early childhood education," said Karen Vance, a former kindergarten teacher who is now principal of Rosa Parks Elementary School in Tulsa. When we asked Vance what lessons the nation could draw from Oklahoma, she said: "Look at the remarkable difference you've made in these children's lives by starting early." Other teachers and school administrators echo the point, and everybody seems to think the effort is worth it. Some seem slightly offended when asked why a red state is a pioneer in early education. "This isn't a liberal issue," said Skip Steele, a Republican who is a city council member in Tulsa. "This is investing in our kids, in our future. It's a no-brainer."

That's also the view of the United States military, which has a model day care program for service members, and of many other countries. Finland's school system is often regarded as one of the best in the world: it provides subsidized public day care and pre-K for children from birth to age six, and 97 percent of children age three and over attend one of these programs. Likewise, Shanghai is a top performer in standardized tests worldwide and is often hailed as a model school system; in Shanghai, 98 percent of children are enrolled in preschool.

Let's acknowledge that this area of early childhood education is controversial, and that some Americans see it as intrusive big government getting its foot in the family door. It's also true that many programs succeed as experiments and then don't work as well when scaled up. Some enthusiasts see early childhood interventions as a silver bullet to fight poverty—but there are no silver bullets in this area. Everything is more complex and difficult than it seems. Yet a broad range of evidence from the United States and other countries, backed by the latest findings about brain development, support the argument that the earliest interventions are the most cost effective. James Heckman, the University of Chicago economist, writes: "We can invest early to close disparities and prevent achievement gaps, or we can pay to remediate disparities when they are harder and more expensive to close. Either way, we are going to pay."

S o how can you make a difference in this battle? Obviously, the average person is not going to sponsor a Head Start program, but you could put a child through two years of Reach Out and Read for $40.

We have all seen private philanthropy make a difference in the world of private schools and universities. Yet major donations have largely bypassed the pre-K years. One of the few preschool programs that has managed to get strong business and community support is the Cincinnati Early Learning Centers, a cluster of seven early childhood centers in Ohio that support needy kids. Business executives and civic leaders have recognized the organization as a pillar of the community, and that's a model of civic support that could be adopted in other cities.

Another dimension, of course, is advocacy. You can join RESULTS and learn how to help expand pre-K across the country. Another organization on the forefront of pressing for early childhood interventions is the First Five Years Fund. You and your church or civic association could urge your city council to help launch reading programs at the local public schools. You can encourage your member of Congress to support early childhood initiatives, or write a letter to the editor urging that the Nurse-Family Partnership be invited to work in your city. It may seem an uphill task, but you'll have something important on your side: evidence that it works.

Some have stepped up. A group of 300 business leaders, including former CEOs John Pepper of Procter & Gamble and James Zimmerman of Macy's, have formed an organization called ReadyNation, to demand that the federal government invest more in children. "More and more business people are supporting the need for additional funding for early childhood," Zimmerman says. "Why? Because investing in early childhood achieves the best ROI for our country. Currently more than 90 percent of our education dollars are spent after age five, yet 85 percent of a child's core brain structure is developed before age five. This should have nothing to do with politics and everything to do with good business decisions." More business leaders, civic leaders, and citizens could step up and make that case.

A Summer Springboard for Kids

Fresh out of Harvard in 2009, Alejandro Gac-Artigas joined Teach for America and found himself teaching a first-grade class in a low-income school in Philadelphia. When he tested his class in October, hoping to see great progress that would confirm his aptitude as a teacher, he was crushed to discover that his kids were actually well behind where they had been at the end of the previous school year in June. They had suffered "summer slide."

This is something that mostly affects low-income children. While middle-class children, prodded by their parents, gain ground over the summers or at least hold steady, low-income children often regress because their homes don't have books and home conversation is less enriching. Some research suggests that by eighth grade the accumulated "summer slide" for low-income students accounts for two years of the gap between high- and low-income children. Put another way, two-thirds of the achievement gap between low-income and high-income children in high school may be due to cumulative "summer slide."

It took until after Thanksgiving—eighty-three days from the start of school—for Gac-Artigas's pupils to regain the reading skills (recognizing letters and the like) that they had attained the previous spring. "That angered me," said Gac-Artigas. "It felt as if my kids were already dealt a tough deck. The fact that they can't play their hand for three months of school, where those same losses are not happening to that extent in higher resource communities, it felt wrong." He resolved to do something about it.

Gac-Artigas's father is a Chilean playwright and former political prisoner who survived torture. His mother is Puerto Rican and the first in her family of twelve to attend college. Alejandro had been told from a very young age that education was the key to moving

up in life. He encountered prejudice as a poor Hispanic child growing up in the South, and after his parents moved to New Jersey, he
wrote a book—at age twelve—called *Yo, Alejandro* about his immigrant experience. That brought him speaking engagements first at
neighboring schools, then in schools around the state and eventually
around the country.

After his first year teaching, Gac-Artigas took an internship at
McKinsey & Company, the management consulting firm, to gain
insights into how to run an organization and maybe even how to
tackle summer slide. "So I finished teaching on a Friday, started
McKinsey on a Monday," he recalls. "Finished McKinsey on a Friday,
started back teaching on that Monday."

McKinsey offered Gac-Artigas a full-time job after Teach for
America, and he was tempted by the money, as it would help his
financially struggling family. But he was drawn to education—even
at McKinsey he would spend his lunch hour tracking down education
officials in Philadelphia to discuss ideas. So he turned down McKinsey and formed a nonprofit called Springboard Collaborative to chip
away at the summer slide problem. He won a fellowship from Echoing Green, an organization that supports social entrepreneurs trying
to make a better world, and devised a five-week summer camp that
teaches reading and works with the children's parents to promote
reading at home. The program was piloted for low-income children

Alejandro Gac-Artigas

in kindergarten through third grade in eight Philadelphia schools—the first time in recent history that the Philadelphia school district awarded such an opportunity to a start-up. Aside from the in-class summer school, parents and students attend a workshop once a week to practice home reading. Teachers visit students' homes and earn bonuses based on how many visits they make. At school during the day, students have daily and weekly goals. If they meet the goals, they earn school supplies and books. If they exceed goals, they may even get laptops.

Gac-Artigas at first considered partnering with an existing summer school program but decided to break out on his own because he insisted on involving parents. "Summer learning loss is a symptom of the deeper problem that kids in low-income communities aren't learning at home or in school," he said. "We focus on training the parent and teacher to collaborate over the summer—essentially training the parent to be the kids' reading teachers at home." In its first year in operation, with 340 students, Springboard Collaborative replaced a 3-month reading loss with a 2.8-month reading gain. In the second year, the reading gain was 3.3 months—at a cost of just $850 per stu-

SHERYL WUDUNN

David Williams and his two boys, both
students in the Springboard Collaborative
summer program in Philadelphia

dent. Because of matching funds, a donor can sponsor a child's participation all summer for just $300.

The program now begins with pre-kindergarten, targeting children such as five-year-old Byata, who didn't recognize letters. "Essentially, she hadn't held a book before," explained Gac-Artigas. "She didn't know what the front cover was, she didn't know the right way to hold it, she couldn't identify the first word on a page."

Byata turned out to have been traumatized by problems at home. She had been physically and sexually abused, and her biological mother gave the girl to a great-aunt, who became her legal guardian. The great-aunt has a host of relatives and friends around her who all help raise Byata, and over the summer at Springboard the girl learned the alphabet and made other progress. Most of the children in Springboard are older, such as ten-year-old David Williams Jr., who is in fifth grade, and his eight-year-old brother, Daiquin, in third grade. David moved ahead by five months during the camp, while Daiquin accelerated by twelve months—a phenomenal gain that had their single dad brimming with pride. Both boys received laptop computers as rewards for their progress. In a tiny home in a rough part of North Philadelphia, their dad, David Williams, raises his two sons on the small hourly wage he gets as a home health aide. Before his kids joined Springboard camp, the elder Williams would try to read to his kids three or four times a week, but these sessions were tense, with them resisting and him frustrated.

"I learned a lot of secrets," said Williams. "Just the whole process as far as how to pick a book, making sure you pick a book at the right level. The things we do before we read and the things we do after reading. Those things help me."

Williams, who is African American, knows firsthand the risks that boys like his face in the inner city. He himself spent six months in jail for narcotics offenses. Afterward, he paid $12,000 in tuition to a program to learn how to be an electrician, before becoming overwhelmed and dropping out. Now Williams is trying to pay off his tuition debt and hopes to return to his studies someday. He obtained custody of his boys seven years ago because their mother had a hard time managing her household.

Every day, Williams reads about twenty minutes with each son and deploys the techniques he learned in the Springboard workshops.

He and his son preview the title and the pictures to predict what the book is going to be about before starting to read; they summarize and adjust their predictions as they read; then at the end of a session, Williams asks his sons about what they have read. All this makes a huge difference, he says.

"Before it was like, 'Ahhhh, I don't want to read.' 'Get in there and read, you got to!'" he says. "Now it's like, 'You're about to go read.' 'All right, cool!'"

Give struggling parents guidance, and very often they embrace it because of their yearning to do their best for their kids. That's the case with Williams, who is enormously grateful to Springboard Collaborative for giving his children the chance to soar in school. "Honestly, me trying to transition over to being a single father, and just wanting to see the best for my kids, and finally, after all these years of me poking, and trying, and trying this and trying that, I am actually seeing some real progress," he said. "I love this program." He puts the importance of school in perspective: "I know that out there in this world if you can't read, they're building jails. A kid that's not educated, there's not a future for him."

CHAPTER SIX

Who Grabs the Marshmallow?

Our greatest glory is not in never falling, but in rising every time we fall.

— CONFUCIUS

Our brains shape not only IQ but also what we think of as character—persistence, pluck, conscientiousness, grit, and optimism—which a growing body of research suggests is also immensely important in breaking the cycle of poverty. Although these character traits benefit all young people, they are particularly critical for low-income children, who will spend more of their lives struggling. One of the first scholars to focus on character traits as an escape route from poverty was James Heckman. He studied young Americans who receive the GED high school equivalency degree and found that in knowledge and IQ they do just as well as high school graduates. But their earnings are only at the rate of high school dropouts. The reason, Heckman says, is that "as a group, they drop out of everything they start—college, marriage, jobs." In short, the GED gives them book learning but not persistence.

Although early childhood education may be the single most cost-effective window for intervention, later childhood and adolescence can also be turning points. The message is that there are steps we can take to help young people muster optimism, learn self-discipline, and transform their own trajectories. A starting point is developing grit.

What does grit look like? Essentially, it looks like Khadijah Williams, an African American girl who grew up homeless in California with her mother and younger sister. In childhood, Khadijah shifted from town to town, school to school, shelter to shelter. She attended only half of kindergarten, missed all of first grade and half of second grade, then attended third and fourth grades but missed half of fifth grade and all of sixth grade. In seventh grade she bounced among several cities, and in eighth grade she attended school for only two weeks. But Khadijah knew she was smart—she had tested in the 99th percentile in third grade—and she read books, newspapers, and anything else she could get her hands on, even as obstacles were piling up around her. When living on the streets or in shelters, she tried to tidy herself and ensure that she didn't smell, and in high school she decided that she would have to get help to realize her ambitions. She sought assistance from teachers and counselors, as well as from programs such as Upward Bound and School on Wheels, and people did what they could to lend a hand to a smart girl who dreamed of going to college. "Once I understood that school could serve as a permanent solution to my life of poverty, I basically latched on to education like a life vest," she said. "I had the focus. I had the knowledge set. Education was going to literally set me free."

Khadijah enrolled for her junior year of high school at Jefferson High School in Los Angeles and resolved that she would stay put in one school until graduation. While living with her mom and sister in a homeless shelter at the Orange County armory, she rose at 4:00 a.m. each day, commuted by bus to school, and after classes participated in academic competitions, track and field, and the debate team. Then she would take the bus back to the shelter, returning by 11:00 p.m. She scored the highest in her grade on SAT tests, and earned just shy of a 4.0 grade point average.

One of the organizations that Khadijah reached out to is South Central Scholars, a foundation that helps needy kids in the Los Angeles area. It was founded after Miles Corwin, a former *Los Angeles Times* crime reporter, learned of the killing of a fifteen-year-old boy by gang members. The slain boy's only identification was a returned exam on the French Revolution, at a school for gifted students. On top of the test, the teacher had written a big A. That murdered boy, smart and talented and yet unable to escape the violence, inspired Corwin to write a book, *And Still We Rise,* about children who miraculously surmount the slums. An orthopedic surgeon, James T. London, and his wife, Patricia, read the book and decided to help. They founded South Central Scholars to support the college ambitions of overlooked strivers, and the organization visited Khadijah's school and connected with her.

When Khadijah was writing her college essays in the fall of senior year in high school, the Londons invited her to move into their home in Rancho Palos Verdes so she could have a calmer environment in which to finish her applications. Khadijah wrote powerfully about her experiences and applied to Harvard, which accepted her on a full scholarship. Harvard introduced her to Rita Nethersole, a local woman who became a host mother during her college years when Khadijah needed someone to lean on.

"There is a ladder and at the top you know is success, but some people have more rungs than others, or the ladders are broken," said Khadijah. "You can't climb a ladder if it's broken. You need support. For me, that support was through mentors or strangers, and two I want to identify as being incredibly important to me are the Londons and my host mother, Rita."

Khadijah graduated from Harvard in 2013, getting a special shout-out from the commencement speaker, Oprah Winfrey. It's clear that Khadijah has remarkable intellectual gifts, and unsurpassed grit and self-discipline, but she also triumphed because so many people helped her.

"It's all about taking that first step," said Khadijah. "People really do underestimate how much difference they can make in someone's life. What Rita and the Londons did is they felt there was a need and they stepped up and did what they could. There are so many students out there who need that support who aren't getting it, and there are so many people who are willing and able to give that help, but they don't feel like they're the right person or in the right place. The truth is that they are and they can really make a difference and just do that by putting aside those fears."

Khadijah's success is a reminder of how outside support can make all the difference for a young person who is blessed with talent but lacks the backing that is routine in middle-class homes. Yet there is an acute shortage of such mentors, especially men for teenage boys. Whether the guidance is through Big Brothers Big Sisters or Experience Corps, iMentor, or a local organization such as South Central Scholars, it can have a transformative impact on a young person's life.

Khadijah's case is unusual, of course. She not only had dreams, but she also recognized the value of education early on, maneuvered with

Khadijah Williams with her Harvard degree

grit and drive to achieve those goals, and found mentors who could support her financially and emotionally as she applied to college. The roots of this kind of prodigious persistence seem to develop early, as Walter Mischel found in his famous "marshmallow tests," conducted at Stanford University in the 1960s. Mischel conducted the first research in this area on the island of Trinidad, where he offered children a 1-cent candy immediately, or a much nicer 10-cent candy in a week's time. He then examined what factors made children more willing to delay gratification, and he found that the most important factor was coming from an intact family. Later, at Stanford, Mischel conducted further research on self-control and eventually tested 653 children between the ages of three and a half and six years, all from the Bing Nursery School near Stanford, between 1968 and 1974. A child was put at a desk with a marshmallow (or sometimes an Oreo cookie) and told that in exchange for waiting fifteen minutes without eating it, he or she would get a second marshmallow.

Some ate the marshmallow immediately, but most tried to hold out and earn the second. They struggled, looking away, pulling their hair, closing their eyes, or finding some other way of distracting themselves. About one-third of the children managed to wait the full fifteen minutes. Years later, researchers looked at the outcomes of those children and determined that self-control when faced with a marshmallow is a marvelous predictor of success at life. The children who delayed eating the marshmallow did much better as teenagers and earned significantly higher SAT scores than those who gave up and chomped on it; children who waited the full fifteen minutes scored 210 points higher than those who gave up within the first thirty seconds.

A brilliant young University of Pennsylvania psychology professor, Angela Duckworth, conducted her own follow-up experiments in self-control and goal setting. Duckworth is a Chinese American who has absorbed the Confucian passion for education, diligence, and hard work. She found that self-discipline of eighth graders, based on a self-assessment survey, was a better predictor of high school grade point average than IQ. That fits right in with the Confucian world's understanding of success. In opinion polls, American kids say that the students who earn the A's are the smart ones, the "brains." In China and Japan alike, students say that the ones who do best are those who work the hardest. Duckworth called this elusive drive for success "grit," which she defines as passion and perseverance for long-term goals, and that seems about right. She devised a simple set of questions to measure a person's grit, and it tended to predict success at college better than SAT scores did.

Grit may also be the best explanation for the remarkable achievements of three particularly successful groups in modern American history: Jews, Asian Americans, and West Indian blacks. Richard Nisbett, a University of Michigan psychology professor, points to these groups as underscoring the gains available from the right "nurturing." Jews, he notes, have won about one-third of all Nobel Prizes in science awarded to Americans. Asian Americans account for about one-sixth of students admitted to Harvard and other Ivy League schools. And West Indian blacks (like Colin Powell), whose roots are in the Caribbean, are one-third more likely to graduate from college in America than other blacks and have incomes about one-third higher, even though they are more recent immigrants. Professor Nisbett argues that these achievements are not born of an innate advantage in intelligence. He cites a study that followed Chinese Americans who in early years lagged slightly behind white counterparts on IQ tests. Then, beginning in elementary school, the Chinese Americans were outperforming their peers, apparently because a focus on education led them to work harder. As adults, 55 percent of the Chinese American sample entered high-status occupations, compared with one-third of whites. To succeed in a profession or as a manager, whites needed an average IQ of about 100, while Chinese Americans needed an IQ of just 93. In short, Chinese Americans took the same intellect and squeezed more success out of it.

The common thread among these three groups is a cultural emphasis on diligence or education, linked to an immigrant drive. Jews and Chinese have a particularly strong tradition of respect for scholarship, with Jews said to have achieved complete adult male literacy—the better to read the Torah—some 1,700 years before any other group. In China, the parallel force was Confucianism and its reverence for education. Among West Indians, the crucial factors for success seem to be the classic diligence and hard work associated with immigrants, and intact families. The upshot has been higher family incomes and fathers more involved in child rearing.

Grit seems in part to reflect brain architecture, which is shaped in early childhood. Recent scans of the brains of those who underwent the marshmallow test found differences, particularly in the prefrontal cortex (the area associated with impulse control). But Duckworth has also been trying to develop ways to teach grit. She has been working with KIPP, a charter school network that has achieved outstanding results in troubled school districts, to coach students to build their self-discipline. This focus on character traits, including optimism and self-control, has led some KIPP schools to roll out "character report cards" along with academic report cards.

Duckworth carried out a research program of three hour-long sessions that taught seventy-seven students in fifth grade how to set goals, build "if-then" action plans to identify obstacles and ways to overcome them, and work hard. They found that these students performed better on three measures—grade point average, attendance, and conduct—than a control group merely taught "positive thinking."

As Mischel had earlier found in Trinidad, grit also correlates to being raised in an intact family. There's overwhelming evidence that poor kids have much better outcomes when they are raised in two-parent households (that's not necessarily true of middle-class kids who can get plenty of support from a single parent). Children in single-parent households are more than three times as likely to grow up in poverty as children in two-parent households. Researchers have yet to clarify the connections between strong families and grit, but it may be that such families are better placed to nurture and transmit traits like self-discipline and cooperation that are broadly useful for children growing up—including when they form their own families as adults.

There's little doubt that working-class families have been fragmenting in ways that compound poverty. In 1965, Daniel Patrick Moynihan published his clarion warning about a "tangle of pathologies" affecting the black family and leading to poverty. In the half century since his report, the share of black children born to unmarried mothers has tripled, and today the share of white children born to unwed moms is the same as it was for African American children in Moynihan's day. There's also a strong correlation with socioeconomic class. Among white women in the United States with only a high school education, the proportion of children born out of wedlock has risen from 6 percent in 1970 to 44 percent today. As a study for the Urban Institute concluded: "These demographic trends are stunning. . . . That the decline of traditional families occurred across racial and ethnic groups indicates that factors driving the decline do not lie solely within the black community but in the larger social and economic context."

There are many reasons why a child living in poverty may do better with a two-parent family. There may be more supervision, more grandparents to help out, fewer blow-ups by a frazzled parent at the end of her tether. In recent years, there has also been evidence that boys in particular do better with a dad at home as a role model, perhaps in part because moms talk more with young daughters and dads more with young sons. There is a far greater risk of physical and sexual abuse of children when there's a stepfather or stepbrothers, or when the mom has a boyfriend who spends time in the house. Aside from sexual abuse, a child may also face beatings or other physical abuse from a stepparent or boyfriend who is less patient with a child than a biological parent would be. It's difficult to know how frequent this kind of physical or sexual abuse is, but our sense is that it's distressingly common, though often unreported.

Liberals sometimes feel squeamish about promoting marriage for fear that they are being intolerant or else stigmatizing those in non-traditional arrangements. Conservatives sometimes assume that the solution to poverty is marriage promotion, but the George W. Bush administration funded such efforts, and by and large they didn't work. One called Family Expectations helped just a little, but most wasted millions of dollars. A careful evaluation of one, Supporting Healthy

Marriage, found that the per-couple cost was $9,100 and that it had no impact on whether the couples stayed together. Moreover, marriage promotion can propel single mothers into problematic marriages that don't last: one study found that single moms who marry and then divorce are worse off financially than if they had never married.

A critical underlying problem has been a jobs crisis for unskilled men, as trade unions have collapsed and manufacturing jobs have fled abroad. Low-skilled men are much less able to support a family today than a generation ago, and perhaps as a consequence are more likely to turn to crime and substance abuse. It may be that the decline of marriage has less to do with men who refuse to commit themselves and more to do with women who don't think that an unemployed man with a criminal record brings much of value to the household. Women may perceive these men less as life partners than as sperm donors.

In programs involving child poverty, we face a basic choice. Do we invest in the front end, trying to break the cycle of poverty by providing family planning and helping children when they are young and malleable? Or do we pay at the back end, after the problems of poverty manifest themselves, through the criminal justice system and hospital emergency rooms? As must be clear by now, our argument, drawing on the views of most experts, is that it's far more cost effective—and fair—to prevent problems from arising in the first place. As Derek Bok, a former president of Harvard University, once said: "If you think education is expensive, try ignorance." But, in fact, since the 1970s the United States has mostly tried the opposite approach. We've invested minimally in early childhood to prevent delinquency, but enormously in the criminal justice system as we quintupled incarceration rates.

States now spend $50 billion a year on the prison system, up from $9 billion in 1985. The United States has 5 percent of the world's population and 25 percent of its prisoners, and the proportion of Americans ensnared in the criminal justice system is twice as great today as when Ronald Reagan was president. One study found that by age twenty-three, 49 percent of black males have been arrested, along with 44 percent of Hispanic males and 38 percent of white males. It's increasingly recognized in red and blue states alike that this effort to solve our social problems by criminalizing them has failed, particularly with regard to youths.

When economists examined 35,000 juvenile offenders in Chicago, they learned that all else being equal, those sentenced to detention centers (rather than to, say, home monitoring) were 22 percentage points more likely to end up in prison as adults. The reason seemed to be straightforward: youths sent to juvenile detention met up with other offenders and formed social networks of the criminally inclined. America detains children at a rate five times greater than any other country. Much of this is not only counterproductive but also economically unsustainable, and both Democrats and Republicans are supporting efforts to use alternatives to prison for nonviolent offenders. Among the leaders in this effort are Connecticut (which halved the number of children in jail), New York, California, Missouri, and Texas. California spends $216,000 per year on a juvenile delinquent in custody, and that money could be far better used on preventive programs.

Granted, preventing youth delinquency and educational failure is far easier said than done. But to see how it's possible to ignite youthful passion and grit so that kids want to succeed and have the tools to do so, visit New York City's Intermediate School 318. Rising like a fortress over a tough neighborhood in Brooklyn, with grates and bars over some windows and doors, it's a middle school where 70 percent of students are poor enough to qualify for free or reduced-price school lunches, and four out of five pupils are black or Latino. As you arrive, the tired school building seems to exhale surrender.

Yet a triumph has unfolded at IS 318 since 1999, when a tiny nonprofit called Chess in the Schools paid for a tutor named Elizabeth Spiegel to teach chess part-time to the students here. Spiegel challenged her students and infused them with her own passion for chess. Soon the school chess team under her direction began to soar at middle school tournaments. The success excited the school, and more students began to sign up. In 2006, wanting to take advantage of student enthusiasm, the school recruited Spiegel as a full-time chess teacher and coach of the chess team.

The chess room, which she oversees, is like any other classroom, except that hundreds of chess books line the shelves. Among those that seem particularly well-thumbed: *The Ruy Lopez for the Tournament Player, Understanding Chess Middle Games, Casablanca's Best*

*Elizabeth Spiegel, left, plays through and analyzes a student's
tournament game from the previous weekend.*

Games, The King's Gambit, and *How Life Imitates Chess.* On the door
are posted the latest chess ratings of all the club members, from masters to lowliest novices. The room itself is in genial chaos, with students arguing about the relative merits of various grandmasters as if
they were NBA stars. The students divide their time between practice
games with one another and sitting together for a lesson at which
Spiegel uses a chess board projected on a large screen to coach them
to think ahead.

"So what's the best move for white here?" Spiegel asks a chess
class, pointing to the screen. Today's lesson is about how to use a rook
to achieve a checkmate, and she coaxes the students to suggest various options. Then she plays them out to see which would work. "Can
I make the box smaller?" she asks. "We're trying to get the king in a
corner, because it's much easier to checkmate him there." The students are leaning forward, engaged, as if they're watching a sports
event.

The results are astonishing, particularly in a chess world that is
dominated by private schools and white suburbs where some children have had chess tutors since the second grade. In contrast, a representative IS 318 chess club member is Carlos Tapia, an eighth-grade
Mexican American whose dad is a housepainter and whose mom is a
housemaid. They can't play chess or afford a chess tutor for him, and
Carlos doesn't have his own room in which to study. But Carlos and
the other students throw themselves into chess, taking classes on the

game with Spiegel during the school day and staying after school to practice. The IS 318 kids like Carlos live and breathe chess twenty hours a week or more. "They're very motivated to get better," Spiegel says. "It's the cool thing to do. People look up to you if you're a good player."

Spiegel herself learned chess at the age of four and is one of the thirty best women players in America. The game gave her self-confidence when she was struggling in school, and now she works to replicate the process with her students. "One of the things that motivates me is that when you go to these tournaments, it's mostly a white, private school game," Spiegel says. "I'm so glad these kids are from a public school, kids of color."

In sixth, seventh, and eighth grades, IS 318 routinely crushes opponents. Since 2000, it has won more chess championships than any other school in America. In 2012, its kids not only won the middle school titles but also competed in the senior high school division against kids who were mostly four years older. IS 318 ended up winning the national championship for high school students, the first time a middle school had ever done so.

Even with all this success, the school chess program is struggling to stay afloat because of budget cutting. At tournaments, other schools go to restaurants; IS 318 students survive on homemade peanut butter sandwiches. Organizers of chess tournaments, rooting for these scrappy kids, often waive the entrance fees so that they can participate. The school has reached out to businesses, seeking sponsors, but bankers' kids don't go to IS 318 and no one has seemed very interested in helping.

"We've tried to reach out to hedge fund folks," says John Galvin, the school's assistant principal and protector of the chess team. "We haven't had much success. I don't have their names in my Rolodex. That's why poor kids often don't have as much success. Their parents don't have the Rolodexes."

Even so, IS 318 bursts with pride. The school phone message brags about its status as a national chess champion, and a documentary called *Brooklyn Castle* highlighted the students' success. The chess club has grown to about 100 members and is extraordinarily diverse. Rochelle Ballantyne, who was raised by a single mom from Trinidad, soared at IS 318 to become one of the best young women players in the country. Now a student at Stanford University on a full scholarship, she aims to become the first African American female chess master. You get the sense that what the chess team brought the IS 318 students isn't just expertise on the chessboard, but a gritty self-confidence and the belief that if they work and sacrifice, they can have a better life than their parents.

That's what the IS 318 chess club is, one of innumerable and inexpensive initiatives that don't by themselves erase poverty but do create opportunity and extend horizons. If you love chess, or even if you don't; if you love kids; if you love kids with grit; and above all, if you want to make a difference, back programs that inspire children to realize that they can grow up to be more than pawns.

Mrs. Grady and the Boy Who Made Her Cry

Sometimes the chance to make a difference comes in unexpected ways and places. Most of us encounter people in our daily lives who could use a hand—yet too often we don't reach out. Perhaps it's because we're embarrassed, we're running for a train or bus, we're grabbing groceries to make dinner, or we don't know quite what to offer. Perhaps we think contributions of one sort or another can't make a difference. But they can.

In the late 1950s, Olly Neal was a poor kid with an attitude and no obvious prospects. He was rebellious and resisted help. But his story is a reminder of the power of role models and mentors, particularly informal ones, and the dividends that can accrue from reaching out even to adolescents who seem beyond redemption.

Olly's father was a farmer with a second-grade education, and Olly was one of thirteen brothers and sisters living in a cramped house in rural Arkansas with no electricity. Olly attended a small school for black children—this was the segregated South—and was always mouthing off. Carolyn Blakely, then a new teacher at the school (now a retired professor who taught at the University of Arkansas), remembers Olly as an at-risk kid prone to challenge authority. At the time, teachers in the high school addressed the students as "Mr." or "Miss," and the students were expected to reciprocate. Olly disrupted class by addressing his teacher as "Carolyn." To deal with troublemakers like him, Blakely recalls, "I'd go home and stand in front of the mirror and practice being mean."

"He was a free spirit," Blakely recalls of young Olly Neal. "Olly had so much talent, and so much energy, and so much curiosity about things. But if it hadn't been directed into the right path, he could have gone in a bad direction." That's what seemed to be happening. A regular shoplifter, Olly Neal was finally caught stealing from the store where he worked part-time. He was fired from his job and seemed headed for a life in trouble. Then one day in 1957, in the fall of his senior year, Olly skipped Carolyn Blakely's class and wandered into the library, set up by an English teacher named Mildred Grady. Grady was an earnest, dedicated African American woman who had seen Olly as a smart kid with potential, and so she tried to reform him. He responded by mocking her and reducing her to tears.

"I was not a nice kid," Olly Neal recalls. "I had a reputation. I was the only one who made her cry. She would have had good reason to say, 'This boy is incorrigible.'"

That day in the library, Olly idly browsed the small book collection and spotted a book with a risqué cover of a scantily dressed woman. The book was *The Treasure of Pleasant Valley,* by Frank Yerby, a black author, and it looked vaguely appealing. Olly wasn't a reader, and he didn't want word to get out that he had checked a book out of the library, for fear of undermining his tough-guy image.

"So I stole it," he says.

He tucked the book under his jacket and read it at home in secret — and he loved it! Novels weren't a tedious bore, he discovered, but vehicles to transport him to new worlds. After finishing *The Treasure of Pleasant Valley,* Olly sneaked it back into the library and returned it to its place. And there, on the shelf, he noticed another novel by Yerby. The temptation was too great: he stole that one as well. This book too was riveting, and to Olly's surprise, when he returned it to the shelf after finishing it, he found yet another book by Yerby that he somehow hadn't noticed before. Four times this happened, and by then he was a devoted reader. "Reading got to be a thing I liked," he says. He soon graduated to literature, including novels by Albert Camus. He began reading newspapers and magazines as well, and became engaged in the social and political issues of the day. He began to dream, and his hopes became self-fulfilling when he went to college and ultimately law school, emerging as a pioneering black lawyer in Arkansas and an important figure in the civil rights movement.

In 1991, Neal became the first African American to be appointed district prosecuting attorney in Arkansas. A few years later, he became a judge, and then an appellate court judge. Throughout his distinguished legal career, Neal was a determined defender of the underprivileged, working to advance the health, literacy, and welfare of the needy. His daughter Karama absorbed the same spirit: after earning a doctorate in genetics, she taught bioethics at Emory University and now runs a community development program in Arkansas.

As one of his school's great successes, Neal always attended high school reunions. At one of those reunions, he got to chatting with Mildred Grady about how those books in her little school library had changed his life. She nodded, and confessed that she had spotted him stealing that first book. Her first impulse, she said, had been to confront him and reproach him for stealing a book that he could easily check out. Then, in a flash of insight, she had realized that he was embarrassed to be seen as a reader. So Mrs. Grady had kept quiet. And then the next Saturday, she had driven seventy miles to Memphis to see if she could find another novel by Yerby. There was no budget for gas or for books, but she was willing to use her own meager pay as a teacher at a segregated black school to buy a book in hopes that it would open Olly Neal's heart and mind. The first bookshop she had tried didn't have any books by Yerby, so she had visited a second and then a third. Finally, she had found one, bought it, and put it on the library bookshelf.

Mrs. Grady, who has since died, told Olly how thrilled she had been to see him steal the second book as well. Twice more, this bighearted woman spent her Saturdays trekking to Memphis to buy books by Yerby. As an African American woman denied opportunities because of her race and sex, Mildred Grady had plenty of reason to be bitter

Olly Neal, left, being sworn in as an Arkansas
circuit judge on January 1, 1993

at being stuck as a teacher in a rural segregated school with impertinent kids who didn't appreciate books or education. Instead, she
poured her soul into her students—and Arkansas really should name
a school after her. For Olly Neal was just one of many children whom
Mildred Grady transformed, offering opportunities that they ultimately seized.

"There are some kids who can't be reached," Judge Neal acknowledges. "But there are some that you can reach every now and then."
And he was one of them.

CHAPTER SEVEN

Coaching Troubled Teens

Act so that you treat humanity . . . always as
an end and never as a means only.

—IMMANUEL KANT

In Tulsa we watched a classroom of eighth graders, half boys and half girls, engaged in a curriculum focused on avoiding teenage pregnancy. Developed by a New York education expert, Michael Carrera, it is rated a "top-tier" program by the Coalition for Evidence-Based Policy and has been adopted in schools in low-income areas in twenty states. In the class we watched, the kids were discussing in a very non-didactic way how to deal with a boyfriend or girlfriend who pushes for sex. The teacher, Rebecca Breuer, asked the class what someone might say to pressure another into sex, and a bunch of boys and girls immediately raised their hands.

"If you don't do it, I'll break up with you," suggested a Latina girl in back.

"If you really loved me, you'd do it," offered an African American boy on the other side of the room. Heads nodded sagely with each comment.

"What's that called?" Breuer asked.

"Sexual coercion," several students piped up. Breuer nodded and began talking about how students can deal with a zealous partner when they're not ready for sex.

When writing about grit, we mentioned that using the criminal justice system to address the pathologies of poverty has been largely a failed strategy, particularly with teens. But an array of strategies have been shown through rigorous evidence to lift adolescents out of poverty. A starting point is family planning, in particular the effort to reduce teen pregnancies. Some 77 percent of American teen pregnancies are unintended, and outcomes are often grim when children have children. The mom may drop out of school, and the child is more likely to be raised in a stressful, high-poverty environment. In Tulsa, we met a family in which the matriarch had her first child at thirteen. Her daughter in turn had her first child at fifteen. And that woman's child gave birth, while on drugs, at age thirteen.

The world desperately needs to help kids avoid unintended pregnancies—for their sake and for the sake of their children. That means more comprehensive sex education programs in schools, and more publicly funded clinics to provide contraception. One study by the Guttmacher Institute found that without publicly funded contraception, the rate of unintended pregnancies among teenagers in the United States would be 73 percent higher. Public investment in pregnancy prevention is enormously cost effective, for unintended pregnancies cost taxpayers $12.5 billion a year—and that includes only the first year of health care for the infant. Each dollar invested in contraception programs pays for itself many times over, yet federal funding for family planning through Title X (the main United States source of such funds) is, after inflation, less than one-third what it was in 1980. There are many ways to get involved, from volunteering at a family planning clinic to joining one of the many Planned Parenthood initiatives, such as its college campus program.

The Carrera curriculum for middle schools and high schools is one of the most impressive efforts to deal with these issues. Devised with the help of the Children's Aid Society in New York, it aims to arm disadvantaged kids not just with condoms but with skills and self-confidence as well. The program runs from sixth grade through senior year of high school, and it includes discussions of health and sexuality and also of jobs, bank accounts, and financial literacy. The students get help opening their own savings accounts, and they get medical and dental care, vision care, and eyeglasses—even braces if they need them. All this encourages kids to sign up, and in socially conservative communities it reduces the sensitivity of the program as "sex education." It's an elective that students sign up for, and their parents have to consent because of the discussions about sexuality.

Dr. Carrera argues strongly that single-intervention approaches don't work very well, because one of the underlying reasons for pregnancy is fatalism and hopelessness. As he sees it, pregnancy prevention isn't just a technical matter of preventing eggs from meeting sperm; it's also about giving kids hope and determination so that they have a stake in the future and positively want to avoid pregnancy. "Wisdom in our work begins," Dr. Carrera says, "when we give up giving up."

Back in the Carrera classroom in Tulsa, the conversation segued to what happens when the sexual coercion comes not from a boyfriend or girlfriend but from an adult, and Breuer played video clips in which young people described their confusion as they were preyed on by family friends or other trusted adults. What followed was a remarkably adult conversation among eighth graders about erections and lubrication, and how a conflicted young person could feel a measure of physical arousal without consenting to sex. Breuer emphasized that whatever the arousal, consent is always necessary, and that "no" always means "no." Afterward we chatted a bit with the students, and one girl, Gabby, said she found the instruction enormously useful. Her older sister, she said, had given birth as a teenager—but maybe wouldn't have if she had been in the Carrera program. The Carrera program is expensive (in Tulsa, it costs $2,300 per student per year), but that's nothing compared to the multibillion-dollar cost each year of 750,000 teen pregnancies in America. Carrera classes are mostly paid for by school districts or foundations, but the program eagerly accepts donations as well. A $50 gift, for example, covers the cost of seeding a savings account for a student as part of the financial literacy component of the Carrera curriculum.

There are other initiatives that have been invaluable in reducing unwanted babies, aside from provision of family planning. A Chicago organization, Options for Youth, has worked with 4,000 adolescent mothers and tried to get them back into the education system. A ten-year evaluation found that only 3 percent of these young women had a repeat pregnancy as a teenager, much lower than among comparable girls. Meanwhile, more than 70 percent of the girls in the program graduate from high school, twice the national average for teenage moms.

Beyond pregnancy prevention, schools are an important way to reach troubled children and turn their lives around, and a good teacher can have a remarkable impact even in a troubled school system. A Harvard study found that in a large, urban public school system, a particularly good elementary school teacher improves long-term outcomes enough to raise the lifetime earnings of a classroom of kids by $700,000, compared to an average teacher. Some teachers do this consistently year after year. Yet the most effective teachers often work in upper-middle-class schools that least need an advantage, while inner-city kids of color are more likely to get the least effective teachers. A Los Angeles study suggested that if African American students had a teacher from the top 25 percent, instead of the bottom 25 percent, of effectiveness, and if results accumulate for four years in a row, the race gap might even disappear. To attract and retain more top-flight teachers in inner city schools, we must pay them more or otherwise incentivize them.

We also must rethink the role of schools in low-income communities. For example, according to research, one of the most dangerous times of day for kids living in tough neighborhoods is between 2:00 p.m. and 6:00 p.m. Young girls find themselves at the highest risk of sex leading to pregnancy, and young men get into fights that put their lives at risk. We could dispatch more police to the streets in those hours, or we could better utilize an infrastructure in which we as a society have invested billions of dollars: schools. Too many of them in low-income communities close their doors at 2:00 p.m. or 3:00 p.m.

"They're padlocked, and just outside there are kids living this life of extreme danger," says Luis Ubiñas, former president of the Ford Foundation. "So, what do we do?" Ford's answer is to expand the learning day at these schools. Having helped spawn a wave of programs in early childhood, the Ford Foundation has moved up the age ladder to help struggling schools expand the typical school day and keep kids off the streets. After-school clubs are common in high-income school districts but almost nonexistent in low-income neighborhoods. Ubiñas, who grew up in the South Bronx and found traction as one of the first children to join Head Start in the 1960s, told us that a child in an affluent family may have spent as much as 50 percent more time in school, summer school, or other enrichment activities by age eighteen than a low-income child.

To address this problem, the Ford Foundation supported a three-hour after-school apprenticeship program called Citizen Schools as a "second shift" in middle schools in low-income neighborhoods. Students get tutoring, participate in college and career programs, and receive professional development courses. First started in Boston, the program invites volunteers to come in and talk to classes about their work and white collar life. These volunteers—from companies, universities, or nonprofit organizations—teach ninety-minute classes once a week for ten weeks to expose students to law, business, engineering, science, and other fields. The volunteers also offer a certain amount of coaching about goal setting. Results are encouraging: students gained 8 percentiles on standardized tests in math and 2 percentiles in English, at a cost less than $2,000 per pupil.

In some states, at-risk young people and their families can be coached together. One evidence-backed program is Youth Villages, which is a bit like a Nurse-Family Partnership for at-risk teenagers and their families. A nonprofit founded in 1986, it coaches low-income moms and dads—or some other relative—and gives them support so that they can do a better job of parenting. Today Youth Villages works with adolescent boys and girls in eleven states, offering both residential centers and home support—what it calls "building strong families."

Among those helped by Youth Villages is Fred Burns, one of ten children born to an impoverished couple in Tennessee who struggled with drug addiction and domestic violence. The family moved in and out of homeless shelters and rarely had much food; Fred sometimes had to steal so that he and his siblings had something to eat. Fred grew up with a serious anger and aggression problem, and at age thirteen he was placed in foster care. That led to a roller coaster of eight foster homes in succession, and his behavior problems finally landed him in a Youth Villages residential facility. Mentors began to work with Fred, hearing him out and coaching him on patience in a long-term relationship that deepened into friendship. "You felt like they were really trying to work together and make things better for you," he said. "They supported me and they made sure I kept going."

As Fred calmed down, Youth Villages looked for a relative stable enough to continue raising him. An aunt, Shirley, agreed a bit reluctantly, because she wasn't sure that she could handle a teenager, but a Youth Villages social worker supported them during this adjustment process. Gradually Fred settled down, and Shirley formally adopted him when he was sixteen years old. With this new stability in his life,

Fred Burns addresses his classmates as valedictorian during Wingfield High School graduation ceremonies in Jackson, Mississippi.

Fred began to excel in sports and academics. He became the first member in his family to graduate from high school, and he did it in style: he was valedictorian, with a 4.25 GPA. Fred accepted an academic scholarship to Mississippi State University, was successful as a walk-on to the football team, and later transferred to Jackson State University to major in computer engineering.

Now twenty-three and a college senior, Fred tutors and mentors other youths, coaches football, and gives gifts at Christmas to other families. "The time that everyone has put into me is the reason that I am what I am today," he told us. "I'm giving back because people have been believing in me, and somebody believing in me has helped me believe in myself. I'm doing for others what others have done for me."

The Youth Villages programs, which have been rigorously evaluated, claim a long-term success rate with troubled adolescents of 80 percent, meaning that they are living with families or on their own and have had no trouble with the law. That success rate is twice the national average, even though Youth Villages programs cost only one-third as much as traditional approaches. Youth Villages argues that with the right support and scrutiny, half of the 600,000 kids in America being raised in effect by the state (including foster care) could remain with their families or relatives, saving tens of millions of dollars annually and reducing the trauma and upheaval for those children.

Another school intervention that seems to matter a good deal is working with very bright high school students who don't have the background or home support that puts them into a pipeline to the best universities. Many outstanding high school students don't think much about college, because it is seen as unaffordable or because their families never went to college. They may not realize that it is often cheaper to attend a first-rate private college on a scholarship than to attend a local state university or even community college, and guidance counselors at troubled high schools are often too swamped to be of much help. One solution is the College Advising Corps, which has a model similar to Teach for America and places dynamic recent graduates as college advisers inside low-income high schools to guide students through the process of considering colleges, applying, seeking financial aid, and enrolling. The advisers work for two years and receive stipends. The advising corps is already in hundreds of high schools in fourteen states and is expanding rapidly.

Job-training programs, job subsidies, and other initiatives to move juvenile offenders into the workplace are often good bets. Ronald Reagan had a point when he said that "the best social program is a job." One type of program that has had excellent results is the career academy, which trains at-risk teenagers in specialized careers and gives them practical work experience. Eight years later, those young people randomly assigned to career academies are earning significantly more than those in control groups. Because of their success, there are now 7,000 career academies in America serving 1 million students.

Jobs are crucial not just because of the earnings they provide, but also because of the boost to self-identity and self-confidence. Researchers at Harvard examined why it is that life expectancy has fallen by five years for white female high school dropouts between 1990 and 2008 (a decline surpassed in the industrialized world only by Russians after the fall of the Soviet Union). The scholars examined many possibilities, including obesity, poverty, and marital status. Only two factors seemed closely linked to early death: one was smoking (no surprise there) and the other was not having a job. The researchers suggest that a job brings a sense of purpose to life, a feeling of control over one's surroundings, and social interactions to counteract loneliness and depression.

Make no mistake, these are difficult social issues and we don't pretend that there are easy solutions. Skeptics are right that human behavior is infinitely complex and that government programs can have unintended consequences; it's equally true that resources are limited, and we have to make difficult choices about our priorities for investment. Our argument is that for all the uncertainty, the data suggest that we have underinvested in interventions at the beginning of life—family planning, pregnancy, infancy, childhood—despite growing evidence that they have the highest returns. In contrast, antipoverty investments in America have been disproportionately about supporting the elderly and creating safety nets. Social Security and Medicare have reduced the poverty rate among senior citizens from 35 percent in 1959 to 9 percent today. That's a remarkable success story, attributable to the voting power of seniors. The United States has likewise directed education spending disproportionately at universities. We believe in programs for the elderly, in safety nets, in universities. But we think it is time to raise spending where it goes furthest, in targeting children, and that the earlier the intervention, the better.

Children don't vote (and low-income parents don't vote very often), so child poverty rarely rises on the political agenda—and that's probably why children are the age group most likely to live in poverty in America. But when countries have made a concerted effort to expand opportunity, they have succeeded. Here are a couple of examples with lessons for the United States:

- In March 1999, British prime minister Tony Blair made a historic speech pledging to end child poverty in twenty years. "The announcement startled the journalists, advocates and academics he had invited to hear him," says Jane Waldfogel, a Columbia University professor who wrote a book about Britain's war on child poverty. "Yet once the pledge was made, it took on a life of its own. Overnight, it seemed only right that the government should be aiming to reduce child poverty significantly and to promote more equal life chances for children." Blair promised universal preschool beginning at age three and a community support program called Sure Start for low-income families with children under three. He emphasized efforts to raise wages. Not all the initiatives succeeded, and unforeseen problems arose. But in the first five years, Blair managed to cut the proportion of children living in poverty from 26 percent to 14 percent. Many in Britain will protest that it wasn't enough and that it wasn't sustained; from across the Atlantic, it is an impressive example of what leadership and political will can accomplish.

- Mexico had a dysfunctional antipoverty bureaucracy that focused on providing a safety net through food subsidies, rather than building opportunity. Reformers saw that one of the underlying problems of Mexican poverty was that poor families did not invest in children in the way middle-class families did, and so they devised a program to (in effect) bribe impoverished parents to keep children in school and take them to medical clinics. The reformers field-tested this initiative in 1995, rigorously assessed the results, and showed them to President Ernesto Zedillo. Zedillo bravely took on Mexico's interest groups and phased out the food subsidies, replacing them with a program now called Oportunidades. It has become one of the most admired antipoverty programs worldwide, relying upon "conditional cash transfers" (development-speak for bribes) to families who meet conditions such as sending daughters to school. The World Bank says that Oportunidades raised high school attendance by 10 percent for boys and 20 percent for girls, and the children enrolled in the program gained an extra centimeter in height per year compared to those in a control group. Some studies suggest that Oportunidades will pay for itself by building the human capital to power Mexico's industrial revolution, and by reducing future welfare costs.

The United States can enjoy the same kind of progress as Great Britain and Mexico. What is lacking is political will—and a public outcry.

A Milestone for Jessica

We opened our exploration of building opportunities for children in America with the story of Jessica, our Oregon neighbor. The conclusion of her saga serves as a reminder that, with strong and dedicated support from others, even huge challenges can be overcome.

In seventh grade, Jessica was living in a trailer with her mom and brother, Nathan. Drug-related visitors came and went, the electricity and water periodically were shut off for nonpayment of bills, and there was often no food in the house. Jessica put up with it because she wanted to be with her mother. She rarely went to school but would prowl the neighborhood and break into homes, stealing food and clothing.

For a time Jessica had a boyfriend with whom she shyly held hands. Her mom invited the boy over for the night and put him in Jessica's room, instructing them to share the bed. Jessica kept him at arm's length all night, thinking, *This can't be how most moms behave.* When Jessica mouthed off, her mother would rage back at her. "I was an unbearable kid," Jessica admits, "and my mother would say she wished I'd never been born."

Maybe the worst came when a young man moved into their trailer and was sharing drugs with Jessica's mom. Then he took a shine to Jessica—who had just turned thirteen and was becoming an attractive blonde—and showed up in her bedroom at night. "I want to have sex with you," he told her bluntly.

"No!" she told him.

Then, she says, he held her down and raped her. Jessica says that she told her mother, who didn't want to hear it. Almost every night, the man would show up in her room and force himself on her. That was seventh grade for Jessica.

That year of torment ended when the family was evicted from the trailer for nonpayment of rent. As eighth grade was beginning, Jessica's mom dropped her off with an old family friend, Jeff, an alcoholic prone to rages. He tried to raise Jessica and keep her out of trouble, but she was a rebellious, impertinent troublemaker who talked back. Jeff and his wife steadily turned against Jessica.

"You're nothing!" Jessica remembers Jeff shouting at her one day in a drunken rage. "You're nothing. You're going to end up just like your mom!"

After Jeff, while drunk, punched Jessica in the face one night, she ran out into the darkness. There was a home she used to walk past where two dogs lived, and as she fled, she saw the dogs and crept into the backyard with them. The homeowner heard the dogs barking and called the police, and Jeff wound up in jail. When Jessica went by a few days later to pick up her belongings, Jeff's wife wordlessly handed her a backpack with everything Jessica had in the world. As Jeff's wife saw it, the couple had tried to help—and Jessica had upended the house and caused Jeff's jailing.

This was a low point in Jessica's life, but it also proved a turning point. A social service agency placed Jessica with foster parents, Mike and Lark Ring. Mike is a crane operator, and Jessica already knew Lark as her former school bus driver. The Rings had four grown biological children and over the years had hosted dozens of foster children. Some stayed only for a few days while arrangements were worked out, and others stayed years. At any one time, the Rings usually had about four foster kids in the house.

Lark treated Jessica with a mix of firm discipline and unrelenting love. She told Jessica that she herself had been a foster child and had been through hell. Lark had been just five months old when her mom shipped her off to her dad and stepmother, and later she was handed off to other family members and then a succession of foster homes. Some foster parents sexually and physically abused her, and she remembers being stripped naked at one house and beaten with a hose. Finally, in ninth grade Lark was placed with a foster family that embraced her with love, and she began to turn herself around. As an adult, after she married Mike, she began to take in foster children herself, as a way of paying it forward.

Jessica was a headache but not, Lark thought, beyond redemption. Lark saw Jessica as an echo of her childhood self, and she told the girl, "I survived, and so can you." Slowly Lark began to chip away at the barriers the girl had constructed. There were still some ferocious battles, but Lark could be tough. She barred the girl from wearing tops that were low-cut or showed her belly, and Jessica was grounded when she lied or broke house rules. "I would growl at her," says Lark, "and then I'd go back and tell her that I loved her."

In ninth grade, Jessica was performing a bit better in school, but she was still an obvious loner who didn't always do homework and was capable of much more. In sophomore year, a boy whom Jessica liked made fun of her. Jessica went home and cried. Lark found her and hugged her. "God loves you," Lark repeated to her over and over, and they held each other. As the tears slowed they talked. Jessica came to feel that she did have an ally after all. With that, she began to turn herself around in school. When Jessica worked hard, she found, she could get A's. She was looked at with new respect. This was a novelty, to be regarded as a smart kid. By senior year in high school, Jessica was getting nothing but A's, while also working as a lifeguard to earn money, and she began to dream of becoming the first person in her family to go to college. Jessica persuaded the high school to let her take online college classes and earn credits, to show colleges—which might be skeptical of her early bad grades—that she could do the work.

We were astonished when we next saw Jessica. She had dyed her hair dark brown and her demeanor was completely different. The wild, crazy girl had become demure. She had also begun to forgive her mom, after long, frank, anguished conversations between the two of them. As Jessica puts it: "She gave birth to me. I still respect her for that and I still love her for that. There are some things that I can't forgive, but I still care about her because she's my mother."

Jessica graduated from high school and in 2012 she entered Western Oregon University on a scholarship. She plans on a career in law enforcement, in hopes of working with troubled kids like her old self. She figures that she owes everything to Lark's efforts. "I'd like to help somebody else like others helped me," she said. "I want to help those who can't get here on their own. Maybe I can reach out to them and say, I was there."

After a year of college, Jessica ran out of money and had to drop out to get a job to work and save for a time before returning. It looks as if her college education will be a start-and-stop process as she struggles to pay the bills, but she's determined to earn her degree. Jessica's story is a reminder that even very messed-up teenagers can, with a shoulder to lean on, show stunning resilience, and that poverty in America is not inescapable.

CHAPTER EIGHT

The Power of Hope

To eat bread without hope is still slowly to starve to death.

— PEARL S. BUCK

Jovali Obamza, a bright fourth-grade boy in a remote village in the Congo Republic, a three-day drive from the capital, Brazzaville, was about to be expelled from school for falling three months behind in school fees—or $7.50. He desperately wanted to stay in school and knew that his life's prospects hung in the balance.

Jovali's parents were very, very poor. The father, Georges Obamza, weaves wicker stools out of straw and sells them for $1 each, and he and his wife, Valérie, have six surviving children to support. Two others died of malaria; the family still can't afford a $6 mosquito bed net. The family was eight months behind on their $6-a-month rent and thus faced the risk of eviction and being left homeless in the jungle. Jovali has two other school-age siblings (the other three are younger) and they don't go to school regularly either, because of the $2.50 school fees per child per month.

We've met plenty of Americans who are drawn to help children like Jovali, thousands of miles away, where small donations can often have a larger impact than at home. But these Americans also worry that donations accomplish nothing because people are poor as a result of self-destructive behaviors, from substance abuse to laziness. In this view, helping the poor is like putting a dollar bill into a homeless drug addict's tin can and thinking it will go for food. Whenever Nick writes about programs to help the poor in his *New York Times* column, he gets a torrent of responses to the effect that such programs only reward indolence.

The blunt truth is that this cynical view has a certain foundation: self-destructive behaviors are indeed a factor in poverty at home and abroad. We must acknowledge all the underlying pathologies, including the human capacity to make bad choices. But these issues are far more complex than cynics believe, and the solution is not just to scold the poor. Humans anywhere in the world can be locked in a "poverty trap" of despair and sometimes clinical depression. One way of making a difference is to provide a ray of hope. We think this is an important new area of research, and scholarly understanding of it is still unfolding, but it helps explain a great deal of what we've seen both in the United States and abroad—and ultimately it's encouraging in that it offers tools to make a difference, spreading opportunity to adults as well as children.

Georges Obamza says he goes drinking several evenings a week at a village bar. He figures he spends $12 a month on alcohol, enough to pay rent and Jovali's school fees with some left over. Other villagers said the numbers sounded right but that Georges is actually less of a drinker than many other local men. That is a pattern we have seen around the world; even in Muslim countries such as Iran or Pakistan, where alcohol is theoretically banned, there are speakeasies where men gather in the evening to spend hard-won cash. In central Kenya, a government-backed study found that men spend more money on alcohol than on food. Esther Duflo and Abhijit Banerjee write that the world's poor typically spend 2 percent of incomes educating children. They spend twice as much on alcohol and tobacco as on education in rural Papua New Guinea, three times as much in Udaipur, India, and four times as much in Guatemala. Substance abuse is also a significant factor in poverty in America, of course.

Why are there such self-destructive patterns all over the world? In part they arise because life in an impoverished village or slum is dreary, tedious, and depressing. If we were Georges Obamza, facing eviction and watching his children die of malaria or be expelled from school for nonpayment of school fees, we might seek comfort from a drink, too. Embedded in the human psyche is a yearning for fun, entertainment, and companionship, if only as short-term relief from long-term misery. When in poverty, so many people feel locked in a trajectory of hopelessness, and they sometimes respond in ways

Georges Obamza and his six children in the Congo Republic

that make that hopelessness self-fulfilling and transmit it to the next generation.

Poverty is often accompanied by clinical depression. A 2010 Urban Institute study found that 55 percent of American babies in poverty are raised by mothers who show symptoms of mild to severe depression, which in many cases impairs a woman's ability to attach to her child emotionally. "A mom who is too sad to get up in the morning won't be able to take care of all of her child's practical needs," noted Olivia Golden, a coauthor of the paper. "If she is not able to take joy in her child, talk baby talk, play with the child—those are features of parenting that brain development research has told us contribute to babies' and toddlers' successful development."

In the United States, a Gallup poll in 2012 found that 31 percent of people living in poverty said that they had been diagnosed with depression, compared to 16 percent of other Americans. The problem isn't just lack of money, but also the sense of hopelessness that pervades many low-income areas. When randomly chosen households in high-poverty neighborhoods were able to move to higher-income areas in an experiment called "moving to opportunity," mental health improved as much as could have been expected from the most effective prescription medications.

Abroad, the same pattern holds. Anne Case and Angus Deaton of Princeton University found frequent markers of depression among poor people they surveyed worldwide. Almost one-third of women in Udaipur, India, said that they "cried a lot" some or most of the time, and 49 percent were sad some or most of the time. Across South Africa and India, roughly one-quarter to one-third of those surveyed said they didn't feel like working or eating, had trouble sleeping, and spent a month or longer worried "most of the time." Of those who worried in this way, as many as half said this interfered with normal activity "a lot." Another study, by the University of Queensland in Australia, found that the country with the highest rate of depression is Afghanistan, with the Middle East and North Africa also suffering very high rates.

Poor people like Georges become depressed in part because it's extremely stressful living on the precipice. When we are stressed, as we've seen, we produce more cortisol, and researchers have found more cortisol in poor Kenyans in times of drought. The cortisol matters because, in the prefrontal cortex of the brain, it can interfere with impulse control, and that may be one reason why people under stress sometimes adopt self-destructive behaviors.

Scientists have found that when people are worrying they are drained of cognitive power and self-discipline. When experimenters ask people not to think about a white bear, the brain of course immediately conjures a white bear—and trying to suppress the thought becomes a burden. Afterward, those people choose a less healthy snack than do those who haven't received the white bear instruction. Likewise, Sendhil Mullainathan and Eldar Shafir, coauthors of a new book, *Scarcity,* found that poor people who have been primed to worry about a $1,500 car repair bill do worse on an IQ test than those worrying about a $150 car repair. When people spend their days fretting about eviction, electricity cut-offs, bills, and jobs, they're biologically less able to exert self-control.

In another example of how the stresses of poverty can impair our abilities, Mullainathan administered an intelligence test to sugar cane farmers in India, both before the harvest (when they were worrying about economic pressures) and afterward, when they faced a respite from those pressures. The farmers did much better after the harvest, apparently because their minds were no longer preoccupied with economic challenges. The research found that having to worry about a serious financial problem costs a person the equivalent of 13 points of IQ. The study's conclusion was that the poor "are less capable not because of inherent traits, but because the very context of poverty imposes load and impedes cognitive capacity."

Some insight into the pathologies of poverty comes from a set of experiments in the mid-1960s that, fortunately, no review board would permit today. These started at the University of Pennsylvania as a variant of Pavlov's famous work with dogs. Instead of getting dogs to associate bell-ringing with feeding, researchers aimed to make dogs link a high-pitched tone with an electric shock. The thesis was that if dogs were shocked after they heard the tone, they would learn to react to the tone and flee at once, without waiting for the shock. In preparation for this, the dogs were trussed up and subjected to the high-pitched tones and then the electric shocks. Then the real experiment began, and the dogs were put in crates from which they could easily escape.

To the researchers' surprise, when the shocks began, the dogs didn't try to escape. They just lay there in the crates, whimpering sadly. The experiment seemed a failure. Fortunately, one of the young graduate students freshly arrived on the scene was Martin E. P. Seligman, then just twenty-one years old, and he had an epiphany. The dogs, he realized, had learned futility. They had been conditioned to give up. "During Pavlovian conditioning they felt the shocks go on and off regardless of whether they struggled or jumped or barked or did nothing at all," Seligman writes. "They had concluded, or 'learned,' that nothing they did mattered. So why try?"

Seligman launched a new series of experiments. Some dogs were exposed to shocks that they could turn off by pressing a lever with their noses, and they quickly learned to do so. Other dogs, the control group, were not given shocks. A third group of unfortunate dogs was exposed to shocks that they could do nothing about. The result? When the dogs from these various groups were put in the crates and exposed to shocks, those in the control group that had not previously been shocked promptly jumped out. So did the dogs that had learned they could turn off the shocks. But the dogs that had been exposed to shocks over which they had no control just gave up, lay down, and whimpered.

"Clearly, animals can learn their actions are futile," Seligman writes, "and when they do, they no longer initiate action; they become passive." Seligman called this response "learned helplessness," and the general principle has been confirmed in many other studies. The phenomenon has been found not only in lab animals but also in humans (in the case of humans, of course, not with electrical shocks).

Is there an analogy to poverty? To be poor often means that bad things regularly happen that you cannot avoid or control. This is particularly true where racism or other prejudices seem to make escape impossible—as with blacks historically in the United States or with the burakumin minority in Japan. The burakumin are ethnically the same as other Japanese but constitute an occupational minority (descendants of those who handled dead bodies or were in other "unclean" jobs) and were confined to particular neighborhoods and barred from intermarriage. Among the burakumin, rates of crime and alcoholism have been high; many of Japan's yakuza gangsters are burakumin or from the ethnic Korean minority, which has also suffered widespread discrimination. When groups are not only poor but also see no way to a better life, they more easily surrender.

Interventions that create hope, such as microsavings schemes and entrepreneurship training, can shatter this cycle.* Seligman found that learned helplessness can be unlearned. When people or animals learn they can escape their situation, they lose their passivity. They take responsibility.

Esther Duflo and Abhijit Banerjee were conducting a randomized controlled trial of an antipoverty initiative initially developed by BRAC, a highly regarded Bangladeshi aid group, when they discerned the power of hope. The initiative, in this case implemented by an Indian microfinance group called Bandhan, involved finding the poorest of the poor in a village, then offering these families a pair of cows, a small herd of goats, or a flock of chickens, and helping them build a small business. Duflo and her colleagues meticulously studied the impact of this program and discovered something puzzling: it was *too* successful. It produced wealth even in areas seemingly unrelated to the livestock. The families in the study earned seven times as much money from livestock as they had before, which made some sense, but they also

---

* So can giving more control over purse strings to women. Only about 1 percent of land titles are in the hands of women, and there's evidence that when women own assets the money generated is more likely to support children's education. An organization called Landesa, based in Seattle, has done excellent work gaining property rights for more than 100 million poor people around the world, in particular women. Simply ensuring that widows and daughters can inherit property when men die may be a step toward reallocating funds from alcohol or drugs to children's education.

earned 50 percent more from nonagricultural businesses, even though these weren't part of the program. They earned three times as much from tending their own fields, which also hadn't changed. The families were eating significantly better and had more savings, and were more likely to be giving food to other people. The magnitude of the improvement in living conditions couldn't be explained by the value of the gift of goats or a couple of cows. They now had more money than seemed plausible. Similar findings had emerged at half a dozen sites worldwide, so it wasn't a mistake. What was going on?

One clue is that after eighteen months, those who received livestock reported significant improvements in mental health. They showed fewer signs of stress, anxiety, and depression and said that their overall health had improved (although there was no apparent outward improvement in physical health). Another clue: recipients of livestock were now spending 28 percent more time working. Their children were also devoting more time to studying.

"What we hypothesize, although we cannot directly confirm it using this data, is that this improved mental health is what gave participants the energy to work more, save, and invest in their children," Duflo explained. When lack of hope creates a "poverty trap," she says, the proper response is to inject hope. Duflo noted that skeptics have long cautioned that microcredit would lead to families spending more money on "temptation goods"—soda, alcohol, tobacco, candy—but that in fact careful monitoring suggests that microfinance leads families to spend less on frivolities. Once families discern a pathway to a better life, they find it easier to save and invest for a brighter future. We believe that many successful aid programs, like the gifts of livestock, work not so much because of the gift itself but because they create hope that turns passivity into action.

One bit of evidence for this may come from child sponsorship programs, the kind where an American sends $30 a month to support a child in a needy country. More than 9 million children are sponsored in this way, and we ourselves have sponsored children through Plan USA in Sudan, Haiti, Philippines, and the Dominican Republic.* Many other organizations have sponsorship programs as well, includ-

---

* We have visited our sponsored children in Sudan, Philippines, and the Dominican Republic and strongly encourage it, particularly as a family journey. It's truly wonderful to visit a child whom you have been writing letters to, and seeing photos of, for years. Both sides find it pretty exciting.

ing World Vision, Save the Children, and Compassion International, though their models vary. We have always liked the way Plan USA focuses on developing the entire village rather than just the child, partly to avoid creating jealousies and partly because it's often more efficient to build a new well or school for an entire village than to nurture a particular child. Compassion International, on the other hand, is a Christian organization that focuses on the individual sponsored child. It emphasizes building hope, self-confidence, and spiritual growth. The sponsored children in Compassion International get at least eight hours a week of special tutoring and counseling, attend special retreats, and get coaching in goal setting.

In 2013 Bruce Wydick of the University of San Francisco published a meticulous six-country study of more than 10,000 children who had been sponsored through Compassion International, comparing their outcomes to siblings who were slightly too old to be eligible for sponsorship. He found that sponsored children gained more than an extra year of schooling and were significantly more likely to finish high school and even college. They eventually rose to more sophisticated jobs, such as becoming teachers. It was the best evidence yet that child sponsorship accords a lifelong benefit to children and communities, but Wydick found that the impact came not from the general development work but from the focus on raising individual aspirations and self-esteem. The sponsored children had greater expectations for themselves, more self-confidence, and less hopelessness. They were more likely to aspire to a solid education and a good job, and they were more optimistic in general. "Child sponsorship strongly and positively impacts a wide array of psychological measures in children," the researchers found. Wydick concluded that antipoverty organizations didn't focus enough on addressing psychological impediments such as passivity and lack of self-esteem. As he put it to us:

> Traditionally, development has focused on the relief of what economists call "external constraints": people need fresh water, so we build a well; they need schooling, so we build schools; they need credit, so we provide microfinance. But the "internal constraints" of the poor are perhaps even more important: helping the poor, especially children, to expand their view of their own capabilities, to develop goals, new reference points, and aspirations. It may be that when a belief in self-efficacy and aspirations have taken root, the

Bruce Wydick with Compassion International
children in Indonesia

poor learn to develop ways to deal with the external constraints on
their own, and these other issues begin to take care of themselves.

Wydick worries that leading aid groups "train people to become
receivers, instead of givers," and adds: "This may neutralize well-
intentioned efforts to help the poor." Wydick himself runs a small
nonprofit in Guatemala, and he says that this line of research has led
him to focus less on "opening up the goodie bag" and more on nurturing self-confidence and optimism. "I am coming to believe," he says,
"that this idea of 'bringing hope to the children' isn't so much a trite
phrase, but embodies something quite profound."

A common problem with aid programs, we've found, is that locals
don't feel "ownership." Outsiders come in, identify problems, and tell
everybody what to do. One of the wisest observers of global development is Josh Ruxin, an American public health expert who has lived
for many years in Rwanda. In his book *A Thousand Hills to Heaven*
he recounts that a colleague of his once asked community leaders
what their biggest problem was. Ruxin thought it would be lack of
food, the need for electricity, or problems with schooling. His colleague reported differently:

"They said alcoholism. The men are using what productive fields
they have for bananas for banana beer and it is holding the community back!"

"Did you ask them how to fix that?"

"They think it is all about despair. If we convince everyone that prosperity is possible, they will change. They will not drink or use their fields for that."

Ruxin and his Rwandan colleagues tried many strategies to overcome that despair, and overall they succeeded. But one of Ruxin's seemingly good ideas serves to illustrate how important it is to involve local people in decision making. Ruxin's idea was to introduce a high-value crop, pomegranates, which were ideally suited for the soil and climate and could be sold for very high prices. Ruxin contacted POM, a maker of pomegranate juice in California, and obtained a donation of 600 pomegranate plants to create a large cooperative in rural Rwanda. This seemed such a promising notion that the U.S. African Development Foundation invested in the project, hiring consultants and taking over the initiative while Ruxin and his wife, Alissa, were back in the United States. That's when everything went wrong:

> The lead consultant thought that the co-op workers should be paid for preparing the land, multiplying the stock, and overseeing the office. Instantly, the U.S. funds became the harvest and the co-op's president took control of all financial transactions. Those who were not getting paid refused to help plant or prune. It became about the job and the money in hand, not about the future of the community. . . . Anger doomed the project, and it was mostly abandoned.

The notion of ensuring local buy-in overlaps with warnings against creating dependency from many leaders in the developing world. "Charity is no solution to poverty," warns Muhammad Yunus of Grameen Bank. "Charity only perpetuates poverty by taking the initiative away from the poor." Likewise, President Paul Kagame of Rwanda has worried aloud to us that too much aid leads to overreliance on outsiders and insufficient drive and gumption. Obviously, it's not simple: the gifts of animals in the BRAC program were charity, yet they worked wonderfully.

One of the debates in the antipoverty community is about programs that simply hand cash to the poor, on the theory that they know better than outsiders what to do with it. These "unconditional transfers" have exceptionally low administrative costs, because they don't entail much more than handing out money. An American group called GiveDirectly aims to give 90 cents of every dollar donated to an extremely poor family in Kenya. The families use the money to replace a thatch roof with tin, buy school uniforms, buy land, or do whatever else they choose—the money is theirs. The grants are not renewable, which may guard against dependency. We were initially wary of this approach, partly for fear that money would go toward the purchase of alcohol or drugs, but early evidence is promising. A randomized controlled trial found that the gifts of cash reduce hunger and increase investments in livestock without increasing spending on temptation goods such as alcohol. People were happier and their bodies had less cortisol. This is an experiment worth watching.

On balance, we think there are ways to make aid magnify hope and curb dependency, such as requiring local people to invest their own sweat equity in a project and take ownership of it. We also think that some of the most important kinds of assistance are those that create jobs so that the poor can earn their own way to a better life. The best three-letter weapon against poverty is spelled not A-I-D but J-O-B.

Americans sometimes hint that it's not worth saving people's lives in poor countries because then they'll just have more kids: *Until families curb the number of children they have, the sad truth is that there's no reason to try to save lives from malaria or TB or hunger.*

We disagree. That Malthusian argument is a canard. In fact, it's increasingly clear that one reason people have large families is because they expect some children to die. Give them hope that their children will live, and they'll have fewer kids. The history of demography is that after child mortality rates drop, birth rates tumble as well, after about a twenty-year lag. Indeed, we're already seeing fertility rates dropping sharply in poor countries. Indian women, for example, now average just 2.6 babies—down from almost 6 in 1950. Bangladeshi women average just 2.3 babies, and Mexican women 2.2 babies. The United Nations Population Fund calculates that the number of children under the age of fifteen will end the century no higher than it is now.

It's true that we have to do better at providing comprehensive family planning in poor countries (and also in the United States, especially among at-risk teenagers), and it's a tragedy that some

220 million women around the world don't want to get pregnant but lack access to contraception. We need to do a better job in the field making contraceptives available and developing contraceptives that are cheap, effective, and don't require medical personnel to use. Nonprofits such as the Population Institute in New York and Path in Seattle are developing new contraceptives, such as a vaginal ring that a woman can use without her partner necessarily knowing; it can protect not only against pregnancy but against HIV as well. We need more of these efforts to support contraception, but it would be wrong to refuse to help people until birth rates drop. The way to deal with population pressures is to reduce child mortality and support family planning and education, while planting hope.

A Kenyan Named Kennedy

One of the largest slums in Africa is Kibera, a vast agglomeration of winding mud alleys and makeshift shacks in Nairobi. Crime is widespread; garbage and sewage are everywhere. People sometimes defecate into plastic bags and then dispose of them by hurling them into the distance—so-called flying toilets. Life here can be smelly, scary, and depressing, and you see young men sprawled in the dirt alleys drunk or drugged into a stupor. They've given up.

This is where Kennedy Odede grew up. He was born to a fifteen-year-old unwed mother, and the community discussed killing him at birth, for such was his tribe's tradition for male babies born out of wedlock (to prevent them from making claims of paternity and inheritance against other families). But the elders decided to spare this baby for two reasons. First, a drought had just ended, and it was considered auspicious that Kennedy's birth coincided with the much-anticipated rains. Second, he arrived by a breech birth, with no medical help, and there was a local tradition that a baby who arrived feet first and survived would grow up to be a leader. So the elders decided to let the boy live and named him after a person who to them exemplified leadership—President John Kennedy—while also saddling him with the middle name Owiti, meaning "unwanted."

Kennedy Odede's mother was illiterate, and he never knew who his father was. By all odds, Kennedy should be one of those unemployed men in a stupor, for he was the eldest of eight children and received no formal education himself. He was lucky to get one meal a day. "We could not be full, so we would drink lots of water," he remembers. At the age of seven he was selling peanuts in the market to help his family survive. His mother then married a man who was brutal to her and to Kennedy, and the boy noticed that his presence made his stepfather beat his mother more. So at the age of ten he ran away from home and began living on the streets, sleeping under stalls in the marketplace.

Yet somehow young Kennedy was imbued with a mysterious confidence in the future, perhaps because he knew that elders expected him to become a leader. "I think some people are simply born as hopeful people—it sounds funny to say so, but I can't think of any other explanation," he says. "I always woke up especially early, around 4:00 a.m., determined to make each day better than the last." Then he would watch the sun rise as he thought about something his mom would tell the children when they were especially hungry: *You should be grateful for things that are given to rich and poor in the same measure, like the light of the sun.*

For a few months, the boy attended an informal street school and learned the alphabet. After he had to drop out for want of school fees, he kept looking at words and trying to sound them out. A neighborhood boy, Omondi, who was an excellent student at a government school, taught Kennedy what he learned in class. Kennedy was obsessed with learning and desperate to read. When he found scraps of old newspaper in the market he would struggle to read the words, asking people for help. A Catholic priest in Kibera admired the boy's passion for literacy and gave him an English dictionary, which became a means for further self-improvement, and then a nun took Kennedy in and tutored him privately in reading.

The boy's optimistic nature was regularly tested. One of his best friends, Boi, was shot dead by the police after he was caught stealing: "Because he was from the slums, they just killed him," said Kennedy. Another of his best friends, Calvin, grew tired of endlessly looking for work in an area with 80 percent unemployment and turned to drugs. One day Kennedy visited Calvin's home in the evening and no one answered his knock. He pushed the door open and found Calvin hanging from a noose in the middle of his shack. He had left a note: "I can't live this way anymore."

Kennedy was probably spared a life of crime in part because of his ineptitude at thievery. At the age of twelve, sickened by hunger, he tried to steal a mango from a shop and was caught. A mob of vigilantes, enforcing market justice, beat the boy severely and might have killed him if a pastor in the crowd hadn't pitied him and paid for the mango. Kennedy was so terrified that he never dared steal again.

He impressed foreign visitors to Kibera with his passion for learning. When he was fifteen, a visiting researcher gave him a biography of Nelson Mandela. Kennedy was mesmerized. He dreamed of being like Mandela. A couple of years later a visiting American gave him *A Testament of Hope: The Essential Writings and Speeches of Martin Luther King, Jr.* Kennedy struggled through the complicated English but was riveted by the idea of bottom-up community organizing. He was inspired to make a difference himself, to try to start a movement. By this time he had been lucky enough to find a job loading and unloading propane gas cylinders for ten hours a day, for $1. He bought a cheap soccer ball and started a youth soccer club to unite young people, give them a purpose, and help them tackle local challenges.

"We talked about the lack of jobs, crime, the abuse women face, and poverty," Kennedy recalls. "All of this negativity had already killed the hopes of many. Many of these young people didn't believe we could start a movement without money, and they said it would be foolish to try. I told them there were many things we could do without money. We could do theater in the streets to call attention to issues, or lead community cleanups, or start our own community development."

Kennedy knew that he wanted not just a soccer club but a real movement, like the ones that Mandela and King had led. He searched out his friend George Okewa, a leader in Kibera, and they brainstormed about what to call the movement. "I told George that I thought there is one disease that kills even more people than poverty," he says. "George thought I meant HIV/AIDS, but the disease I was talking about was hopelessness. George thought about that for a moment, and then he agreed—this is what our community suffered from the most and in many ways caused all of our other problems. I decided I wanted to name my new movement something related to hope." They tossed a few ideas back and forth, including Shining Hope for Kibera. But Kennedy had the ambition to change more than one slum. He decided to call the movement Shining Hope for Communities, SHOFCO for short.

Kennedy wanted Shining Hope to address the sexual abuse of girls, a huge problem in Kibera and one that hit home because two of Kennedy's sisters had been raped and became pregnant by the time they reached sixteen. By some estimates, half of the women in Kibera have their first sexual experience by rape. Shining Hope decided to address the issue through street theater: Kennedy and a group of his friends would suddenly start shouting crazily on a mud lane in the slum, attracting attention, and then would launch into what they called "ambush theater"—an impromptu play decrying rape, or emphasizing that "no" means "no," or simply encouraging men to use condoms. In an area without other entertainment the street theater became the talk of the slum.

These kinds of activities were therapeutic for Kennedy and his friends. They were impoverished, but now they were organizers rather than aid recipients. The boys were learning the power of healing through helping, the strength that comes from being a force for change. Instead of just trying to escape Kibera, they were trying to fix the slum, and this gave them stature in the muddy lanes of their neighborhood. Kennedy was jokingly dubbed by some as the "mayor," and he found immense satisfaction in tackling community problems such as sexual violence and illiteracy, rather than contributing to them. Yes, Kennedy says with a touch of impatience to foreigners who want to help, of course Kibera lacks clean water and good schools and these issues need to be addressed. But the most difficult challenge to overcome is the crippling miasma of hopelessness.

Kennedy was invited to speak about his street theater performances at a conference in Nairobi, and one of those in the audience was a theater director from Denver. The director later mentioned the talk to a friend in Denver, Jessica Posner, a Wesleyan University student who was planning to take a junior year abroad in Kenya. Jessica was intrigued. She wrote Kennedy to ask if she could work on street theater with him. After discussion with his friends, Kennedy agreed. Upon her arrival, Jessica caused a scene by insisting on living inside the Kibera slum.

"No way," Kennedy told her flatly. "There's never been a white person who could live like that." He told her that there was no electricity or running water, and that rats scampered over people as they slept at night. He warned her grimly about flying toilets. Jessica is small and pretty with brown hair and soft features that make her look fragile, and that made everyone worry about her. But she insisted upon staying in Kibera.

"If you can live in those circumstances, I can, too," she told Kennedy. She didn't want to be an outsider living in the aid worker cocoon, and she didn't want to be treated differently because she was white and American. She felt that she would never understand Kibera if she didn't live in it. Kennedy eventually agreed to let her try living with his family in Kibera, sharing a floor with four other people. He figured she would last a day.

Jessica was in fact overwhelmed when she moved into Kibera. The filthy outdoor toilets, the rats—it was all as had been advertised. "I'm not an outdoorsy person; I hate camping," she says, but she had been challenged and was too mortified to back down. She gritted her teeth and persevered, even when she repeatedly became severely sick. Jessica helped Kennedy and his friends write out scripts for their street theater performances, which at the time were improvised, and the young men came to appreciate her good ideas. She might be from a different world, but she had a good heart and mind and was a valuable addition.

Jessica was dazzled by Kennedy, who was two years her senior. He exuded charisma and possessed a brilliant if raw intellect. He confided in her his dream that some day he might get a formal education. But he didn't have money, and he didn't have the background to pass the Kenyan school exams. Posner proposed a solution: he should skip elementary school, middle school, and high school and apply directly to Wesleyan. "They give scholarships," she explained. As she and Kennedy talked about this, they grew closer. Kennedy told her that it was a local custom for a host to walk hand in hand with a guest, so she carefully held his hand as they walked about; when she found out that this "custom" was a fiction, she felt not tricked but flattered, and they slipped into romance.

At Jessica's insistence, Wesleyan's admissions office agreed to consider an application from Kennedy. He had no formal transcripts or scores on the SAT or Test of English as a Foreign Language, so he wrote essays about his background. Wesleyan admitted Kennedy on a full scholarship, and then the United States embassy in Nairobi twice refused him a visa to study in America.* Finally, he and Jessica arrived on the campus in the fall of 2008, Jessica for her senior year and Kennedy for his freshman year.

---

* It's frustrating how often extraordinary young men and women are denied American visas even after admission to good colleges. The entire process of seeking a U.S. visa is so bureaucratic and arbitrary that it tarnishes the image of the United States among those otherwise disposed to admire it. Much of the goodwill that the United States gains with public diplomacy it undoes with its visa policies (which are more the fault of Congress than of the State Department).

Kennedy Odede and Jessica Posner with girls who attend
their school in the Kibera slum of Nairobi, Kenya

If Kibera had been overwhelming for Jessica, Wesleyan over-whelmed Kennedy. "It was my first time to have enough food, my first time to have a shower, the first time food wasn't a big deal," he says. "I had to call my mom to make sure I hadn't died and gone to heaven."

Until this point, Shining Hope was a movement, not a charity. It had existed six years without donations or outside support, and that meant it had negligible resources with which to operate. At Wesleyan, Odede began to talk aloud about his next great dream for Shining Hope for Communities—to start a girls' school in Kibera. He thought one way to fight sexual abuse would be to educate girls so that everyone would respect them, and that a girls' school could be the center of a broader outreach effort in the slum. But this was something that Shining Hope couldn't self-finance; it would have to ask outsiders for help. Posner decided to contribute $3,000, her life savings accumulated through years of babysitting and waitressing.

"My family thought I was nuts," she remembers. Her parents had been skeptical all along about her Kenya fascination, and she had avoided telling them that she was living inside Kibera for fear that they would "freak out." They also had mixed feelings about her romance with Kennedy. On the one hand, he charmed their socks off, and the whole family fell in love with him. On the other hand, Posner was still in college and was falling heavily for a Kenyan slum dweller to whom she was planning to hand over all her savings. "You should stop and consider the practicality of this all," her dad advised. But

Posner browbeat her mom and dad, just as she had bullied Kennedy and the Wesleyan admissions office. Her parents backed down when they saw how important the school was to her.

Kennedy and Jessica won grants for the girls' school from Projects for Peace, DoSomething.org, Newman's Own Foundation, and Echoing Green. In the summer of 2009, they started Kibera School for Girls, with classes in pre-K, kindergarten, and first grade. There was an outpouring of support from Kibera, not least because this was a local project rather than something built by outsiders. Posner and some other white people were involved, but the boss was unmistakably Kibera's own "mayor," Kennedy Odede.

Jessica stayed in Kibera while Kennedy returned to Wesleyan for his sophomore year and tried to manage the project via Skype. On her own, Posner was sometimes out of her depth. "I blew it a lot," she acknowledges. A Kenyan student friend pleaded for help paying school fees. Posner gave her the money—and was taken for a ride. "I was sure that I was doing the right thing," she says, and yet she was just confirming the stereotype of the white person as a naive outsider to be bilked. Posner resolved more than ever to seek local guidance, from Kennedy and others: "I may have the best intentions in the world, but they may not translate."

In 2012, after Odede's graduation, at which he served as the student commencement speaker, he and Posner were married in the United States—and then returned to Kibera. They won more attention, support, and financing, using it to expand Shining Hope for Communities to serve more than 50,000 residents in one way or another. They added a thirty-foot-high water tower to supply chlorinated water reliably to local residents—selling it cheaply, not giving it away, to make sure that the project was sustainable. They started a clinic providing HIV testing, prenatal care, contraception, and cervical cancer screening, relying upon electronic medical records. They used the clinic to launch public health drives to deworm residents and coach new moms on optimal breast-feeding. They added microsavings initiatives, a public library, a community newspaper called the *Ghetto Mirror,* and a job skills training program. Shining Hope even built clean public toilets, including one that produces methane—which provides the gas for cooking at the Kibera School for Girls.

The school became the heart of Shining Hope and the pride of Kibera. There's a reasonable argument to be made that in a place like

Kibera it's better to have a third-rate school that serves thousands rather than a top-notch school that serves dozens. But Odede wanted the best standards possible; he saw the school not just as a platform for education but as a way to produce new leaders and to lift the spirits of all Kibera. He wanted a centerpiece to instill pride, a vehicle to show that Kibera could perform every bit as well as any other place in Kenya. So the Kibera School for Girls gave the children beautiful uniforms and the best teachers and classrooms possible, capping each class at twenty students, even though demand was far greater.

School was free, but the parents had to commit to working five weeks during the year in lieu of tuition. The parents also had to commit to attend monthly meetings. Admission officers looked for two qualities in prospective students: the poorest kids and the brightest ones. The competition was excruciating, with almost 500 children competing for the twenty slots in each new pre-kindergarten class. Word spread about the school, and foreigners dropped by—and left behind large checks. The Mothers' Day Movement, started by a Connecticut woman to honor Mother's Day with something more meaningful than flowers, chose Shining Hope for Communities as its preferred charity one year, and the result was $130,000 in donations that led to construction of a beautiful new school building with twenty classrooms for children from pre-K to eighth grade. Families in the United States often sponsor a girl for $1,200 a year, renewing annually and

The end-of-year party for students at Kennedy and Jessica's Kibera School for Girls. Most of the students test above American grade levels, even though English is often their third language.

exchanging letters and photos with the child. The sponsorship also covers health care for the student's family, as well as financial training and parenting support. Partnerships with American schools are under way, and American students travel each summer to Kenya to work with the students. After the girls finish eighth grade, the aim is for them to attend top-notch high schools in Kenya, or in some cases even the United States, and there's hope that some overseas sponsors may continue to support them through university.

The classrooms in Kibera School for Girls are warm and inviting, very much like the best suburban schools in America, with student artwork on the walls and eager students frantically waving their hands to be called on. Elsewhere in Kibera, the student-teacher ratio is about 80 to 1; in these classrooms it is 8 to 1, and class is in session fifty weeks a year. In a writing class we watched, the girls were coached to write "juicy sentences": they practiced taking drab, formulaic sentences and recasting them with scenes, emotions, and active verbs. In Kibera School for Girls, laughter echoes down the hallways, and the girls are boisterous, self-confident, and excited to see visitors. They call out in English, the language of instruction. Even though English is the third language for most of the girls, the latest assessment showed 86 percent exceeding United States standards for their grade level. Some of the second graders are reading at seventh-grade level. In recent Kenyan exams, the school ranked first in the district, even though the children are drawn from the very poorest families in a slum.

"You have one girl who feels that she should be president of Kenya," says Julia Alubala, a kindergarten teacher. "She asks, 'What should I do to be president?' These girls will be stars. Our girls will be more Kennedys in the future." Shining Hope also uses the girls as ambassadors in the community, spreading the word about the value of education. One of the school songs goes like this:

> *I'm here to tell you: I too have my rights,*
> *A right to live, a right to eat,*
> *A right to dress, and a right to education.*
> *It is through education that I become a pilot,*
> *That I become a doctor, that I become a teacher.*
> *Parents, give me education! Education is the key!*

Some of the problems these children face, of course, won't go away. "Fifteen percent of these kids have been raped," Jessica said in a low voice as the girls filed into class one morning. "One five-year-old girl was being raped each morning." Two preschoolers suffered fistulas because of rape, and one was leaking urine and feces as a result. Doctors had to repair the cervix of one and the uterus of another. Seeing that it was difficult for girls to learn while they were fearful of rape, Shining Hope began an initiative to end the impunity for sexual violence. That included a safe house and also a campaign to encourage girls and their parents to overcome the stigma and report rapes to the police, and then pressuring the authorities to act.

We accompanied Shining Hope advocates as they took girls and their families to the Kilimani Police Station in Nairobi to try to get rapes prosecuted. The family of Ida, a four-year-old girl who had been raped by a neighbor so severely that she needed surgery, took two weeks off work to get the girl medical care and try to have the rapist jailed, but after repeated trips to the police station the only response was a request from one officer for an $11.50 bribe to arrest the perpetrator. The family refused. The police may then have taken a bribe from the rapist's family, for the case remained frozen and the file was perennially missing documents. We watched in disbelief as a police officer threatened to arrest not the rapist but Ida's family, for "neglect" in leaving the girl alone.

On another occasion, we accompanied a Shining Hope advocate and two girls, ages thirteen and fourteen, to the police station to seek justice after a rape by a neighbor. Again, the police seemed to be on the take, for after eight visits by the family—lasting several hours each—the case was still in limbo. The police had the family jumping through hoops, rounding up witnesses and bringing them to the police station—and then paying the police for paper and a pen to write witness statements. Editar Adhiambo, a twenty-five-year-old advocate who herself was raped at age six and again at fifteen, said such charges are common. Editar says that Kennedy is her role model, and she preaches a message of empowerment and education to local girls. "People need to eat hope," she tells people. "Work hard. Stop sleeping. Stop daydreaming. Sit down, relax, and focus on your goals, focus on education. There's no best friend like a book. It cannot cheat you, it cannot lie to you, it cannot tell you, 'Editar, go drink. Editar, go have sex without a condom.' It will tell you, 'When you have sex, use a condom. When you drink, don't take too much, maybe don't even take it at all.'"

Jessica Posner now chatters away with Kibera residents in the Swahili and Luo languages (Odede is a member of the Luo ethnic group, the same one as Barack Obama's father). While Kennedy is the charismatic grassroots leader focused on spreading the Shining Hope model to another Nairobi slum, Mathare, Jessica is the policy wonk who brings rigorous measurement and evaluation to determine what works and at what cost. Kibera remains a sometimes dangerous place, but Posner says she feels completely safe because the community looks out for her. Once, when Kennedy was away, Jessica was staying just outside Kibera in an apartment and robbers tried to break in during the night. She frantically telephoned friends in Kibera for help; they shouted out the alarm, and a posse of Kibera men ran full speed through the night to rescue her. They arrived just in time and chased the robbers away. Posner was shaken but unhurt.

"She has eaten as the locals, she has lived as the locals," explains George Okewa, the community leader. "They see her as one of them." The great strength of Shining Hope, Okewa says, is that it is seen as Kibera's homegrown project, founded by a local person and run by him. You see that all over the neighborhood. People point out the schoolgirls and comment on how "smart" their uniforms look. They watch admiringly as the girls brush their teeth outside after lunch. They ooh and aah over the girls' fluent English. A vegetable seller shakes her head and says: "You would never know that there could be a school like that inside Kibera."

Kennedy and Jessica ultimately would like Shining Hope to work in many cities in East Africa as a bottom-up organization providing not just education but also hope. "It's a starting point for changing your life, and for changing a community," Kennedy says. "One of the most devastating realities of Kibera for me has always been this sense of tremendous wasted human potential. Hope will not solve all of the problems we face, but it reminds us of the promise of imagination and ingenuity—something I know poor people have in abundance."

CHAPTER NINE

A Doctor Who Treats Violence

As long as you're breathing, it's never too late to do some good.

— MAYA ANGELOU

It began as lovemaking and ended in murder. Martavia Lambert and Anthony Brown climbed into bed planning to make love for the second time that day, but the caresses and giggles didn't last. Brown, twenty-three, a local chief of a Chicago street gang, the Vice Lords, suggested that Lambert, his wife, was cheating on him with a neighbor. Lambert hotly denied it, saying that she had resisted the man's advances. It was 3:00 a.m. in a second-floor apartment in a decrepit African American neighborhood of boarded-up windows, vacant lots, and gang graffiti on Chicago's West Side, where the wee hours are periodically shattered by screams and gunshots.

Brown and Lambert had been married for two years. Both had been raised in the slums, alongside drugs, gangs, and violence, and no one had ever stepped in to intervene. Fights were common and mostly ended up badly for Lambert. She was five feet four inches, no match for Brown, a stocky five feet eight inches and 200 pounds. On other occasions, he had broken her ankle, punctured her eardrum, and badly injured her arm. This time, as Lambert and Brown shouted at each other, their two small children woke up and began crying. Brown threw an electric fan at Lambert, hitting her and the infant beside her. Lambert grabbed a pair of scissors and stabbed Brown in the side of the head, above the ear. Bleeding but not gravely injured, he ran out. When Brown returned to the room, shouting, Lambert stormed forward. Her grandmother, Linda Harris, who owned the apartment and who was trying her best to raise five grandchildren and great-grandchildren there, tried to get between Brown and Lambert but was tossed aside. Harris then ushered the small children to safety in another room.

Brown threatened Lambert, according to the police report. In response, Lambert grabbed a butcher knife with an eight-inch blade from the kitchen and held it in front of her.

"Bitch, that knife don't scare me," Brown said, and he began to kick and punch her. She plunged the knife into his chest. Brown screamed. "She stabbed me," he said, collapsing on the floor and bleeding from the mouth. Lambert, suddenly horrified, dragged her bleeding husband outside and into her car, then raced to the hospital. There he soon died. Police arrested Lambert and charged her with first-degree murder.

It was one of three murders in Chicago that day, and it was reflective of the kind of inner-city violence that constitutes an enormous problem in America and other countries alike. Most studies find that each murder in America leads to costs of between $10 million and $12 million, including police and prison bills and social services for families of victims and perpetrators. The University of Chicago Crime Lab calculates that gun violence costs every Chicago household about $2,500 a year. Crime and violence not only create an economic burden but also exact a toll on poor neighborhoods, for businesses don't want to invest in such areas, and children find it difficult to concentrate on school when they're afraid of being shot or beaten on their way home. Indeed, researchers have shown that children in high-violence inner cities suffer the same post-traumatic stress disorder that haunts many veterans of the Iraq and Afghan wars.

As we've emphasized, the most cost-effective way of dealing with these problems is a range of early childhood interventions, for it's easier to turn around an eighteen-month-old toddler than an eighteen-year-old drug addict. Crime and violence are part of the price we pay as a society for failing to intervene effectively early on. The violence then harms entire communities, making other interventions more difficult.

One promising effort to curb such blights is Cure Violence, inspired by an infectious diseases specialist, Dr. Gary Slutkin, whom we met earlier. Dr. Slutkin, who has taken a public health approach to curbing murders in Chicago's most dangerous neighborhoods, has enjoyed such success that the program has been replicated around the United States and in many other countries.

Slutkin grew up in Chicago, the son of a research chemist father and an accountant mother. His dad equipped him with a love of science—Slutkin's childhood bedroom contained an oversize model of a human eye—while his mom ingrained in him a social conscience. These carried Slutkin to medical school. He tried research, thinking he would do a joint M.D./Ph.D. program, but found lab work unexpectedly tedious. To give himself time to figure out what to do, he took a year-long break with a few friends, driving from Algeria through the Sahara Desert and then to the Central African Republic, Congo, and South Africa. Throughout his trip, Slutkin encountered a degree of disease and suffering that he had not imagined, and he pondered how to use his training to greatest effect.

Returning to medicine, Slutkin took a medical residency in infectious diseases in San Francisco, focusing on tuberculosis. At thirty-one, he became medical director of the San Francisco Department of Public Health Tuberculosis Control. Many patients he treated were from Vietnam, Cambodia, or Laos and didn't speak English or trust Western medicine. So Slutkin hired Vietnamese immigrants as outreach workers to track down TB patients and ensure they took the medicine he had prescribed. This was an unorthodox approach, as the workers had no medical training and were barely literate in English, but it worked: the program helped to essentially eliminate tuberculosis in the city.

Slutkin then moved to Somalia, one of the poorest countries in the world, intending to work on tuberculosis there. But a cholera epidemic struck the refugee camps soon after his arrival, to staggeringly lethal effect. "We were all completely over our head, and we did a lot of crying," Slutkin remembers. There were only six doctors for one million displaced people in forty camps, so Slutkin and his colleagues began training Somali birth attendants and low-level health workers to recognize cholera and provide basic treatment. Once more, local outreach workers helped contain an epidemic.

For a decade Slutkin worked on infectious diseases in Africa, including a stint with the World Health Organization setting up some of the first AIDS programs. By 1994, he was burned out and returned to Chicago, where he found inner-city violence to be a challenge as intractable as any medical pathology he had struggled against over-seas. If anything, this was tougher to wipe out. The Vice Lords gang, for example, had been founded in 1957 and remained as active as ever in local violence. Chicago already had some of the toughest gun control laws in the country, but they had not been effective in eliminating guns. "It was like trying to get rid of mosquitoes in Africa," Slutkin said.

The more he pondered urban violence, the more he felt it had been misdiagnosed as solely a moral problem or a criminal issue. He decided it was in many ways more like a disease epidemic. Contagions spread among people who have low resistance, and that seemed true of violence. A large body of research has also shown that people exposed to violence are more likely to engage in violence. In effect, Slutkin mused, they have compromised immune systems. Slutkin knew how to halt an epidemic. The first step is to detect new infections and interrupt their spread so that they won't be transmitted to others. That was what he had done with tuberculosis, cholera, and AIDS. Now he decided to attempt the same thing in Chicago, forming a nonprofit eventually named Cure Violence to treat violence as an infectious disease. He hired outreach workers, mediators, and then "violence interrupters" who could stop an infection in its tracks. These individuals were local pillars of the community—which, in gang-controlled neighborhoods, often meant ex-convicts with rap sheets two feet long and gang tattoos on their hands. They were to be the equivalents of Vietnamese refugees in San Francisco and birth attendants in Somalia.

Slutkin convinced Chicago grant makers and the Robert Wood Johnson Foundation, which focuses on health issues, that crime is a public health challenge, and they took a chance on him. He started by focusing on a block in the West Garfield Park neighborhood of Chicago, the community that at the time had the highest number of homicides. One of those he hired as a violence interrupter was China Joe.

An African American, China Joe doesn't actually have any Chinese blood, but his eyes look somewhat Asian—perhaps because his mother was half Cherokee. When he was a kid, someone called him China Joe and the name stuck, even though his real name is John Lofton. His dad worked in construction, his mom in a bakery, but as a boy China Joe fell into a fast crowd and was dazzled by the allure of quick money in the streets. A light-complexioned man of slight build,

China Joe joined the Vice Lords as a ten-year-old and soon became an expert thief of store cash registers.

Imprisoned in a juvenile detention home for the first time at age twelve, China Joe ended his formal education in regular schools in the fifth grade but earned the equivalent of a doctorate in street hustling. As he rose in the Vice Lords, he committed robberies and burglaries and became legendary for his heists from drug dealers. He knew they carried a lot of cash and might not report its theft to the police. China Joe started his own intelligence network, sending provocatively dressed girls as "honey traps" to attract drug lords.

"They were drooling at the mouth when they saw how I had them dressed up," China Joe remembers with a laugh. "The girls, they were good. They knew how to work it." Each girl would date a drug dealer and report back to China Joe on where he kept cash and narcotics, and when he would be alone and vulnerable to attack. Then China Joe and his team would move in, kidnap the drug dealer, lock him in a car trunk, and steal his drugs and money. A Christmas Eve heist earned him $80,000 in a few hours. Naturally, these kidnappings also earned China Joe plenty of enemies. He was shot once and carried a gun everywhere he went, even to the bathroom. He also became addicted to heroin while sampling the merchandise he stole. He was arrested frequently and spent about half his life after the age of twelve behind bars

China Joe, in the offices of Cure Violence

With time, China Joe grew tired of prison and having to look over his shoulder, and that's when Cure Violence reached out to him, in 2005, when he was in a prison drug rehabilitation program: Would he be interested in giving up crime and working as a mediator to prevent killings in his old gang neighborhoods?

"I was tired of going through the same scenario, using drugs, robbing people," China Joe says. "I said it's time for me to do something different." So he agreed. A Chicago judge, Carol Kipperman, bravely took a risk on him and released him to the streets to work with Cure Violence. (Judge Kipperman told us she has no recollection of this move.)

"That's when the change started taking place," says China Joe, a broad smile tracking across his face. "That's when the caterpillar made its metamorphosis, and I became a butterfly."

When the Vice Lords heard about Brown's killing, they decided it had to be avenged. Linda Harris heard rumors that the gang was planning to attack her apartment and shoot it up. Lambert heard the same thing in jail and called her grandmother to warn her. Harris was trying to work out her relocation when there was a thunderous pounding on her door. "We want to talk to you," a gang leader shouted through the door. Harris shouted back through the locked door that the gang members should talk to the police. She then hurriedly herded the children into a back room in case bullets started flying. She called 911, but when the police didn't show up after a few minutes, she made another call.

China Joe? This is Linda Harris! You gotta come here quick. The Vice Lords, they're banging on my door. Come quick, or we'll all be dead!

The crucial moment came as China Joe was in the middle of mediating a dispute over turf. The altercation had begun between two low-level drug dealers, and each dealer had called in reinforcements. Now a half-dozen gang members on each side, very likely armed, were facing off.

We ain't moving, one gang member snarled.

Oh, you're gonna move.

Man, like I said, man, we staying. We ain't going nowhere. We was here before you.

You wasn't here! I was here before you.

China Joe sensed that neither side wanted a shoot-out, but he knew that neither side could be seen as backing down. He promptly established himself as the alpha male, issuing orders: *Ya'll need to come together and figure out how you gonna do this here. But however you gonna work it out, it's gonna be peaceful. 'Cause ain't no shooting is gonna go down.*

He told both dealers to shift spots a bit and sell their heroin on different ends of the street (this is not the kind of détente that the police can impose). The gangs grumblingly assented, tensions eased, and the prospect of guns blazing disappeared. It was at that moment that Linda Harris called China Joe.

Okay, China Joe responded. *I'm on my way.*

The drug dealers could hear Linda shouting through the cell phone, and they asked China Joe what was happening. He tersely explained that some street punks were ready to shoot up a house and kill a grandma and five kids.

What? someone said. *That's just wrong.*

The others began making similar comments, and China Joe casually asked them if they'd like to come along and help him calm the situation. They said yes. When China Joe and the two gangs jumped out of their cars at Linda's building they found a crowd of angry Vice Lords. All were taken aback to see China Joe arrive, trailed by a cavalry of a dozen gang members from rival cliques.

You know you got no business messing with someone's family, China Joe told them. He pointed out that two of the children in the house were actually Anthony Brown's own babies. *You ain't helping him, you're hurting him!*

One of the gang members whom China Joe had brought with him piped up as well: *You know you ain't got no business messing with nobody's family.*

China Joe remembers it this way: "They were just acting out of emotion. Once you talked to them, they knew it was the wrong thing."

Eventually the Vice Lords drove off, massacre averted. China Joe knocked on Linda Harris's door and told her she was safe now.

"If it hadn't been for him," she said, "I don't know what would have happened to me or my kids."

That's the kind of incident in which Cure Violence and its violence interrupters make all the difference, though much of their work is less dramatic. Cure Violence staff are also undertaking long-term efforts at behavior change, encouraging alternatives to gangs and crime while discouraging any resort to violence. Like China Joe, they make themselves known in their assigned communities and encourage people to call them when they fear trouble. Staff members also trade intelligence among themselves on recent threats, clashes, murders, and possible retaliations. When someone is shot, they go to the hospital room to commiserate with the victim—and counsel against a retaliatory hit. Cure Violence also organizes a community response wherever there is a murder: a protest, a memorial service, or a vigil, meant to shame or stigmatize those behind the violence.

Gary Slutkin has come to feel at home on the roughest streets. One staff member, Alphonso Prater, remembers once watching a few young hoodlums surround Slutkin's car and accuse him and his team of snitching to the police—a way of delegitimizing everything they did. Slutkin had just gotten into his car and was about to drive off, but at that he got out of the car, faced the men, and said that was a lie.

"The doc stood his ground," Prater remembers. "I'd never seen white guys in the neighborhood stand their ground. The doc just stood there. I thought he'd get jumped, and some of them might have had guns. But the doc stood there and talked to them." Prater shook his head at the memory and added in a tone of awe: "I looked at the doc and said, 'You're my man!'"

Outside groups have conducted a series of rigorous evaluations of Cure Violence and found it reduces shootings substantially, at negligible cost. The Justice Department sponsored a 229-page evaluation by four experts who found that the program reduced shootings by 16 to 28 percent, depending on the area. That was a significant achievement for Cure Violence, with a budget in Chicago of $5 million (most funding for Cure Violence comes from local governments, but private donations made on its website help, too); Chicago spends $1.9 billion on "public safety" each year. Cure Violence calculates that every $1 spent on its programs in Chicago saves $15.77 in medical and criminal justice costs alone, and Slutkin thinks that the approach is capable of lowering inner-city homicides by 70 percent. "We've seen that level of effect from this intervention a few times," Slutkin says. "It's a pretty consistent figure with what you're able to achieve in some areas in this way, with child mortality, with TB."

Yet Cure Violence has the funding to operate in only one-quarter of the neighborhoods where it's needed. If only we were as willing to pay for prevention as for prisons.

Cure Violence offers a window into the power of public health programs, which work with large clusters of people as opposed to clinical efforts involving a doctor and a patient. The public health campaign against cigarette smoking, which used cigarette taxes, public education, and warnings to reduce the share of adults who smoke from 42 percent in 1965 to 18 percent today, has saved hundreds of thousands of lives annually. Likewise, the public health campaign against drunk driving and traffic deaths has been one of the great successes of American policy to save lives.

Could a broad public health approach to violence be as effective? We don't know, but we like Gary Slutkin's approach of studying what works and learning from it. It should be complemented by other public health initiatives that try to reduce violence among teenagers, especially boys. One such effort, called Becoming a Man, or BAM, was rolled out in Chicago as a randomized controlled trial with 2,700 at-risk boys in grades seven through ten. They participated in in-school and after-school programs meant to defuse conflict, and the results were very promising. While the program was under way, it reduced violent crime arrests by 44 percent compared to those in the control group, although when the program was stopped the next year, the gains in crime reduction faded. The cost per participant was $1,100, and the University of Chicago calculated that society's savings were more than three times that.

In the long run, the best way to prevent epidemics is to boost people's immunity and change the environment so that infections are less likely to take hold and spread. To do that, Cure Violence also sends staff members like China Joe to give talks at schools, juvenile detention centers, and prisons, delegitimizing weapons and violence while encouraging young people to find status in school rather than gangs.

"They've heard of me," China Joe says proudly. "And I tell them, 'There's better ways of doing things. I don't want you doing what I did. I spent enough time in prison for you. The best thing you need to do is get you an ink pen, get you a book. That's called education; it's your future. There is nothing out here on this corner but a lot of mayhem, prison, or death. You have a choice. You can either pick up the pen or you can pick up the gun. If you pick up the gun, you're going to prison or you're going to the graveyard. Those are your two options.'"

Renaissance Giver

Getting sent away to "the farm" in Arkansas in 1972 was probably a life-saving event for Noel James Oates, but at the time it
was horrible, and the worst of it was the straps. Each supervisor had
one — a length of leather about three feet long, with a wooden handle.
Guards would put you in handcuffs, tie you down, and pull your arms
and legs until you thought you would explode; it was called being
stretched. Then the strap would snap down hard, and there would
always be blood. If it was time for you to leave the farm and you still
had strap marks, they'd add two more months to your sentence to
allow your marks to fade. When visitors or officials came, the straps
would disappear. Oates was being "trained" to reform his delinquent
behavior.

Vivid memories of those years came back to Oates, who goes by
Jim and is now an engineer in San Diego, when he saw someone on
television describing how Cure Violence helps fight inner-city crime
with "interrupters" such as China Joe. For Oates, it made perfect
sense, and it felt personal, for he had almost been sucked into a life of
violence. So he decided to support Cure Violence, backing up China
Joe and the others on the front lines. Oates had come a long way.

His family was well-educated and living in Houston, his mother
a law professor. Still, he was arrested for the first time when he was
twelve years old, for selling marijuana. His Little League coach, a
policeman, intervened, and the charges were reduced so that he got
off with a fine. At age fourteen, in the middle of ninth grade, Oates
left home and hitchhiked across the country. He stole small things to
support himself, and he was arrested in Fort Smith, Arkansas.

"Things were spiraling downhill," he recalls of his own youthful
trajectory. After his arrest, he was sent to "the farm," where the kids'
mail was censored and the strappings began.

"They were a total failure," Oates says of these juvenile reform farms, which existed in several states and were later banned after revelations of deaths of youths in custody. "Complete corporal punishment and a lot of abuse, almost like being a slave."

Oates's lucky break came when the reform school officials discovered his high IQ. With high recidivism for adolescents at the farm, they wanted a success story, so they gave him a job running the machinery for the farm's dairy and enrolled him in high school equivalency classes. Oates ran the milk pasteurizer and homogenizer and also earned his equivalency diploma. In the final months of his incarceration, he learned to prepare architectural drawings and work as a draftsman.

At eighteen, Oates was released. He found his way back to Houston and got a job with Shell Oil Company as a draftsman. He started off smoothly but then fell into a rut. Seeing that he was going nowhere, Oates's mother intervened. *Take a night course and see what you think,* she urged. *You really have it in you to go to college, but you just don't know it.*

Oates took an astronomy course at a local community college, liked it, and earned an A. The next semester he took an algebra class and a second astronomy course and got two A's. "I just took off," he recalls, laughing. "I had a purpose. I was successful."

Oates continued working for Shell during the day while going to

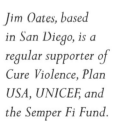

Jim Oates, based in San Diego, is a regular supporter of Cure Violence, Plan USA, UNICEF, and the Semper Fi Fund.

night school. Shell discovered his proficiency at math and trained him in computer processing of seismic data related to oil exploration. Soon the geophysicists found that they could turn to Oates for first-rate processing and they increasingly relied on him. Now enamored with the world of math and science, Oates ended up earning a degree in electrical engineering. Many years later, he discovered that his mother would tell her classes a motivating story about a fourteen-year-old kid she knew who had gone through crises and turmoil in his teenage years only to go to college later and thrive.

Now fifty-nine, Oates lives on the southern California coast with a beautiful view of the Pacific Ocean. He has built his career in the telecommunications industry, most recently at Broadcom, where he tested baseband modem chips for cell phones. After his distinguished twenty-eight-year career as an electrical engineer, no one who knows him today would guess his troubled past—but it still shapes him. When Oates saw that television show about Cure Violence treating gang violence as a contagious disease, he searched the Internet and watched Gary Slutkin's TED Talk and a couple of Cure Violence videos.

"Because of my history when I was younger, it really spoke to me as something I wanted to support right away," Oates says. He began donating $100 every month, by automatic deduction from his bank account. Oates thinks that Cure Violence has an approach that is particularly effective, and the more he learns about it the more he likes it. "For the rest of my life," he says, "I'll be making that monthly donation."

For Oates, Cure Violence builds on his habit of helping others. For twenty years, Oates has supported foster children abroad through Plan USA. He now supports five different foster children—two girls and three boys—including two in Senegal and one each in Egypt, Burkina Faso, and Ghana. "I wanted to support girls because of the obvious hardships girls everywhere encounter," he said. Oates also gives to the Fistula Foundation to support surgeries for women and girls with a childbirth injury known as obstetric fistula. His mother told him about it.

"From time to time I try to do a reassessment," Oates says. "There were times when I was unemployed and living a very no-frills kind of lifestyle, and I had to throttle back on my donations. But I never, ever would stop my support of my foster children."

Oates combines volunteering with his donations. He has a hobbyist's interest in oceanography and the marine environment, and he occasionally gives presentations about oceanography to children in elementary and middle schools. When he went to one school in East Los Angeles, he was taken aback at the eight-foot-high fence topped with barbed wire surrounding the school. Administrators told him they could lock down the school in two minutes and have police helicopters there in five. Some of the kids had lost brothers and sisters to gun violence, and for them tide pools might as well have existed on the moon—yet they relished his visits and the images he showed of sea life. "They get a lot out of it," says Oates. "I get a lot of good feelings out of doing that."

Otherwise, like most upper-middle-class professionals, Oates doesn't hang around much with the poor, and he doesn't have a direct connection to troubled youth, so Cure Violence is his way of helping that community. "We're pretty much the richest people who've ever lived, and if we don't give, who is going to?" he asks. "I try to be really appreciative of what I have, and to the extent I can, I want to share.

"I definitely do believe that giving is its own reward," he says. "I've just had that feeling many, many, many times. You get more than you give, ultimately. Heaven knows our next generations are going to have a tough time, and I'm not so sure we're leaving a better world for them. So I want to do whatever I can to help the creativity, the people who are coming up with solutions to things."

CHAPTER TEN

Attacking Sex Trafficking

You may choose to look the other way but you can
never say again that you did not know.

—WILLIAM WILBERFORCE,
LEADER OF THE ANTISLAVERY CAMPAIGN IN
GREAT BRITAIN BEGINNING IN THE 1780S

Reverend Becca Stevens, an Episcopal priest newly arrived at
Vanderbilt University in Nashville, was looking for an issue of
social justice for her congregation to tackle. She picked sex trafficking, partly because sexual abuse of minors was a concern that resonated very personally with her. When Becca was four years old, her
dad was killed in a car accident caused by a drunk driver. Her mom
was left with five children and was grateful as the church and community stepped forward to help. Among those who assisted was a family
friend. Once, during a spaghetti dinner at church, this man led Becca
to an upstairs room, closed the door, and sexually abused her. "I just
remember thinking, If I drop this plate of spaghetti, I'll get into so
much trouble," Becca recalls. So she put up with it—and the man continued to abuse her for the next two years.

Growing up in a supportive middle-class family, Becca over-
came that trauma and graduated as a Phi Beta Kappa in math from
Sewanee University. She is human testimony to the principle that
when bad things happen to us, they sometimes give us special insights
or empathy that can be harnessed for good. Because of the abuse
she endured, Becca could relate to sex trafficking victims who had

*Reverend Becca Stevens in the café she runs to help female
victims of sexual trafficking find employment*

experienced so much abuse themselves. "Those couple of years were
a huge gift to me," Becca says. "The gift is that I get why people end
up out on the streets. I get that it messes you up in relationships." The
roots of sex trafficking, she says, lie in rape of children, pointing to
research indicating that a majority of prostitutes have been sexually
abused as children.

Human trafficking was a most appropriate target for Becca's congregation because it remains one of the most brutal and widespread
human rights violations in the world today—including in the United
States. UNICEF estimates that 1.2 million children are trafficked every
year around the world, and the International Labor Organization
calculates that almost 21 million people are victims of forced labor
worldwide, including 4.5 million who are in forced prostitution. India
probably has more girls sexually trafficked every year than any other
country, and Pakistan, Bangladesh, Nepal, Malaysia, Cambodia, Vietnam, Moldova, Romania, and Mexico also have enormous numbers.
Human trafficking exists to some degree in almost every country
worldwide.

Within the United States, estimates of sex trafficking vary immensely. We subscribe to an estimate by Ernie Allen, former president of the National Center for Missing & Exploited Children, that at
least 100,000 juveniles are sexually trafficked or prostituted each year
(out of more than 1.6 million children who run away or are kicked out
of their homes each year, according to a Justice Department study).

Some of those cases last just a few days or involve minors trading sex for food, shelter, or protection. Our own calculation (based on arrests, data for online prostitution advertising, and results of surveys of men about purchasing sex) is that on any one day there may be 100,000 women and girls (about 10 percent of them underage) selling sex in the United States, both willingly and unwillingly. But we estimate that over the course of a year, several hundred thousand women or girls pass through the sex trade in the United States at some point.

Forced prostitution is as stubborn a social problem as any today, yet it is gaining increased attention in the United States and around the world in part because of vigorous advocacy by civil society and religious organizations. In the United States, one of the leading organizations is Polaris Project, founded in 2002 by two Brown University students, Katherine Chon and Derek Ellerman, after they read a newspaper article about a horrific brothel nearby. Polaris Project now operates a national human trafficking hotline (888-373-7888) and supports efforts to pass antitrafficking legislation around the country. In New York City, a survivor of trafficking named Rachel Lloyd runs an outstanding program called GEMS Girls, which helps girls who have been trafficked, and in Washington Andrea Powell runs an organization called FAIR Girls that prowls the streets to look for girls needing help escaping from pimps. In the international sphere, a Christian organization called International Justice Mission has been active in India, Cambodia, the Philippines, and other countries, working with the police to make traffickers pay a price for prostituting children. All these groups are beginning to make the world more dangerous for traffickers, and they need not only financial support but also volunteers to help women and girls trying to start over. Citizens also need to ask police chiefs and prosecutors why it is that they always go after prostitutes, almost never after pimps or johns.

Reverend Stevens and her congregation have excelled in building this kind of coalition to fight sex trafficking in Nashville. It started when she realized that one of the bottlenecks is a lack of beds for women seeking to escape pimps, and she organized a fund-raising campaign to acquire a private home in which women can live for two years while trying to overcome prostitution and narcotics. Stevens is charismatic, well connected, and relentless—which explains why her congregation at Vanderbilt has grown from 10 when she arrived to 300 today—and Nashville responded enthusiastically. The church acquired a large house that could accommodate about a half-dozen women, forming the kernel of Magdalene, a two-year residential program for women fleeing prostitution and, usually, narcotics and alcohol. Magdalene offers therapy, but it also offers hope for these women: a holistic program that integrates therapy, job training, and help staying away from drugs, alcohol, and bad old friends. The women must submit to random drug testing while at Magdalene, and they pledge to avoid their old pimps and acquaintances from the streets, at least until they're ready to handle them. The women in the home run it themselves; those who have been off the streets longer offer help to the newcomers.

One of the first women whom Becca helped was Clemmie Greenlee, an African American woman who had been raped repeatedly beginning at the age of five and then systematically pimped from the age of twelve. Clemmie began drinking at age eight, dropped out of school in the fourth grade, and soon became a heroin addict and an expert at robbing johns. On one occasion she did more than steal. A customer was beating her badly, so she pulled out a knife and stabbed him. "I didn't see blood, so I stabbed him again, four more times," she said. He almost died, but fortunately for Greenlee he was a married man who begged the police not to press charges, and without his testimony they didn't have a case. She was freed.

By 2001, Greenlee was a gaunt eighty-five pounds, sleeping on the streets or in abandoned buildings, all of her money going to crack cocaine. She had had a son who was killed in gang violence. She was seen as having so little commercial value that pimps abandoned her. An old friend from the streets found Greenlee in a crack house and dragged her over to see Reverend Stevens at Magdalene.

"I met Becca and saw the program, and Becca hugged me," Greenlee remembers. "That hug changed my life." Greenlee entered the Magdalene program, flourished with the help of volunteers, stayed clear of drugs and alcohol, and became an invaluable counselor to younger women trying to flee their pimps. To her astonishment, she met a man she loves, and they're now engaged. She also has tried to take on other issues, and after seeing a television program about Cure Violence in Chicago she started a similar program in Nashville to honor her murdered son. Because of her civic work in the community, she was named Nashvillian of the Year in 2007—a remarkable step for a woman who six years earlier had been a junkie and a prostitute. Greenlee has moved on to New Orleans to run a program there called Eden House that is modeled on Magdalene. It is one of about a dozen sites around the country trying to scale up the Magdalene model.

There are a couple of major misconceptions that people often have about sex trafficking. The first is that it primarily entails foreign women smuggled into the United States. That does happen, of course, and there are horrific brothels with Mexican women and girls in major cities targeting working-class Latino men in transactions for as little as $30. There are also massage parlors with Korean and Chinese women who, when they bought their way to America, were told they would be working as waitresses. But by far the most common victims of human trafficking in the United States are home-grown girls like Greenlee. Most traffickers in the United States are simply pimps.

The second major misconception is that women and girls are overwhelmingly selling sex voluntarily, working cooperatively with pimps to make money. Sure, some women do sell sex without coercion. But many do not, and even when a woman is now selling sex consensually, she often entered the sex trade involuntarily, typically as a minor. The Justice Department estimates that the average age of entry into juvenile prostitution in the United States is thirteen or fourteen, and the age of entry is similar abroad. Greenlee notes that pimps routinely give girls a quota that they must earn each day, say $500 or $1,000, and they are beaten if they fall short. "If you're putting a whip on my back because I'm not picking enough cotton," she says, "or if you're beating me because I'm not earning my quota, it's the same thing. It's slavery."

There's a view that the best way to tackle prostitution is to legalize and regulate it, a policy that has been implemented in parts of Nevada and in Amsterdam, Germany, and New South Wales, Australia, among other locations. This approach does have advantages. In a legal brothel, social workers can ensure that sex workers are over eighteen and working voluntarily, and health workers can check that they don't have HIV or sexually transmitted diseases. In a formal brothel, women are also safer than on the streets. Yet in practice, this system doesn't work so neatly. A jurisdiction that allows legal prostitution attracts sex tourists, creating a parallel market for underage or trafficked girls. In Nevada, the women in legal brothels are eighteen or over, but there are also plenty of younger girls working outside the brothels. Even in Sydney, Australia, there are reportedly four times as many illegal brothels as legal ones. In Amsterdam, only 4 percent of prostitutes are estimated to be legally registered.

The approach that has been gaining ground around the world is the Nordic model, pioneered by Sweden in 1999. It focuses on prohibiting the purchase of sex and the trafficking of women; in practice, this means that women who sell sex are offered social services but not arrested, while men are arrested and fined when they try to buy sex. This crackdown on the johns has significantly reduced prostitution in Sweden; the total number of people involved in street prostitution has been halved by some calculations. The Nordic model doesn't function perfectly, and critics say that it drives sex work underground, but polls suggest that Swedes regard it as a success, and there has been increasing adoption of this model in other countries as well.

In Nashville, Reverend Stevens has worked with the authorities to put together an approach that likewise isn't perfect but seems to address trafficking reasonably well. One component similar to the Nordic model is that men are arrested for soliciting prostitutes. Those who are first offenders are fined $300 each, with the money going to support programs such as Magdalene, and then dispatched to a "johns school." This is a day-long session in which the men are warned about sexually transmitted diseases and robbery and listen to former prostitutes like Greenlee describe the brutality of the business. Part of the aim is to stigmatize the purchase of sex, and that seems to be slowly happening in America. Surveys suggest that about 15 percent of American men have purchased sex at some point in their lives, a considerable drop from earlier decades when fathers sometimes took sons to a brothel to lose their virginity.

In the Nashville model, when women are arrested for prostitution there is a serious effort to get them help. In lieu of a prison sentence, prostitutes are offered the chance to attend a day-long program in which Becca and others from Magdalene explain what their treatment options are. The sex crimes prosecutor, Antoinette Welch, an ally of Becca's, warns the prostitutes of the dangers of AIDS and violence if they stay in the sex trade. We attended a session and watched as Welch passed out horrifying photos of corpses of prostitutes who have been murdered in Nashville. "I don't want this to happen to any of you!" Welch said as she fought back tears. "I'm so afraid that if you go back to the streets, this will happen to you."

One of Becca's insights was that women need not only a safe house but also a suite of services that touches all facets of life and ties them together into a comprehensive program. They need not just a place to live but also a living, not just therapy but also friendship, not just classes but also role models. To train them for jobs, she started a social enterprise, Thistle Farms, which employs about fifty women. They make candles, soap, and fragrances, selling them on the Internet and in several hundred stores, including Whole Foods. More recently, Thistle Farms opened a café to offer former prostitutes jobs as baristas and waitresses. There has been strong support from the community, including flooring donated by the Al Gore family from its old family barn, and a local magazine soon named one former prostitute as the best barista in Nashville.

Central to the project has been a force of 300 local people whom Becca has recruited as volunteers. They donate their time, working in the café, helping Thistle Farms sell its goods, or providing professional expertise of some kind. They teach the women to read, use a library, find a job—advising them on what to wear and how to speak in a business setting—and access services such as family planning or tattoo removal. These middle-class volunteers work side by side with women who until recently were drug addicts selling sex; it's a powerful learning experience for both sides.

Becca and her volunteers certainly haven't solved the problems of sex trafficking, and some of the women they try to help falter or suffer relapses. One, Julia Baskette, joined Magdalene for nine months before a family member invited her home for a visit. While home, she relapsed into drugs and prostitution. At a truck stop, she climbed into the truck of a twenty-four-year-old married man, Kendrick Merritt. Her nude body, showing signs of torture, was later found nearby, and Merritt was convicted of the killing. Julia's family donated a family table in her memory to the Thistle Farms café.

Yet overall Becca's success rate is remarkable: 72 percent of the women who enter Magdalene graduate two years later, clean and sober and ready for a new life. More than 150 women are now graduates of the program. Magdalene has steadily expanded and now has six houses in Nashville with twenty-eight beds. That's a fraction of what's needed, and there's a long waiting list. "I could fill 1,000 beds," Becca says. She notes that it's far cheaper to keep the women in Magdalene, even with lavish services, than to keep them in prison—and Magdalene's outcomes are far better.

Shana's Comeback

Reverend Stevens oversees Magdalene and Thistle Farms, but the people who actually spend their nights trying to coax women and girls away from their pimps are survivors such as Shana Goodwin, who herself endured decades of prostitution.

Shana's trajectory is fairly typical. Her mother was a drug addict, and Shana was born with heroin in her system. As an infant, she was sent to live with relatives, one of whom molested her. "I don't know how early it started," she says. "I just remember him being in my bed every night." Shana later moved back in with her mom, who was trading sex for drugs. Strange men would come tramping through the house, and Shana would sometimes lock herself in the bathroom to stay safe. After dropping out of school, barely literate, in the seventh grade, Shana was taken by her mom to a stranger's house at age thirteen for her initiation into prostitution. To make the ordeal more

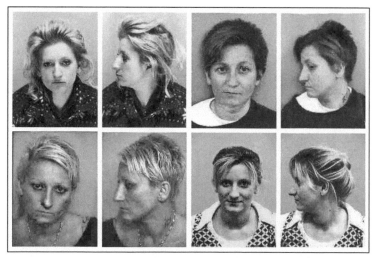

Police mugshots taken of Shana Goodwin after her arrests for prostitution

bearable, her mom first injected her with heroin. "I just remember falling back on the waterbed," Shana says. "My fear was gone."

Shana ended up controlled by a pimp named Nitty, who ran a "stable" of seven women and girls selling sex. Every penny that Goodwin and the other girls earned went to Nitty, which is how it usually works. Pimps routinely have prostitutes tattooed with their names and symbols, and Goodwin has sixteen tattoos, including a dollar sign on her face, "Daddy's Girl" on her buttocks, and "Trust No One" in big letters across her chest. "It's like tagging cattle, so you can know which cow is yours," Goodwin explains today. Pimps sometimes sell women to other pimps for cash, and Goodwin was once sold to a pimp in Memphis for a typical price—$1,500. A couple of times Goodwin tried to run away, and Nitty beat her when he recovered her. She never sought help from the police, partly because she had learned to distrust them: she had been arrested 167 times; her pimp, never.

By the time she was thirty-five, Goodwin had been using drugs and involved in prostitution for more than two-thirds of her life. Then she was in prison—which gave her a chance to get clean of drugs— and was offered a place in Magdalene. She jumped at it. Once there, she received therapy for what doctors diagnosed as post-traumatic stress disorder, similar to what some war veterans experience. She took computer classes. She slowly recovered. A prominent cosmetic surgeon in Nashville, Dr. Brian S. Biesman, agreed to remove her tattoos without charge. (When Goodwin sat in the waiting room, she would startle well-to-do Nashville women who were there to get their wrinkles erased.)

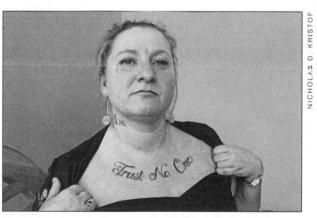

NICHOLAS D. KRISTOF

Shana Goodwin today, with tattoos that she wants removed

Goodwin is pained most by the gulf separating her from her four children, all born with narcotics addictions and given up for adoption. She telephoned her oldest child, now a young man, to see if he wanted to meet. He cursed her and hung up. Still, she's glad that she didn't try to raise them. "If I had kept them, imagine what they would be like," she said, and then there was a moment of wistfulness before she added: "I broke the cycle."

Shana Goodwin has now been off drugs and alcohol for four years. She is thriving in a sales job at Thistle Farms, selling candles and other products made by women who previously sold sex. She's taking college classes. On the side, she volunteers daily to help young women get off the street and escape their pimps. We followed her through Nashville's seedier districts and the hotels where pimps keep girls. She asked some of the women if they needed help, telling them that she could arrange shelter if they needed it. Her dream is to find donors and supporters and start a program for young women in trouble, using her own experience to minister to others who need help. She explained: "I just want to help other women."

PART TWO

Reforming the Art of Helping

CHAPTER ELEVEN

Charity

In Search of a Revolution

We can't solve problems by using the same kind of
thinking we used when we created them.

—ALBERT EINSTEIN

Charities save lives, promote literacy, and reduce hunger, but for
all the good they do, they could accomplish far more if they were
better organized. Nonprofits still have one foot in the eighteenth-
century preindustrial economy, for they are atomized into tiny and
inefficient players, held back, as we'll see, by public resistance to businesslike steps that would allow them to scale up and modernize. It's
time to rethink what a charity should be.

One of the leaders in this rethinking is Dan Pallotta, a nota-
bly ambitious presence on the Harvard campus when Nick arrived
there as an undergraduate in 1978. Pallotta wanted to become president of the United States and was already a budding politico, having been elected to the school board in Melrose, Massachusetts, at
the age of nineteen. Pallotta is gay, which unfortunately complicated
his political ambitions. Searching for an alternative avenue of public
service, he organized a bike ride across America that raised $80,000
for Oxfam, and parlayed this into a part-time fund-raising job for
that organization. After graduation, Pallotta moved to Los Angeles,
where he found a job as a fund-raiser for charitable causes, largely
in the Los Angeles Jewish community (Pallotta learned to cover the

crucifix around his neck when he made visits). At this time, he was in his twenties and living a wild life of partying and sex addiction. The wildness ended after Pallotta caught a serious illness and thought it might be AIDS. (It was not.) The scare sent Pallotta into therapy that helped turn his life around. He used a fund-raising consulting company he had started, Pallotta TeamWorks, to sponsor a long-distance bicycle ride to raise money for AIDS in 1994, involving 478 people bicycling from San Francisco to Los Angeles.

Soon Pallotta TeamWorks was organizing AIDS rides all over the country, netting millions of dollars for medical services at AIDS charities. In 1998, Pallotta TeamWorks expanded into holding three-day fund-raising walks for breast cancer, and these proved even more successful. The first one, a sixty-mile hike from Santa Barbara to Malibu, brought in more than $4 million. Soon Pallotta TeamWorks was holding these fund-raising events all across the United States and even abroad, and it was moving into other causes including suicide prevention (a former boyfriend of Pallotta's had killed himself, making the issue particularly important to him). Dan does nothing halfway, so he poured money into marketing, advertising, and logistics to ensure that the events ran smoothly.

"People don't imagine the scope and the scale of it," Pallotta says. "People at the time would say, 'Is that a full-time job?' " In fact, Pallotta had more than 350 full-time employees in sixteen U.S. offices. The team included a sixty-member traveling crew that followed each bike ride or multiday walk to erect a mobile city each evening — including tents, toilets, kitchens, showers, medical units, and dining halls. Pallotta TeamWorks had another fifteen people in its internal advertising agency, including media buyers, graphic designers, a photographer, and a published poet. For capital, it set up a multimillion-dollar line of credit. Pallotta recruited the best people and paid generously — including a salary of $394,500 to himself in 2001. "We did what we believed would work," Pallotta recalls. "We advertised our events the way Apple advertises iPads."

Some activists in the stressed and contentious AIDS community accused Pallotta of profiteering. For one AIDS ride in the east, Pallotta TeamWorks had chosen as beneficiaries three AIDS groups working in Philadelphia. But there were ninety-one AIDS organizations in Philadelphia, and eighty-eight of them felt aggrieved. Some of them were focused on minority groups and accused Pallotta

TeamWorks of discrimination and racism. They threatened to hold a "die-in" at the beginning of the bike ride. That depressed participation by cyclists, which reduced the event's income, and the Pennsylvania attorney general ended up fining Pallotta TeamWorks $110,000 for generating a small percentage return and failing to register as a professional solicitor. The attorney general's opinion did not suggest any deception, but critics pointed to the fine to raise doubts about Pallotta.

Pallotta TeamWorks continued to grow, attracting 182,000 people as walkers or bicycle riders in its events. It accumulated an even more astonishing 3 million donors. By 2002, these events had raised $582 million, which Pallotta plausibly describes as "more money raised more quickly for these causes than any other events in history." Harvard Business School chose Pallotta TeamWorks for one of its formal case studies, and the company moved into a new 50,000-square-foot headquarters with state-of-the-art facilities. In 2002 Pallotta netted — after expenses — $81 million for AIDS and breast cancer services and research, a sum equivalent to half the annual giving of the Rockefeller Foundation at the time.

The charity world is notorious for its feuds, and Pallotta's flamboyance made him an increasing target. Some resented the way his name seemed to be at the center of everything. Some critics would say: *It's about him, not AIDS or cancer.* Others were aghast at the high salaries for people running charity events: *Why should ordinary workers contribute to charitable events run by people earning hundreds of thousands of dollars a year?* Logistics, marketing, and administrative expenses swallowed up about half of each dollar donated, and this drew additional fire. In 2001, Pallotta tried to expand too quickly, holding more AIDS bike rides than the market could bear, so the amount going to charity on those rides dipped to 21 percent. One rider sued, and outrage at Pallotta spread among some AIDS activists.

AIDS Community Donor Action ran an advertisement with the headline "Ask Pallotta TeamWorks Will Their Upcoming AIDS Vaccine Events Save Anyone's Future, EXCEPT THEIR OWN?" One critic denounced Pallotta's "greed and unabashed profiteering off the good intentions of others. People with AIDS do not need his services." Even Bill O'Reilly got in on the act, warning on Fox News that "the executives of this company are getting very wealthy off this."

Avon, which was Pallotta's partner in the cancer walks, announced it would cut its ties with him and hold its own fund-raising walks for breast cancer. Without a partner, Pallotta TeamWorks collapsed. It owed money to the bank, and now it had no way to make payroll or pay the rent. Pallotta describes that day as the worst in his life, and his voice still breaks as he tells the story. "It was just a horrible period in my life," Pallotta recalls. "To have lost all that family of 350 people and this beautiful new headquarters and this incredible business that took so long to get to this place. And then this lawsuit and the creditors. My God! It was just terrible."

Those who criticized Pallotta as a profiteer believed that without the glitz and advertising more money would be available for AIDS and cancer research. Indeed, the California AIDS bicycle rides continued under new management, in a more understated way—but without the promotional spending, the amounts raised for charity plunged. Net returns to AIDS charities dropped more than 70 percent in one year, from $6 million in 2002 to $1.6 million in 2003. The San Francisco AIDS Foundation laid off twenty-eight employees, and the Los Angeles Gay and Lesbian Center eliminated fifty-five jobs. More than 48,000 people participated in the last year of Pallotta TeamWorks walks for breast cancer; the next year, 8,000 people joined the Avon walks. The net amount raised for breast cancer grant making fell from nearly $71 million under Pallotta in 2002 to $11 million under Avon in 2003.

We tracked down one of Pallotta's most fervent critics back in 2002, Craig Miller, of AIDS Community Donor Action. "I stand by those criticisms," he said. "A tremendous amount of money was being raised by events produced by Pallotta TeamWorks. The money was being raised in the name of AIDS charities, but very, very little of the money raised was actually going to AIDS charities. The vast majority of it was being consumed by very high event production costs." As it turns out, Miller has been doing some of his own AIDS fund-raisers, including walks to raise funds for AIDS charities. Overhead for his 2012 walk in San Francisco ate up 58 percent of revenue—worse than Pallotta's average performance—and the event netted $1.2 million for AIDS charities, a paltry sum compared to the amounts raised by Pallotta.

After Pallotta TeamWorks collapsed, Dan salved his wounds by writing a book about his experience, *Uncharitable,* and in a TED Talk he cites his experiences to argue: "The way we think about charity

*Dan Pallotta leads his father on a Pallotta
TeamWorks AIDS Vaccine Ride in 2002.*

is dead wrong." He's right. There are basic problems with how we perceive and judge charities. These public judgments constrain the charity industry and limit its ability to do good.

When the public considers whether to support a nonprofit, one of the basic bits of information people look for is its Charity Navigator ratings and the proportion of its revenues consumed by administration, particularly salaries. Many people feel that employees at nonprofits should not be paid at private sector levels; psychic rewards should satisfy them. They also see overhead and marketing as a drain that should be absolutely minimized. Administrative expenses can indeed be relevant—we don't want to donate to an organization so that it can build itself a marble lobby—but what truly matters is not overhead but impact. There's no point in funding an AIDS vaccine effort that saves on overhead by using unreliable third-rate laboratory equipment. Would it have been better in the 1950s to finance a polio charity that used 99 percent of its funds to push survivors around a park in wheelchairs, or one that swallowed up half its money in salaries for talented scientists and lab equipment and ended up financing Jonas Salk's invention of the polio vaccine?

One shortcoming of Charity Navigator ratings has been that charities often respond by systematically underinvesting in anything overhead related. Charity Navigator is trying to figure out ways to measure impact, but its focus on overhead metrics has encouraged charities to skimp on computers, personnel training, evaluation, marketing, and talented people. And when you are starved of resources, you often underperform. The fervor of young people for humanitarian work is remarkable—a tribute to youthful idealism—and it's heartwarming that brilliant young people with Peace Corps experience, master's degrees from top universities, and superb language skills are competing for the chance to live in tents in South Sudan or Chad for $45,000 a year. But the enthusiasm often wears off over the years as family responsibilities grow, so turnover is high. We asked Charlie McCormack, who formerly ran Save the Children, about overhead at nonprofits, and he was blunt:

> Our uncompetitive salaries make it almost impossible for people to develop real careers; our under-investment in staff development hampers performance; and our creaky knowledge management and information systems undermine potential results. . . . Nevertheless, donors are more than resistant to funding these kinds of activities and consider pie chart ratios to be proxies for organizational quality. These and other pressures really do hamper results.

Forced to squeeze their overhead, aid groups cut corners in ways that undermine the mission. Without the funds or expertise to do rigorous evaluations, they're often groping in the dark to determine what works best. They also hugely underinvest in marketing, so they are hobbled in getting the word out. For example, scores of aid groups have made videos about the needs of women and girls, and most of these are so earnest and boring that they have zero impact. In contrast, the Nike Foundation prepared two videos called "Girl Effect" with the help of Nike's outside advertising agencies—the ones that get you to pay for a swoosh on a shoe. The Girl Effect videos have been watched 15 million times, spread on countless platforms worldwide to share the message about the importance of educating girls in the developing world. Any aid organization that had tried to invest in such professional work would have been denounced for wasting money.

Nike and other companies have clear metrics, such as net profits and share price, to judge their performance and to justify the success of marketing campaigns. It's more difficult in the case of a nonprofit, and perhaps that's one reason for the lack of investment in growth strategies like marketing—and a reason for the atomization of the sector. Researchers from the Bridgespan Group wrote in the *Stanford Social Innovation Review* that more than 200,000 nonprofits have started since 1975, but that by 2008 only 201 had reached annual revenues of $50 million. In a similar time frame, more than 46,000 for-profit corporations broke the $50 million barrier. Nonprofits almost invariably grow more ploddingly than for-profits, partly because they don't invest resources in building infrastructure, which means that they rarely gain economies of scale. There are no charity analogues of Google or Facebook.

When the spotlight is on overhead ratios, charities sometimes fiddle with their bookkeeping. A fund-raising appeal will include a paragraph about the challenges, so that a chunk of the mailing cost can be allocated to advocacy rather than fund-raising. Purchased in bulk on the international market, generic albendazole pills (for deworming) cost about 2 cents each. Major aid groups account for them at about $2 each (and, until a few years ago, at $10 each), because if the group is delivering 1 million pills, it sounds much better if it can boast that it's overseeing a $2 million deworming project, rather than a $20,000 program.

Nonprofits are often afraid to take risks or acknowledge failure for fear that failure will antagonize donors: *Why donate to an aid group that wastes its money?* Yet risk taking is the only way to improve, and it has been central to growth in for-profit companies. Unfortunately, while shareholders reward corporations for taking smart (and profitable) risks, donors punish nonprofits for deviating from the norm. In Silicon Valley, tech companies almost boast of their failures, as a tribute to their risk-taking cultures. But aid groups have an incentive to hide failures, and that makes it difficult to learn from mistakes. To its credit, a group called Engineers Without Borders that does excellent work on water, sanitation, and civil works around the world has started a website, admittingfailure.com, in which aid workers tell stories about what they did wrong.

In a complex world, initiatives sometimes need to fail at first in order to find an eventual path to success. One excellent international program, for example, provides free meals at schools in impoverished countries for only about 25 cents per child each day. This was originally conceived as a way to improve child nutrition and learning: with full bellies, the children would finally be able to concentrate. But when UNICEF and the World Food Program rolled out this school feeding program in poor countries, the nutritional gain was disappointing. Parents, knowing that their children could eat at school, fed them less at home. But parents were now more enthusiastic about keeping children in school, to reduce food costs at home, and so dropout rates declined. Since then the program has evolved to include special bonuses for girls who attend school regularly, such as a bottle of cooking oil to take home at the end of the month, and this has increased girls' attendance significantly. In short, what was conceived of as a nutrition program arguably failed in that sphere, but it succeeded brilliantly as an education program.

Dan Pallotta is now lecturing and writing widely about how, as he puts it, "our system of charity undermines the causes we love." Pallotta particularly resents criticism of salaries of leaders in the nonprofit industry. "We don't want people making money in charity," he says in a recent book, *Charity Case.* "Want to make $50 million selling violent video games to kids? Go for it. But if you want to pay the right leader half a million dollars to cure kids of malaria, you and the leader are parasites yourselves."

The nonprofit industry needs rethinking because it underperforms. And while we want to encourage charity, we think it's important to acknowledge the downside of the charity world as well as the successes. In a world of little accountability, giving money away to the greatest effect can be very challenging.

We make mistakes, too. In the first edition of our book *Half the Sky,* we endorsed the work of Greg Mortenson building schools in Pakistan and Afghanistan, beautifully described in his book *Three Cups of Tea.* Later it turned out that a chunk of the money donated to his organization went to buy copies of his book and to fly him around to give speeches. That was unacceptable. We visited Greg's schools and programs in Afghanistan and were impressed by them, but we wouldn't have commended his charity to readers if we had understood what many of the donations were going for.

As we see it, there are a few fundamental questions facing the charity sector:

First, how do we encourage charitable giving that actually helps the needy?

Not one of the fifty biggest donations to charity in 2012 in the United States went to an organization that principally serves the poor at home or abroad. Of all the money donated in America, only about one-third goes to the needy. At the top 200 universities, which get much of educational philanthropy, only 15 percent of students come from the bottom half of the income distribution.

The arts are certainly underfunded, gaining only about 5 percent of charitable donations, and they need our support. But gifts to museums lead to bidding wars among rival institutions that redistribute who owns the art and elevate prices of art in private collections—and is that the best way to help people?

The ultimate ornament is a membership on a board of directors. Stephanie Strom of *The New York Times* found that gaining a seat on the board of the Metropolitan Museum of Art often requires a donation of about $10 million, and joining the board of the Museum of Modern Art can require the same. These board seats are useful for making business connections that redound to the advantage of the donor. Meanwhile, these self-interested contributions are tax deductible, which means that they are subsidized by plumbers and nurses. When a tycoon donates a building named after himself to a business school, all taxpayers are subsidizing it while the tycoon is saving on taxes, earning a public relations benefit, and ensuring his grandchildren's admission. Is this really what charity is supposed to be about?

We strongly believe in giving to arts organizations and to universities as well. We proudly write checks to our alma maters each year, and serve on their boards. We encourage others to do so, too, but let's be clear-eyed—most of these donations are not helping the neediest people.

Second, how do we encourage generosity among the wealthy so that it helps the needy in the right ways?

The eighty-five wealthiest people in the world have approximately the same net worth as the bottom 3.5 billion. Even in the United States, the top 1 percent have a greater net worth than the bottom 90 percent. So while philanthropy can't be "the solution" to the world's problems, or America's, it can accomplish more than it does now.

That may be happening, as more billionaires focus on addressing the needs of the world's poorest people. A breakthrough resulted when Ted Turner, the businessman and founder of CNN, was invited in 1997 to give a speech at a United Nations gala. "I was on my way to New York to make the speech," he later told us in his characteristic drawl. "I just thought, 'What am I going to say?'" In impetuous Ted Turner form, he stunned and delighted his audience by announcing a $1 billion gift to United Nations causes such as fighting global poverty. In nominal terms, it was at the time the biggest single gift ever made. When we asked him why he made the gift, he said, "If I was going to speak to the UN, I had to say something!"

Turner paved the way for Bill Gates and Warren Buffett to donate billions of dollars to assist the world's neediest people, and then to recruit others for the "giving pledge," which commits billionaires to give away at least half their wealth. (Not everybody got the message: Donald Trump has given paltry sums and isn't even the largest contributor to his own foundation.) Tycoons such as Turner and Gates have brought to this field not only their wealth but also their business sensibility, emphasizing metrics and returns on investment. Partly because of Bill and Melinda Gates (and many other players, including Rotary International), the number of polio cases has dropped by 99 percent, the death toll from malaria is dropping sharply, and there is hope for scientific advances that will stop the spread of AIDS. Bill Gates's most important legacy may well be not software but the conquest of disease and hunger around the world.

Third, how do we create accountability so that we know our money is doing good? How do we move from celebrating the mere fact of giving to focusing on the impact a gift has?

Charities may start out with excellent intentions, and we don't begrudge their executives for living well if their organizations continue to do good. But that fine balance is not always easy to determine. A highly paid talented marketing executive focused on fund-raising numbers might push the envelope too far in an organization's tactics. And when is lavish spending too much or spending on the needy or on philanthropy too little? These aren't easy questions, but some critics have tried to answer them.

The *Tampa Bay Times* and the Center for Investigative Reporting compiled a list of what they called "America's Worst Charities," based on the amounts spent on fund-raising—including nineteen that allocated less than 1 percent of cash amounts received to those they were supposedly helping. Most of these had evocative names or sounded like established charities, such as Children's Cancer Recovery Foundation, American Association of the Deaf-Blind, or the Police Protective Fund. One enterprising family has profited by starting a dubious charity chain that includes Cancer Fund of America, Children's Cancer Fund of America, and the Breast Cancer Society.

People sometimes think that they can ensure money is well spent if they donate to a religious cause. That may explain the success of Paul and Janice Crouch, a married couple who used donations from well-meaning Christians to help build Trinity Broadcasting Network, the world's largest Christian television network. The Crouches pulled in $93 million in donations in 2010 alone, adding to more than $800 million in assets they had accumulated with the help of viewers over several decades. Alas, with that money, the Crouches built his-and-her mansions one street apart in a gated community in Newport Beach, California. Janice then shunned *her* house, with its tennis court and pool, preferring another home she was provided in Orlando, Florida. The couple also acquired lavish homes in Texas and Tennessee, as well as corporate jets valued at $8 million and $49 million each. The Crouches enjoyed thousand-dollar dinners with fine wine, also thanks to donations, according to Erik Eckholm, who wrote in *The New York Times* about a lawsuit filed for financial improprieties against the couple. Religious donors helped Janice rent two side-by-side rooms in the deluxe Loews Portofino Bay Hotel in Orlando—one for herself and one for her two Maltese dogs, according to two lawsuits. She kept the rooms for close to two years while she was building the Holy Land Experience theme park in Orlando, the *Times* said.

Secular charities sometimes don't do better. Breast cancer is a disease that needs attention and resources, so the Coalition Against Breast Cancer would seem a perfect cause. Yet the New York State attorney general filed suit against the coalition, charging that it raised $9 million and allocated less than $45,000 to fight breast cancer.

Almost everything can backfire. Western tourists to Cambodia, for example, often spend a day or two volunteering at an orphanage. But because well-meaning Americans fall in love with the kids and then make donations to support their education, a new business model has emerged among ruthless Cambodian entrepreneurs: round up half-starved but cute Cambodian boys and girls, take them away from their parents, and put them in a dilapidated building with a sign reading ORPHANAGE; then invite American tourists to visit, somberly ask the tourists to make donations to improve the facilities and pay for the kids' schooling—and then pocket the money, while continuing to starve the children. As a result, some aid groups now ask tourists to stay away from Cambodian orphanages.

The public compounds the problem through giving habits. As Daniel Borochoff, president of Charity Watch, puts it: "One reason people give is that they're asked. And the groups that do the asking are usually the ones that are least efficient." For example, you may be approached on the street by an earnest young woman asking you to make a donation for a food crisis in Africa. You imagine that she is a volunteer donating her time. Often, the aid organization has hired a company that pays people to ask passersby to contribute. These people are called "chuggers," short for charity muggers. Many charities say these professional fund-raising groups help bring in new donors, but they also often keep on average half or more of the money raised. While it can be hard to say no to a friendly pedestrian, you may want to first check on the charity's impact and, if you're impressed, donate directly to the organization. Or say you get a phone call from a firefighter association, asking you to donate $25 for firefighters' widows, and you imagine that the caller may have to put the phone down at any moment to go answer a fire alarm. Actually, a company hires men to make the calls, and they are neither firefighters nor volunteers. Maybe some money will go to firefighter widows, but a significant share will go to the company that makes the calls. Even those charities that place jars by the cash registers in shops, meant as repositories for your spare change, often must pay the store for placement, so a significant share of those coins will go to the shop owner rather than to those adorable kids pictured on the jar. You may like the pitch and the convenience of donating on the spot, but be aware of the donation chain. You can also go home and donate online.

So what is a donor to do in a world of fraud and manipulation? Here are two straightforward bits of advice:

First, don't give just because someone asks you to. Be particularly wary of marketing phone calls, emails, or mailings, or of a chugger who approaches you on the street. If a solicitor pressures you to give immediately, or to give cash, or is vague about anything at all, be particularly suspicious or ask the person to send you literature.

Second, conduct research. In this book we've introduced some organizations that we admire (many appear in the List of Useful

Organizations in the back), and they may be a starting point. But by no means limit yourself to them. If you hear about a nonprofit that appeals to you, look it up on the Web. Check out a prospective organization on Charity Navigator, Charity Watch, or GuideStar (and its ranking site, Philanthropedia), or take a look at the organization's IRS Form 990 and the Better Business Bureau's Wise Giving Alliance to help make sure it is not a scam, but don't be obsessed by percentages of revenues spent on administration and fund-raising. Watch out for charities that adopt a name similar to that of a well-known organization and try to piggyback on its reputation.

You can also support foundations that use evidence-based research to identify and invest in programs to help the poor, such as the Robin Hood Foundation. This foundation, a hedge-fund favorite, folds its network of business experts into programs it funds to fight poverty in New York City. Robin Hood draws on a team of smart and experienced managers to help nonprofits with challenges such as improving brand recognition, streamlining financial reporting, recruiting talented employees, and negotiating better leases. It is also starting Robin Hood clubs in high schools to encourage well-off teenagers to help fight poverty. As with charity:water, Robin Hood has certain donors pay for overhead costs, so that all other donations go directly to antipoverty programs.

We don't want to pretend that there are perfect answers to the problems we've raised. We're frankly conflicted in writing so bluntly about the problems with nonprofits. As we've said, we want to encourage giving, not breed cynicism. We just think that giving requires a foundation of transparency, accountability, and honest talk that doesn't always exist now. Billions of dollars and decades of work have been spent trying to chip away at poverty in America and around the world, and the progress—though real—is unsatisfying. We can do so much better.

Some of this may be dispiriting, but there are countless reminders that aid is sometimes transformative even in settings that might seem hopeless, and that American and overseas organizations can cooperate in ways that are breathtakingly successful. A case in point is Dr. Hawa Abdi, a Somali woman who is equal parts Mother Teresa and Rambo. Sixty-six years old, she is a diminutive woman with a brown complexion and a warm smile that conceals nerves of steel. She wears colorful dresses and head coverings, and day in and day out she works in one of the toughest environments for a doctor in the world. When she was twelve years old, her mother died in childbirth, so she resolved to become a doctor and save the lives of other pregnant women. An excellent student, Abdi while still a teenager won a scholarship to study medicine in Russia. She earned a medical degree, specializing in gynecology, and also a law degree, and then in 1983 she opened a one-room clinic on her family land. She offered medical help to impoverished Somali women. The number of patients steadily grew, and so did the clinic.

When Somalia fell into civil war, Dr. Abdi turned her land into a displaced-persons camp as well as a medical center. Eventually 90,000 people — 1 percent of Somalia's population — crowded onto her 1,000 acres of land, and her one-room clinic grew into a 400-bed hospital. She managed the entire encampment and started schools for children that were so well run that students were three grades ahead of those in the capital, Mogadishu. Worried that handouts would breed dependency, Dr. Abdi taught displaced people how to plant new crops and even started training former animal herders to fish in the sea. She advocated tirelessly for an end to female genital mutilation, which in Somalia takes a particularly extreme form, with a girl's genitals entirely cut off when she is about ten years old and the vaginal open-

Dr. Hawa Abdi

ing sewn up with wild thorns. This is excruciatingly painful and also makes childbirth more dangerous when the girl grows up. Dr. Abdi promoted women's empowerment in every way she could, and even ran a small jail in her encampment—for men who beat their wives.

Somali Islamic militants were appalled at the idea of a woman running such a large enterprise, so a warlord from the hard-line Hizb al-Islam, or Party of Islam, ordered her to hand over operations to his men. Dr. Abdi refused. "I may be a woman," she said, "but I'm a doctor. What have you done for society?" The Party of Islam then attacked the hospital with 750 soldiers, destroying equipment and the operating theater. Over the following days, there was growing outrage among Somalis at this assault on one of the country's few functioning institutions, and the warlord—taken aback at the furor—backed down. He now ordered Dr. Abdi to run the hospital under his direction. She refused. Each day for a week, the militia demanded that she obey, and she steadfastly refused to budge. Indeed, she insisted that the militia should not only leave at once but also write out an apology.

"I was begging her, 'Just give in,'" recalls Deqo Mohamed, her daughter, also a doctor. "She was saying, 'No! I will die with dignity.'" It didn't come to that. The Party of Islam grew tired of being denounced by Somalis at home and abroad and eventually slunk off—and wrote the apology that Dr. Abdi demanded. With the help of Vital Voices, an aid group for the world's women that Hillary Rodham Clinton had helped found, Dr. Abdi rebuilt her hospital and went back to helping her people.

The partnership of Vital Voices and Dr. Abdi is a useful model. Typically, it's the local people on the ground, such as Dr. Abdi, who have the knowledge and connections to get the most done, and in places such as Somalia they also don't raise sensitivities about foreigners imposing alien values on a local culture. Locals also tend to operate much more cheaply than foreigners, for they don't need convoys of SUVs and international flights for home leave. The locals may lack the back office skills in accounting, public relations, and fund-raising, as well as the most recent research on what interventions work. That's where the marriage between an international group such as Vital Voices and a local leader such as Dr. Abdi can be very effective. Vital Voices can raise money for Dr. Abdi, provide administrative and research expertise, and generate international outrage when she is threatened, and she can do the work on the ground, where she has the edge.

We've seen many examples of indomitable courage, but it's hard to beat Dr. Abdi and Vital Voices for the combined strength they bring to their work in Somalia, and for the change they accomplish together on the ground. And if one indefatigable woman can make a difference for tens of thousands of people even in a war zone, that should renew our own fortitude. Sure, charitable organizations need to get better, but no one who has seen an eager Somali child studying in a refugee camp school can doubt the good that they can achieve.

The Biggest Bang for the Philanthropic Buck

In 2006, Elie Hassenfeld was being well compensated for working long hours as a young analyst at Bridgewater Associates, a hedge fund based in Westport, Connecticut. He and some of his colleagues were making more money than they needed, and they talked about contributing some of what they earned to charity.

As investors, they wanted "bang for the buck." If they sent money to a water organization, they wanted the best water organization, where the wells work and the clean water is improving the community's health. But they didn't know much about charities, so they started looking into which organizations deserved their dollars. A total of eight Bridgewater analysts started meeting every week to discuss their findings. Pretty soon Hassenfeld and one of his colleagues, Holden Karnofsky, found themselves increasingly frustrated. They saw that existing charity evaluators were focused on financial ratios and organizational overhead. No one seemed to be reporting on charitable impact.

"The information we were looking for was not available to individual donors like us who want to give a few thousand dollars," said Hassenfeld, thirty-two years old. "Holden and I got very excited about doing research. We were staying up late Friday and Saturday nights sharing notes on which charities were doing well, and it struck us that while we liked our jobs, I wasn't excited staying up late studying the bond market." So Hassenfeld and Karnofsky started GiveWell, which uses rigorous evaluation of the kind that is common in the financial sector but applies it to charities. The idea is that investments in charities should be just as meticulously made as investments in stocks. GiveWell is part of a movement called "effective altruism," an attempt to bring more analytical rigor to charitable donations so as to have the greatest possible impact. Peter Singer of Princeton University has provided the philosophical foundation for the new movement.

Holden Karnofsky, left, and Elie Hassenfeld

In its early years, GiveWell looked at charities in the United States and abroad: KIPP schools, Teach for America, and the Nurse-Family Partnership were among its recommended charities at one point. But in early 2011, GiveWell switched its focus to international charities because Hassenfeld and Karnofsky found that staggering cost differentials allow donors to have more impact overseas. Most of their recommended charities are now working in global health, such as the Against Malaria Foundation and the Schistosomiasis Control Initiative (which combats a parasitic disease widespread in Africa, Asia, and Latin America). Throughout the year they write blog posts about their due diligence trips, mistakes, and reflections. GiveWell.org is an excellent place to get ideas about good international organizations to support.

GiveWell's donors and users tend to be young, and the organization is inspiring others to examine charities with the rigor applied to investments. Once only foundations or very wealthy individuals could apply sophisticated financial analysis to charity, but now anyone can piggyback on the work of GiveWell and other new players. "It's still a nascent movement," said Hassenfeld. "And not nearly as strong as I hope it becomes."

CHAPTER TWELVE

Madison Avenue Helps the Needy

It's not enough that we do our best;
sometimes we have to do what is required.

— SIR WINSTON CHURCHILL

Brian Mullaney had made it big on Madison Avenue. After rising to the top of an advertising agency, he quit and formed his own advertising firm. Soon he found himself rolling in cash, $2 million a year. He lived in a Manhattan penthouse, drove a Porsche, wore Armani suits, and had a gold Rolex watch on his wrist. He had everything in life—except a purpose. That's when he became involved in reconstructive surgery for disfigured children and soon learned about cleft lips and palates.

The human lip is formed in the second month of pregnancy. But sometimes the tissue doesn't come together properly and there is a slit or hole in the upper lip, going toward the nose. That's a cleft lip, and it's sometimes accompanied by a cleft palate, in which there's a hole in the roof of the mouth. No one knows quite why a cleft occurs, although it probably results from a combination of genetic and environmental factors (a mother who smokes is a risk factor). In the West, clefts are surgically repaired in the first year of life, but in poor countries the children often remain hideously disfigured. They may also have difficulty eating and speaking.

Inspired by how fixing a cleft, which is so simple, can change a life path, Mullaney became involved with a charity called Operation Smile, which provides surgical reconstruction for children with clefts around the world. He traveled with American surgeons to Vietnam and China and saw the transformation in children who had cleft lips and cleft palates repaired, and he began to dream of change on a grander scale. Operation Smile was running into its own problems, and Mullaney realized that, in any case, it often made little sense to fly American surgeons and tons of equipment halfway around the world for a week of work; local doctors could perform the surgery. He also calculated that by paying local surgeons for the same work it would be possible to save money, improve efficiency, and build the local skill base. He approached Charles B. Wang, an entrepreneur and the founder of Computer Associates, who agreed to put up the initial investment. Wang personally invested $27 million to back the effort in 1999, and he and Mullaney oversaw a new initiative they called Smile Train. The first two presidents they hired had nonprofit experience but lacked the business sensibility that Mullaney and Wang wanted. When they found themselves looking for a third president in two years, Mullaney agreed to take the helm himself for twelve months on an interim basis. He has never returned to the corporate world.

A business-driven, smart marketing approach led Smile Train to grow at an extraordinary pace. Mullaney focused on fund-raising by advertising and direct mail appeals, sending out mass mailings and carefully measuring which kinds of messages and photos worked best to generate donations. He studied which zip codes responded most generously. He compiled responses by name, learning that someone named Alyson will on average give more than someone named Suzie. While continuing to expand Smile Train at a breakneck pace, marching into new countries, and mastering the science of direct mail appeals, Mullaney began to think that a movie about Smile Train's work would surely help.

"I went to Hollywood; I couldn't get any meetings with anyone," Mullaney says. "So I come back and I go, 'Screw those people, let's do a documentary and try to win an Oscar.'" Smile Train hired two first-rate filmmakers, one of whom had already won an Academy Award, and sent them into the field to document cleft repairs and compete for the short documentary category in the Oscars. One of the directors, Megan Mylan, went to India and focused on telling the story of Pinki, an eight-year-old girl from Varanasi with a grotesque gap in her upper lip, extending to her nose. It was so disfiguring that it was hard not to feel revulsion, and villagers mocked and teased the girl for her deformity. Other children sometimes threw stones at Pinki, and she was reluctant to leave her hut. But her parents didn't have the money for an operation. That's when Smile Train stepped in and, as cameras rolled, helped Pinki get this life-altering surgery. Mylan finished the documentary just a week after the Oscar deadline had passed, so Mullaney put it in the drawer and waited until the time was right to roll it out for film festivals and compete for an Oscar. If it could get Oscar consideration, good things would accrue.

Countless aid groups have made promotional films and videos, usually watched by no one other than aid workers and their mothers. But this thirty-nine-minute film, named *Smile Pinki: A Real-World Fairy Tale,* was different. Powerful and triumphant, it was broadcast by HBO in the United States. *Smile Pinki* cost around $300,000 to make and was watched by millions of people, mostly in India, where it generated huge attention and sympathy for children with clefts. It also raised millions of dollars for Smile Train.

Pinki was flown to Hollywood to walk the red carpet and attend the Academy Awards ceremony; it was the first time she had worn shoes. Indian newspapers documented her departure for Los Angeles, accompanied by her father and the surgeon who had performed the operation, and villagers spent two days at the local Shiva temple praying for her to win an Oscar. When it came time for the broadcast, Pinki's mother and other villagers crowded around the only television in the village, in the home of a local official. Pinki herself sat

Brian Mullaney with a Smile Train patient near Kolkata, India

star-struck in her seat in the Kodak Theatre auditorium in Hollywood watching the celebrities around her, but then, exhausted by her trip, she fell asleep. She was dozing when it was announced that *Smile Pinki* had won the Academy Award. In her acceptance speech, Mylan declared: "Thank you, Pinki! Thank you for letting me tell your incredible story!" By then Pinki was awake and drowsily appreciative.

Mullaney used the success of *Smile Pinki* to help take his operations to new heights. Smile Train soon had a staff of forty-four people—raising more than $100 million a year. Mullaney's aggressive marketing techniques helped Smile Train raise about $700 million on his watch, reaching the major leagues of American charities.

Although Mullaney strongly agrees with much of Dan Pallotta's recommendations for the charity world, including the need to pay executives more and to use modern (and expensive) marketing, he thinks it's almost hopeless to convince the general public of this. So he just does what he thinks is necessary. Mullaney's compensation at Smile Train reached $750,000 a year (he was later required to give some back after a legal dispute), and he tended to recruit top-notch, business-minded executives, whom he paid very well by charity standards. "Charities by and large for whatever reason tend to hire large numbers of low-paid people," he says. "Smile Train hired very small numbers of highly paid people." He acknowledges that the appearance of these arrangements can have a negative impact but it's difficult to dispute his fund-raising results.

Over time, Mullaney began to believe that the challenge of cleft lips and cleft palates was diminishing. Smile Train and improved health care in China, India, and around the world were making a difference. The global cleft problem could be solved, he says, and local hospitals were developing better tools to manage the needs. But while the Smile Train board wanted to focus on bringing down the average age at which clefts were fixed, Mullaney wanted Smile Train to branch out to address other problems, such as burns, clubfoot, and blindness. Charles Wang, Mullaney's partner and financier, resisted, and in 2010, Wang and his board colleagues voted to move Mullaney out of Smile Train. The organization ended up caught in an uproar that led to feuding, resignations, and legal battles. Mullaney left to start a new organization where he would use the same direct mail techniques to tackle an array of other surgical health problems that plague poor countries and tug at donors' heartstrings.

One problem Mullaney focused on is clubfoot, aiming to help the 220,000 children born annually with feet turned inward—children like Rashida Yayé in Niger. Another was cataracts, a huge source of blindness affecting up to 20 million people worldwide. Yet the surgery to solve it is simple and can cost $90 or less in parts of the developing world. A third target for Mullaney has been burn injuries. This is a huge problem in the developing world, where one often sees children who never received treatment after falling into an open fire or being scalded when a pot of boiling water tipped off a wobbly stove. Villagers sometimes bandage the wounds so that skin tightens in ways that compound the injury; with a burned hand, for example, the fingers may end up fused together. Mullaney calculates that some 15 million children suffer from such burns and need corrective or cosmetic surgery.

These are relatively straightforward problems (burn injuries can be more complex) that are widespread and easily solved but can crush people who don't get assistance. A person who is blind can't work, and a child may have to drop out of school to lead him or her around, so cataract repair is often transformative for two people. And it makes economic as well as humanitarian sense, since the formerly blind person can then return to work and become an economic asset.

Mullaney called his new venture WonderWork, and it's a marketing machine, a charity conglomerate that is the umbrella and back office for a set of focused charities working on surgical problems in the developing world. One, 20/20/20, will offer free surgery for those with cataracts. FirstStep helps children with clubfoot. BurnRescue helps children with burn scars. Other charities focus on repairing holes in the heart or water on the brain. WonderWork has little surgical experience in these areas (although it does have a first-rate advisory board of medical experts, such as Atul Gawande), but it finances aid groups that do have that experience. CURE, a tiny nonprofit in Lemoyne, Pennsylvania, that we mentioned earlier, is weak at fund-raising. So Mullaney raises millions through WonderWork under the FirstStep brand, and much of the money is channeled to CURE. Remember how Mullaney's mailing led Shoshana Kline, the California woman, to write a $250 check to help Rashida with her clubfoot?

The half-dozen charities within WonderWork operate with the same marketing and fund-raising machine, sharing overhead to keep costs down, almost like General Motors offering a range of cars. If you respond to one blindness mailing with a check for $50, you may get a letter from FirstStep asking you to help kids in India with clubfoot.

Mullaney is a genial, enthusiastic man who exudes infectious pleasure in what he's doing. A few days before we sat down with him in his midtown Manhattan office suite, we happened to have received a fund-raising appeal for his blindness charity. As we began talking, we pulled out the mailing and asked Mullaney to explain it from a marketing perspective.

The most eye-catching feature of the envelope is a large photo of a toddler with the characteristic white spots on the pupil that suggest blindness from cataracts. The little boy is biting his lip and looks frightened: you look at him and want to reach for your wallet. He's also white, which might seem a bit odd for a charity that is focused on helping children in Asia and Africa. But Mullaney says the boy is from Russia, where Smile Train also works, and the picture is the result of careful market testing. With Steven Levitt, an economist at the University of Chicago and champion of "Freakonomics," Mullaney tested forty-nine children's faces of every possible complexion and expression to see how the public would respond. Perhaps because most potential donors are white, the biggest response is to white kids showing pain, with their health problem visible. In the lower left corner of the envelope is an emotional appeal: *One donation from you can restore the eyesight of a blind child.*

Mullaney intrigued us because he seemed so successful at the art of emotionally connecting Americans to distant suffering—a challenge that frustrated and eluded us. During the genocide in Darfur, Nick traveled through massacre sites, talked to a woman who had survived being set on fire because of the tribe she belonged to, and interviewed a man whose eyes had been gouged out with a bayonet. Yet although Nick was seared by what he saw, he felt as if his columns were shrugged off by readers. Meanwhile, New Yorkers were galvanized by another moral outrage. A red-tailed hawk nicknamed Pale Male had been nesting in a luxury apartment building on Manhattan's Fifth Avenue, beside Central Park, but the building managers tired of the bird droppings and dismantled the nest of Pale Male and his mate, Lola. New Yorkers could accept a faraway slaughter, but evicting two hawks was unacceptable: Bird lovers organized protests, reporters rushed to cover the story, and there was an outcry. The building managers eventually caved in, allowing the birds to return, and Pale Male became an international celebrity, the focus of a pop song and of two documentaries. We kept wondering: *How is it that Nick can't get people as riled up over genocide as they get over two homeless hawks?*

That acute frustration led us to investigate why it is that people respond to some moral appeals and ignore others. One pioneering expert on this issue is Paul Slovic, a psychology professor at the University of Oregon. Together with Deborah Small of the University of Pennsylvania and George Loewenstein of Carnegie Mellon, Slovic

Paul Slovic

conducted a series of experiments by raising funds for Save the Children using different strategies and carefully measuring the results. One approach was to offer a rational appeal emphasizing the scale of the global hunger crisis with a placard noting that "more than 11 million people in Ethiopia need immediate food assistance" and that "food shortages in Malawi are affecting more than 3 million children." That failed. People did not connect to impersonal statistics. Another strategy was an emotional call to help one particular girl:

> Rokia, a 7-year-old girl from Mali, Africa, is desperately poor and faces a threat of severe hunger or even starvation. Her life will be changed for the better as a result of your financial gift. With your

support, and the support of other caring sponsors, Save the Children will work with Rokia's family and other members of the community to help feed her, provide her with education, as well as basic medical care and hygiene education.

Rokia's photo accompanied the text, and people rushed to donate. We're invariably more moved by individual stories than by data.

This research underscores that decisions about helping others are largely emotional and intuitive, not guided by rational assessments of where the needs are greatest. Indeed, rational analysis seems to decrease generosity. Professor Small's group carried this idea a step further, "priming" research subjects by having them perform simple arithmetic calculations such as: "If an object travels at five feet per minute, then by your calculations how many feet will it travel in 360 seconds?" Subjects who answered five of these problems correctly, and who were thus thinking in a more rational, logical way, were much less generous to Rokia without becoming more generous to the larger group of hungry Africans. Thinking logically, it seems, can actually impair giving.

One of the most persuasive advocates of generosity is Peter Singer. His signature thought experiments include this one:

On your way to work, you pass a small pond. On hot days, children sometimes play in the pond, which is only about knee-deep. The weather's cool today, though, and the hour is early, so you are surprised to see a child splashing about in the pond. As you get closer, you see it is a very young child, just a toddler, who is flailing about, unable to stay upright or walk out of the pond. You look for the parents or babysitter, but there is no one else around. The child is unable to keep his head above the water for more than a few seconds at a time. If you don't wade in and pull him out, he seems likely to drown. Wading in is easy and safe, but you will ruin the new shoes you bought only a few days ago, and get your suit wet and muddy. By the time you hand the child over to someone responsible for him, and change your clothes, you'll be late for work. What should you do?

In response, nearly everyone says that the passerby should rush into the pond to save the child. Nobody is so crass as to inquire, *Well, how expensive are those shoes that would be ruined?* Yet, as Professor Singer notes, all the time we allow children to die—not in front of us, but half a world away—because we don't want to make a donation for, say, vaccinations or antimalarial bed nets that save lives at modest cost. To underscore his point, Singer called his excellent book on this topic *The Life You Can Save.*

Slovic, like us, has always found Singer's argument compelling, so in an experiment, he had people read about the drowning child dilemma before they were exposed to the appeal for Rokia. He figured that it would make people more generous. Instead, those who were exposed to the Singer construct donated less to Rokia. Slovic concludes that the drowning child thought experiment is like the math problems: it exercises the rational side of the brain and represses the intuitive moral feelings that might otherwise help a needy child.

The comedian Stephen Colbert captured the contradiction when he invited Nick on *The Colbert Report* to talk about Darfur. Colbert had been nervous about the show because, after all, how do you make fun of genocide? To his credit, he wanted to use his spotlight to help call attention to the slaughter, and he perfectly captured the zeitgeist by looking bored as Nick spoke about mass murder. Colbert then brightly interrupted: "Have you ever thought about writing about something less depressing? Because I was reading the *New York Post* the other day and they had a picture of a cat whose head was caught in a boot and it was adorable. And that's something I could care about, because it was an adorable picture. And it was so cute and I wanted to help that cat so badly."

The human attachment to individuals like Rokia and indifference to large groups is called the "identifiable victim effect," and it's confirmed by a plethora of research. Tehila Kogut and Ilana Ritov of Hebrew University found that people were willing to donate 75 percent more to a child in need of medical treatment when the child was identified by age, name, and a photo, compared to when the person in need was simply described as a child. They also found people more willing to donate toward a $300,000 treatment that would save a single child's life than toward a $300,000 treatment that would save eight children's lives.

The daughter of Jonathan Schooler, a psychologist now at the University of California at Santa Barbara, had an aquarium with tiny sea monkeys. When there were many of them, they appeared to be an undifferentiated swarm, so none of them was particularly interesting. Then they began dying off, until there was only one sea monkey left in the aquarium. Schooler noticed that now he and his children felt much more connection with it. They perceived it as playful and imbued it with personality; they were also much more concerned for its survival. As a result of that experience, Schooler and a colleague conducted experiments that found we generally impute higher-level intelligence to an individual than to one of a group. Indeed, the research found that we're more respectful of a person if he's dressed differently from others around him; put him into a uniform along with those around him, and it's harder to feel empathy for that person.

All this underscores what Stalin supposedly said (but historians suggest he probably didn't), "A single death is a tragedy; a million deaths is a statistic." Aid agencies and journalists alike tend to focus on large numbers of people who need help, and that may be one reason why such appeals often don't get traction. As Slovic puts it: "The more who die, the less we care."

A separate line of research suggests that the focus by aid groups and journalists on needs that aren't being met can also be counterproductive. Scholars find we give because we want to be a part of something happy and successful. If all we hear about the global poor is that they are starving and dying of AIDS, we may simply be turned off.

Humans are also not good at responding to needs when responsibility is diffuse, which is pretty much always the case with poverty and injustice. In one experiment, students were waiting to participate in a market research study when a woman went behind a screen and then appeared to climb on a chair to get something, only to tumble down. She moaned and cried out that her ankle was injured. When the waiting student was alone, he or she helped 70 percent of the time. But when there was a second person who pretended not to care in the room, the student helped only 7 percent of the time. We take our cues in part from those around us, and if the general response is apathy, we're more apathetic ourselves. There's no doubt that these ideas have substantial real-world effects. In the 1980s, activists fighting apartheid in South Africa were struggling to get traction. They tried slogans like "Free South African political prisoners," and people yawned. When they tried "Free Mandela," a global movement was born.

The foibles and irrationalities of our brain create a huge challenge.

Bill Gates expresses frustration that the global health world doesn't convey how thrilling it is to save lives. As he puts it:

> I remember going to Davos some years back and sitting on a global health panel that was discussing ways to save millions of lives. Millions! Think of the thrill of saving just one person's life—then multiply that by millions. Yet this was the most boring panel I've ever been on—ever.... What made that experience especially striking was that I had just come from an event where we were introducing version 13 of some piece of software, and we had people jumping and shouting with excitement. I love getting people excited about software—but why can't we generate even more excitement for saving lives?

To do that, we need to get better at storytelling to build connections and push for change. We know that *Uncle Tom's Cabin* made slavery real to many northerners, and Anne Frank's diary and Elie Wiesel's *Night* have provoked more outrage at Nazi brutality than have scholarly analyses. We need to tell the same kinds of stories about hunger and infant mortality, trafficking, and homelessness.

B y sending out millions of direct mail appeals and tracking the response rates, Brian Mullaney has developed his own expertise in building connections through empathy, and what he has found corresponds to the results of Slovic's academic research. Mullaney emphasizes storytelling about individuals, always showing how change is possible. In his letters about surgeries that cure blindness, Mullaney doesn't mention the term "cataracts," partly because he fears that Americans associate it with the elderly and don't understand that it can cause complete blindness. "Doctors are pissed at us about that," he says. "But consumers don't want to know that crap."

Within aid groups there has been a backlash against grim photos of suffering children—sometimes called "poverty porn"—but Mullaney is unapologetic. Cheerfully exaggerating, he mimics a UNICEF official: "We don't want to show any unhappy kids. No kids with flies." He shakes his head: "It's so antiseptic and artificial. It's like they're dancing around a little village. Why is that? Well, because the managers who are white who work at UNICEF, they go, 'I feel uncomfortable with that.'" Mullaney pauses and shakes his head emphatically. "If you want to raise money, you have to show a problem and suffering."

When we asked Mullaney about the economics of the mailing that we received, he surprised us with a revelation: he expected it to lose money. A first mailing, he says, always loses money, because for every 75,000 direct mail letters sent out to potential new donors, Mullaney says on average 323 new contributors are found.

Overall, Smile Train says it cost $1.79 to raise a single dollar from a new donor in 2012. Mullaney is finding the figures are a little better at WonderWork, but it still costs him $1.45 to raise a dollar from a new donor for clubfoot. Mullaney is willing to lose money the first year with a new donor because he feels he can raise money cheaply in subsequent years. For second and future mailings, the response rate is about 6 percent. After about five years, each $1 invested in direct mail has raised a total of $5 or so.

Like Dan Pallotta, Mullaney argues that charities should operate like businesses in the sense that they should pay for marketing and advertising if that will help the organization achieve scale and have a greater impact. It frustrates him that so many charities scorn professional marketing. "They look at marketing as beneath them: 'It's dirty work, it's slimy, it's sleazy,'" he says. "People come in and go, 'Direct mail? No. I'm going to grow my charity on the Internet because it's free.'"

Mullaney is regularly invited to make presentations to boards of other nonprofits. The conversation usually goes downhill when he explains that the millions he raised were from direct mail:

BOARD MEMBER: *I'm not comfortable spending millions of dollars on direct mail.*
MULLANEY: *Oh, I'm sorry, let's cut that budget in half, and help half as many kids! Would that make you more comfortable?*

"They reject everything," Mullaney protests. "It's a complete waste of time because they don't have the marketing background." He says that charities get by with weak productivity records that would lead General Motors or Ford to go bankrupt and shut down, but with a charity, the refrain is: "They're doing God's work. Aren't they great?" Mullaney notes that there were more than 500 car companies in the early twentieth century, but then a consolidation led to the survival of just a few big ones that could enjoy economies of scale. The same is needed in the charity world, he argues; instead of 1.4 million charities in America, he says there should be no more than 5,000.

Brian Mullaney is brash, and his marketing sensibility can rub traditional nonprofit leaders and donors the wrong way. For example, some might argue that using pictures of a white boy to raise money that goes overwhelmingly to kids in Asia and Africa is misleading. But as long as a charity is true to its mission and showing significant impact, selling a cause is also important.

Mullaney's approach recalls a truth attributed to P. T. Barnum: "Without promotion something terrible happens—nothing!" We flinch at selling blindness and clubfoot as if they were potato chips or laundry detergent, but we're even more troubled by the sight of children who are blind or have clubfoot and aren't getting treated because organizations aren't efficient at raising the money to treat them. You see children with clubfoot dragging themselves through the traffic at intersections in cities around the developing world, begging for money from passing cars. That's a thousand times more undignified than using their photos in mailings. Mullaney may be paid a hefty salary, but he has helped vast numbers of children all over the world—and by using local doctors in developing countries, he figured out how to lower costs, serve more people, and build local capacity. At the end of the day, Mullaney helped start an organization that provided a million free surgeries for cleft lips and cleft palates around the world, giving kids such as Pinki new lives—and helping eliminate cleft in much of the world. And now Mullaney is starting all over again to do the same with burns, cataracts, clubfoot, and more.

The blunt fact is that people working on urgent causes such as poverty or disease too often fail to make their case effectively, in part because they feel that "marketing" is beneath them. When we were both at *The New York Times,* every day we received thoughtful, professional pitches from companies about products that in the end matter very little to the world. Meanwhile, groups working on life-and-death issues such as AIDS would send out unprintably dry press releases to the wrong address. Altruists may flinch at the idea of marketing, but it's more important to "sell" vaccines or girls' education than it is to sell a hamburger.

As it happens, just as we were writing this chapter we got a mailing from the United States Fund for UNICEF, an organization we admire. It contained a tote bag gift for us. When we get these kinds of gifts from aid organizations we gnash our teeth at the waste. Likewise, when we receive a mailing with a stamped return envelope, we grumble about the money squandered on stamps. We remark to each other that we wouldn't want our own donations going to send address labels, nickels, stamped envelopes, or tote bags to random people in a database. We called Caryl Stern, the president of the United States Fund for UNICEF, to grouse about getting the tote bag. But she explained that the tote bag goes only to their best prospects for donations, and that it doubles the response rate. The upshot is that more money is raised for vaccinations, school feedings, and all the other work UNICEF does. Stern noted that the United States Fund for UNICEF has been in the vanguard of experimenting with direct mail for many years, and in 2002 it became perhaps the first aid group to put a nickel in mailings, visible through a glassine window on the envelope. The response rate in the mailings rose from 0.78 percent without the coin to 1.47 percent with it.

"While we did get criticized, it was one of the most successful direct mail campaigns we did," Stern told us. "We're here to raise money to save kids' lives. If at the end of day I'm raising more money and saving more lives, I'm sleeping well at night."

Lessons from a Master Pastor

In national polls of pastors, the church they often choose as most influential in the United States is Willow Creek Community Church, located in a suburb of Chicago. A nondenominational megachurch, it was founded by the Rev. Bill Hybels in 1975 and now attracts more than 25,000 people to weekend services. Hybels, sixty-two, is soft-spoken and understated, a centrist in the religious world who has made social justice issues a pillar of his church. Rick Warren of Saddleback Church in Southern California has embraced social causes as well, as have other megachurches around the country. They can be a towering force to create opportunity in the United States and abroad.

Willow Creek brings ministers from poor countries—including Guatemala and Malawi—to Chicago, where they stay in the homes of church members and make lifelong friends. Soon those Chicagoans on business trips to London are traveling on to Malawi. In Africa, Willow Creek has focused particularly on fighting HIV/AIDS, and its volunteers travel together to Africa to work with local churches on community projects and bridge building. Willow Creek has also increasingly focused on empowering women and fighting sex trafficking at home and around the world. It has a sex trafficking reading group and also works on prison justice issues, encouraging members of the congregation to volunteer in prisons. When we were visiting Willow Creek to talk about the importance of empowering women around the world, congregation members were volunteering time to put together 530,000 packets of high-quality seeds for Zimbabwean farmers, largely women. Each churchgoer that day was given a brightly colored knit bag to make offerings for global poverty causes, and one Monday after a service a Fed Ex driver making a delivery at the church office handed over one of the bags.

"I found this in the parking lot," she said. "I think it's a purse that

Bill Hybels

someone dropped." The receptionist explained that it wasn't a purse but a bag to make an offering to help women farmers fight global poverty, and the Fed Ex driver took it back and looked at it with new respect. "I'm not a member of any church and I don't think about religion very much," she said, "but I think this is the kind of church I'd like to belong to."

Willow Creek has also opened a "care center," serving people who live in nearby communities and are down on their luck. Staffed by volunteers, it provides shelter for the homeless, clothing for needy kids, a food pantry with vegetables grown in a community garden, dental care, vision screening, legal counseling, and help preparing a résumé and finding a job. If you're desperate because your car broke down and you can't afford a repair, volunteers will even lift the hood and see what they can do. All this requires a small army of church volunteers, including lawyers, mechanics, and those with green thumbs.

If Brian Mullaney excels in one kind of marketing for nonprofits, the megachurches are masters of another kind. Part of their success is their skill in communications and attention to their audience. They make engaging in altruism an upbeat, pleasant, and rewarding experience. Instead of guilt-tripping congregations, the churches present altruism as an opportunity to make a difference and to learn about the world. All this is a social activity, a way to work with friends and make new acquaintances, and there's no embarrassment about the fact that it feels fulfilling and rewarding. There's plenty for secular organizations to learn from the sense of joy that Hybels and others manage to convey with the act of giving and engagement in a social cause.

More broadly, it would help enormously if secular and religious forces were more willing to work together in building opportunity around the world. Both do some outstanding work in addressing humanitarian issues, and they could accomplish far more — especially in advocacy — if they worked together. The "God gulf" of suspicion makes it harder to forge ahead against the common enemies of humanity. The distrust, partly a function of the toxicity of American politics, means there's not enough cooperation on issues that everybody cares about, particularly domestic poverty.

We think each side bears some responsibility for the God gulf. Evangelicals let their image be shaped by preening television pastors who are obsessed with gays and who are passionate about human life — until birth. One study finds that even among churchgoers in their teens and twenties, the terms most associated with present-day Christianity are "anti-homosexual," "judgmental," "too involved in politics," and "hypocritical." In the late 2000s the Vatican played a tragic role when its hostility to condoms contributed to the AIDS epidemic. Richard Stearns, a committed evangelical Christian who left a successful corporate career to run the Christian aid group World Vision, writes in his moving book *The Hole in Our Gospel* of his distress when he saw AIDS orphans in Uganda. "What sickened me most was this question: where was the Church?" he writes. "Where were the followers of Jesus Christ in the midst of perhaps the greatest humanitarian crisis of our time? Surely the Church should have been caring for these 'orphans and widows in their distress' (James 1:27)." Stearns lacerates "a Church that had the wealth to build great sanctuaries but lacked the will to build schools, hospitals, and clinics."

Yet the secular left is also responsible for the God gulf. Liberals who pride themselves on their tolerance sometimes mock conservative evangelicals and Catholics for their faith, rarely acknowledging the extraordinary good they often do. These secular critics fume about the Vatican's policy on condoms but don't appreciate that the rural clinics in Africa that treat AIDS patients are often Catholic-run — and that the priests and nuns there sometimes distribute condoms themselves in the battle to save lives from AIDS. Travel in remote, dangerous, and desperate parts of the world and you routinely encounter nuns and priests truly living the Gospel. In early 2014, when mobs of Christians rampaged through the Central African Republic, massacring Muslims, it was often Catholic priests who stood up to the attackers and risked their lives to offer Muslims shelter. Likewise, in the 1994 Rwanda genocide, the only American to remain in the capital during the entire slaughter was Carl Wilkens, a Seventh-Day Adventist missionary who sent his family to safety and then sheltered survivors and roamed the city to save lives. Wilkens was sure he would be killed and that even if he somehow survived he would be fired by his church for defying orders to evacuate, yet he would not bend. Such people merit awe, not snide contempt.

In the United States as well, churches are a pillar of support for the poor and homeless in ways that the secular left often does not acknowledge. A vast number of food pantries and soup kitchens around America are run by local churches and volunteers. The same is true of clothing drives to collect winter jackets and distribute them to the needy. Many churches also offer a range of other services, even health and dental clinics, so that in small-town USA much of the help that the needy get is from local churches.

Some liberals falsely assert that Christian aid groups help only those who are Christians (this is not true of the major organizations) and don't appreciate the scale of giving by people of faith. World Vision has 40,000 staff in roughly 100 countries—more than CARE, Save the Children, and the United States Agency for International Development combined. Some secular liberals are pushing to end the longtime practice of channeling aid through religious aid groups, even though that would cripple aid efforts. In the past five years, half of food aid in Haiti went through religiously affiliated organizations, such as World Vision, that have deep networks on the ground. When secular critics sneer at evangelicals, they're displaying the narrow-mindedness of the religious "bigots" whom they criticize. Religious Americans actually donate more of their income to charity and volunteer more of their time than any other group. If secular liberals can give up some of their scorn, and if religious conservatives can retire some of their sanctimony, combined they might succeed in making greater progress against common enemies of humanity.

CHAPTER THIRTEEN

Scaling Social Good

No one has ever become poor by giving.

— ANNE FRANK

B ernard Glassman was an aeronautical engineer with a doctorate in applied mathematics who wanted to make a dent in homelessness. He could have started a shelter or a soup kitchen, but instead, after six months of study, he decided that the greatest need was for jobs. So he set out to start a factory making baked goods in Yonkers, a New York suburb with a great deal of homelessness. Greyston Bakery would be a for-profit factory and would hire any homeless person seeking a job. "Whoever showed up, we took them in," said Glassman. "We did not do any checks on backgrounds. If they did a good job, they'd remain. If not, they'd go." The business won contracts, making cakes for Macy's for a time, but there were challenges.

"There were crack vials everywhere," said Glassman. "People were afraid to come. Next to us was a brothel. We'd come to work. The hookers were finishing up."

This kind of for-profit model to address social ills is gaining ground, simply because it can generate profits that help make it sustainable and scalable. The old distinction was between for-profit corporations and nonprofits. These days, that's no longer the key distinction in the social sphere. Rather, what's considered crucial is impact. If Greyston can sell more and more cakes and pastries around the country, hiring homeless people to make them, that could do more for the homeless than any well-intentioned soup kitchen.

LIZZIE PRESSER

*Bernard Glassman founded Greyston
Bakery to help provide jobs to struggling
residents of Yonkers, New York.*

We've discussed how nonprofits could use help investing in marketing, transparency, and scale, and another fruitful path is building a sustainable model. Here we'll explore socially driven companies that generate revenues to support their costs and earn a return. Later we'll take a look at how some large corporations are helping drive change by applying their expertise to social endeavors, either through joint ventures with nonprofits or by giving employees time for pro bono initiatives. This muddling of for-profit and nonprofit roles puts some people on guard, but it also creates a huge opportunity. When for-profit companies, whether a small bakery or a mighty corporation, tackle social problems, they can have at least as much impact as a nonprofit. We hope that more people will seek enterprise solutions to social problems, and that more companies will dabble in these social ventures and encourage employees to do so.

Another of the pioneers in amalgamating the nonprofit and for-profit worlds is Jacqueline Novogratz, who started as an international banker, then drifted into the aid world in Africa. She became frustrated that many aid projects consisted of handouts that bred dependency and seemed to stifle creativity. In Rwanda, she became involved in a bakery project in which twenty poor women made doughnuts and samosas to sell in the neighborhood. Two charities subsidized the project at the rate of $650 a month—more than $1 per woman each day—and yet the women earned only 50 cents daily from selling the baked goods, too little to survive. Novogratz helped the women transform their bakery efforts from a charity project into a real business in which they turned a profit and each woman earned $2 a day, four times their previous income. Market pressures forced them to become more competitive, too, and they gained new skills. The market was merciless, and everything that could go wrong did: women stole from the business, and they used rancid oil that made people sick. But they finally learned to run a decent business that showed considerable promise—and then collapsed in the Rwandan genocide.

From the ashes of that bakery, Novogratz began to experiment with "impact investing"—applying charitable donations to support for-profit businesses. Novogratz's own Acumen Fund does impact investing around the world, providing funding for small companies that do everything from manufacture antimalarial bed nets to provide medical care in India. Instead of folding business savvy, marketing expertise, or businesslike practices into nonprofit organizations, the way Dan Pallotta does, these enterprises start from the other end of the spectrum by folding a social mission into a for-profit business. "Change the way the world tackles poverty," Acumen urges donors.

A new vocabulary is emerging to describe these hybrids trying to knit social goals into their operations: benefit corporation, blended value, mission-driven, for-benefit, value-driven, venture philanthropy, fourth sector, and hybrid organization. And these businesses are found in many sectors.

Addressing poverty with enterprise, however, is devilishly difficult, because in the business world good intentions alone don't cut it. Greyston's break came when Glassman was in Colorado for a conference and took a walk around Gold Lake with Ben Cohen and Jerry Greenfield, the famous cofounders of Ben & Jerry's Ice Cream. Ben and Jerry were interested in fostering social good and liked Glassman's program at Greyston. They ordered a few of Greyston's cakes and tarts and liked how they tasted. Ben & Jerry's then invited Greyston to try to become its backup supplier of brownie wafers for ice-cream bars. It was a tall order. Ben & Jerry's had tried a few other companies and hadn't found what it was seeking.

Glassman experimented for months, trying different ingredients and methods, hiring eighteen people, and borrowing from the bank to buy machinery the bakers thought necessary. They couldn't quite achieve the desired taste, but Glassman kept thinking of all the employees he could hire with a big client like Ben & Jerry's, and so he wouldn't give up. One day he got a call from a friend whose family was in the baking equipment business. The friend offered a crucial insight: the secret is not to roll brownie batter like a sheet but to pour it from a bowl into the baking pans, he said. That made the difference in texture after baking. Greyston refined its processes accordingly and won the Ben & Jerry's account. That year, after a bit of brainstorming, Ben & Jerry's sprinkled some brownie wafers into chocolate ice cream and called it Chocolate Fudge Brownie. It is still one of the company's most popular flavors.

The priority, of course, wasn't brownie wafers but homelessness and helping low-income families move up the economic ladder. Jobs were necessary, but so were affordable housing options and child care while the parents worked. So Glassman set out to build a foundation that complemented the bakery and offered services to support employees and other Yonkers residents. The profits from the bakery would help finance the foundation. Today, Greyston has 150 employees and the foundation operates 300 housing units to ease homelessness. The bakery has sales of $13 million a year, giving jobs to people such as Dion Drew.

"They called me on a Wednesday," said Drew, who had submitted his application the previous October. "If I hadn't heard by Sunday, I'd have started selling drugs again." Just nine months earlier, Drew had been released from four years in prison. He had been looking for legitimate work in hopes of making a fresh start in life, but potential employers would look at his criminal record and turn away. He was thirty-one and had never had a real job. He had started selling drugs at age thirteen and then dropped out of school when he started making money. On a good day he'd pull in $2,200; on a bad day, $1,200. He had a girlfriend and a nice apartment, and he helped out his mom financially. But he spent as he earned, and he was in and out of jail. The little brother of his best friend got killed. Other friends died. His surviving buddies were in prison. He decided to turn his life around, if he could just get a job. Of course, for ex-convicts that isn't easy: one survey in Washington, D.C., found unemployment among the formerly incarcerated to be 46 percent.

At Greyston, he was given the night shift making packing boxes in which to ship the brownies. "On my first day, I fell asleep on the job," explains Drew. Things improved and he was soon on the day shift, where he's been for four years. He went from earning $7.15 an hour to $13. He is never late, has had no absences, and gets bonuses for good work. Now Drew heads up research and development for Greyston, mapping out plans for testing new products. He helped launch a line of crunchy brownies and a variety of new flavors in brownies: jalapeño, chipotle, chile, and orange.

"My mom, she can't stop smiling," Drew says. He has a wife and a new baby daughter. For his daughter, "I got out life insurance. I opened an account for her. I save $5 a week for her. She's going to college. Maybe medical school."

Greyston has a colorful range of employees working side by side in its small operation in Yonkers—former drug addicts, ex-convicts, and former homeless people; an information technology specialist who once studied Zen; a former Silicon Valley high-tech entrepreneur, Mike Brady, who left technology for the organic food business and now runs the operation. Brady wants to grow the organization so that it can employ more people, but he must always balance its financial and social missions. Brady has hopes to move Greyston to annual sales in the many millions of dollars, which would make it one of the larger companies with what some call a double bottom line— where social good is as important a goal as profit. But historically it has been a challenge for such enterprises to scale up because fundamentally it's not always possible to optimize both profits and mission, and social purpose tends to be paramount.

"They're figuring out on the side some way to maximize revenue," says William Foster, who runs the consulting practice at Bridgespan, which advises nonprofits. Foster sees change coming, particularly in the form of new social entrepreneurs who have much more sophisticated business skills than those of an earlier generation. He predicts that more social enterprises will grow into large companies. One example of an up-and-comer is Change.org, a for-profit company that helps people create online petitions for social causes. In early 2013 it had 35 million users and more than $15 million in revenues after just six years in operation. Boosted by its dynamic founder, Ben Rattray, it raised $20 million in investment from socially minded investors. Another is Warby Parker, founded by graduates of Wharton Business School to sell high-quality eyeglasses online. For each pair sold, it donates funds or another pair of glasses to VisionSpring, a non-profit that trains "vision entrepreneurs" in developing countries to start businesses selling locally appropriate eyewear (access to reading glasses can add many years to a person's working life). More and more, these enterprises are making an explicit statement about social responsibility in their outreach to the public, or they are embedding social responsibility in their products by using organic ingredients, curbing energy use and waste, and addressing social ills.

One of the attractions of the sector is customer demand. Nearly one-third of American consumers want to increase purchases from companies that are socially responsible, according to Good.Must .Grow., which tracks consumer interest in this space. Reflecting the growing interest, Dow Jones tracks a Dow Jones Sustainability Index, which has assessed more than 1,800 public companies based on environmental behavior, labor practices, gender policies, and similar admirable goals.

Among the new players is a for-profit enterprise, Better World Books, that operates quietly on college campuses. It was founded by Kreece Fuchs, a Notre Dame student who was low on money in 2001 and took some of his textbooks to the campus store in hopes of selling them. Except for *Legal Aspects of Environmental Engineering,* though, the store wasn't taking any back. Desperate, Fuchs listed his books on an online site, half.com. He made $500 that first day. A friend, Xavier Helgesen, started selling his books, too, and then the two of them sold their roommates' books. They couldn't believe how well the sales went. "Imagine how many books at Notre Dame were being thrown away," Fuchs said. An idea began percolating. They met with the Robinson Community Learning Center, which does outreach to low-income families and runs after-school activities in South Bend, Indiana. Fuchs and Helgesen organized a book drive, selling donated books online and splitting the proceeds with the learning center. The center's director, Jay Caponigro, thought the students might raise a few hundred dollars.

Fuchs and Helgesen put up posters and boxes in the dorms, and soon used books came pouring in. Dorm resident directors were calling the two entrepreneurs to pick up the boxes, which were overflowing with books. They collected 2,500 books and listed them all on Amazon. A few minutes after finishing all his uploads, Fuchs checked

Kreece Fuchs at the warehouse for Better World Books

his email. He had closed a sale for his first book, *C Programming Language,* for $21.99 to a student at the University of Utah. Excited, he ran out to tell his friends. By the time he had walked back to his computer they had sold another six books. Fuchs borrowed a car, loaded boxes of books into the trunk, and made many trips to the post office. "That was when we realized there was something to this," said Fuchs. "We sold $16,000 worth of books," he added. "The fun was when I presented Jay with a check for $8,000."

By October, one of their former roommates, Jeff Kurtzman, was getting bored with his banking job in New York and found the new venture an exciting prospect. He took his year-end bonus, left the firm, flew to South Bend, and joined Fuchs and Helgesen in their book venture. That fall, the team won the university competition for best social venture and received $7,000, which allowed them to rent cars, trucks, and warehouse space. When they formalized their venture in 2003, they created Better World Books as a for-profit enterprise with a social mission of helping literacy programs. Better World Books places book drop boxes near street corners, college dorms, and other high-traffic locations for readers to recycle their books, and it seeks old books that libraries would otherwise throw out and gives a percentage of what it makes to those libraries. On average, Better World

Books donates 5 to 7 percent of *revenues,* even if it has no profits, to libraries or literacy programs.

The whole cycle creates happy customers. Fuchs argues that the mission and business of Better World Books go hand in hand, because the social mission is the reason people donate books to the company. After two years, the company revenue stood at $1 million. Two years later, revenues hit $10 million. The three partners hired their business school competition judge, David Murphy, as their CEO, set up regional offices, and expanded to 1,500 colleges and 3,500 libraries across the country. They have invested $2 million into developing a proprietary book scanning and inventory management system. After a decade in business, Fuchs is the most actively involved, serving as vice president of logistics and a member of the company's board of directors, while Helgesen chairs the board but is not involved on a day-to-day basis.

Giant trucks rumble across the flatlands to unload about 600,000 books every week at Better World Books' 300,000-square-foot warehouse at the edge of Mishawaka, a town near South Bend in northern Indiana. Workers comb through giant boxes of used books and evaluate them, shelving the good ones and then selling them to used-book buyers around the world. About 60 percent of the books are deemed not saleable and are recycled.

Stacks of books line the entire factory, seemingly as far as the eye can see. Once in a while, a nice surprise shows up. That's what happened to Ryan Van Plew-Cid, a thirty-seven-year-old rare book specialist who works in a temperature-controlled room inside the warehouse. Better World Books had received a collection from a library that had shut down. Van Plew-Cid opened a book published in 1840 and found an early nineteenth-century lithograph copy of the Declaration of Independence, "folded up and tucked away, perfectly preserved as though nobody over the years had opened up that book and pulled it out," said Van Plew-Cid. Better World Books sold the Declaration for $16,000 on eBay, raising a significant sum for its literacy partners.

Though the social mission is woven into the for-profit business, Better World Books is focused on eliminating inefficiency and driving up volume. It is converting to high-density storage, where books are stacked on top of each other rather than side by side. Fuchs is also planning to retool the software management system and to reach out to ordinary consumers with large book collection receptacles on streets all over the country.

Better World Books now processes 120,000 books a day, 40 million a year. It broke the $50 million barrier in revenues in 2012 and is still growing by double digits each year, including 11 percent in 2013. It has donated more than $15 million so far to more than 100 literacy programs. Margins are slim, and while Better World Books is performing a bit better than break-even, it has chosen to reinvest profits into expansion and promotion of literacy.

Most publicly traded companies start out focused on growth and then, after creating a cushion of profits, begin to give back and adopt corporate social responsibility programs. But a few large companies are trying to embed social responsibility into their culture from the beginning, partly to create goodwill among customers. That's how Whole Foods Market survived a catastrophe early in its life. In 1981, less than a year after it launched operations in a new 10,000-square-foot store in Austin, Texas, the city suffered its worst flood in seventy years. The flood wiped out some $400,000 of the store's inventory and equipment—and Whole Foods had no insurance. But it had strong customer loyalty, and so people from the community joined the store's nineteen workers in cleaning up and fixing the place, which reopened twenty-eight days after the flood. Whole Foods recovered its footing and soared.

Three decades later, Whole Foods has spawned a sub-economy of its own, with a sophisticated, far-flung, and complicated supply chain network that includes large providers and local ones. Among Whole Foods' suppliers is Greyston Bakery, which provides—what else?— brownies. Greyston has hired thirty people to expand the Whole Foods brownie line.

Impossible, Possible Task
A Happy, Healthy Meal

In 2006 Kirsten Tobey and Kristin Richmond partnered for a homework assignment at the Haas School of Business at the University of California at Berkeley. They outlined a company that would create, plan, and deliver healthy meals to cafeterias in schools, particularly those with at-risk students living in low-income neighborhoods with no stores selling fresh vegetables. Though the school lunch market is $16 billion nationwide, there are very few suppliers of healthy, fresh meals, especially for low-income students on government-subsidized meal plans. Tobey and Richmond saw a niche for a company that could do well by doing good.

Tobey and Richmond finished the homework assignment but couldn't put the idea behind them. They started a company, Revolution Foods, to test their idea, but reality quickly intruded when they learned that if they wanted to serve underprivileged children, the maximum the government would pay for a school lunch was less than $3 a person. It seemed hardly possible to provide a healthy meal for such a price, but they were determined to try.

Their first hire was a chef, Amy Klein, who had earlier worked at Teach for America. Then they started asking kids why they didn't like the cafeteria food. Tobey and Richmond heard over and over that the food quality and selection were dreadful. Whole Foods helped them build a supply chain and advised them on what equipment to put in their kitchens. Supplies were a particular challenge at the wholesale level. When Tobey and Richmond needed lunch meats without nitrates and nitrites, they could only find them in consumer-size packets.

Kirsten Tobey, left, and Kristin Richmond,
founders of Revolution Foods

Revolution Foods started in a kitchen in Emeryville, California, that it rented from a catering company. "We would come in at 3:00 a.m. and deliver meals to the school and we'd be done at twelve or one o'clock," said Tobey. "Then the catering company would come in." Soon word of mouth spread, the phones started ringing, and more and more schools wanted to work with Revolution Foods.

After expanding to 8,000 meals per day, they opened a kitchen in Los Angeles and then surged from there, so that they now reach twenty-five major cities. Today they employ 1,000 people making one million meals a week around the country, from Newark to Houston. They have discovered that the secret to getting kids to eat is presentation and taste. Kids first eat with their eyes, so if they don't like what they see, they won't touch it. Despite having to keep meal costs down, they buy only breads that are whole grain and foods that have no high-fructose corn syrup.

In 2012, Revolution Foods won a $9 million contract from the San Francisco Unified School District to provide its 114 schools with thousands of lunches, breakfasts, and snacks each day. In just a few weeks the number of children on the school lunch plan jumped 15 percent, from 20,000 students to 23,000.

Although Tobey and Richmond began only in 2006, they hit $70 million in revenues in 2013. They also created a line of meal kits that sell in Safeway stores and are expanding across the country. They aren't turning an overall profit yet—they aim to reach that in a couple of years—but they say that's because they have deliberately invested in growth, rather than taking profits out of the business. Tobey thinks back on the long path they have taken. Their first food preparation site was a former McDonald's restaurant. "We installed our steamers instead of deep fryers," said Tobey. "The irony was amazing."

CHAPTER FOURTEEN

Doing Good While Being Big

The highest use of capital is not to make more money but to
make money do more service for the betterment of life.

In 2005, Franck Riboud posed a question to Muhammad Yunus, the
founder of Grameen Bank in Bangladesh. Riboud wanted to know
what the food company he ran, Danone, could do to help the world's
poor. Danone was cofounded by his father to make yogurt to treat
intestinal disorders, and Riboud was proud of the company's historic
emphasis on social mission. Yunus knew Danone was the leading
yogurt maker on the globe, with brands that included Dannon and
Stonyfield, and he proposed a joint venture. The plan was to manufacture yogurt to reduce malnutrition among Bangladeshi children
while providing hundreds of jobs. Riboud said, *Let's do it*, and they
shook hands on the deal.

They developed plans by email, and then Riboud visited Bangladesh with a team of executives who began looking more seriously
into manufacturing. Danone and Grameen selected one of Bangladesh's poorest and most remote areas—the rural lands around the
northern town of Bogra—for their project. The venture, Grameen
Danone Foods Ltd., which Yunus has called the world's first con-
sciously designed multinational social business, became a test of what
happens when a major for-profit corporation wades into the social
sphere of international development. It turned out to be far more
complicated than anyone had anticipated.

Even at the start Danone experts saw some of the obstacles. In Bangladesh, 45 percent of children suffer from malnutrition, so ideally the yogurt would contain micronutrients such as iron, zinc, iodine, calcium, and vitamin A. But micronutrients sometimes have a bitter taste. Other problems included the lack of high-quality milk and the shortage of refrigeration in rural areas. There was no reliable and consistent source of electricity to keep a yogurt plant running. Bangladeshis also don't have a taste for Western-style yogurt, so it was unclear how much of a market there would be for the products.

Danone's experiment with making yogurt in Bangladesh is a prime example of the growing interest among even giant multinational companies in social responsibility. There are reasons for skepticism, because some of this is about public relations, but on the whole we welcome this push. When for-profit companies tackle social problems they can have a huge impact. Encourage a major Western company to source its coffee beans from impoverished farmers with sustainable practices and those farmers will benefit more than from a thousand small aid projects. And if the company adopts a policy, where possible, of paying the mother of the house for the coffee beans rather than the father, in one stroke school attendance will rise because more of the money will go for school fees and less for banana beer. Likewise, when companies give employees time and space to take on pro bono projects, this can be an important source of expertise and talent for nonprofits. The tendency in the humanitarian world has been to see corporations as part of the problem, but they can also be part of the solution, and we hope more corporate employees will encourage their companies to improve their social responsibility efforts so that they can have far-reaching impact. Indeed, for companies there are selfish reasons to do so. Aside from improving the corporate reputation, these initiatives may create new customers for their products and also help in hiring and retaining employees. Among young people, a company that provides some social benefit is much more attractive as a place to work than a merciless leviathan.

In the end, Danone specialists determined they would have to start at the very beginning of the yogurt-making process—with the milk. Native Bangladeshi cows give very little milk—about one-twelfth the output of a typical European or American cow. Grameen Danone decided to cross-breed Bangladeshi cows with foreign-bred cows. Grameen Danone workers would then visit the farming villages — sometimes on impossibly narrow dirt paths — to collect milk from farmers' buckets soon after the cows were milked. To help camouflage the bitterness of the micronutrients imported from Germany, Grameen Danone had to sweeten the yogurt. Molasses and cane sugar are native, so those were tried, but the quality was uneven. Both sugar and flavoring would have to be imported. Biogas created by the cows producing the milk proved unreliable as an energy source, so a generator would be needed to supplement the local electrical grid.

"In social businesses, plastic is not allowed," Yunus said. "We don't want to see all these plastic cups all around Bangladesh." Danone researchers had used plastic cups around the world but now would have to develop a biodegradable container. The scientists soon tested a Chinese product made out of cornstarch with good results. When Yunus then suggested edible cups, Danone researchers were speechless. "I eat ice cream and the ice-cream cone," Yunus recalls telling the researchers. "They were very unhappy." They are still working on that.

Seeking creative solutions to malnutrition is important because this is a malady that leaves some 150 million children worldwide physically stunted — and often mentally impaired as well. Undernutrition is a factor in 45 percent of all deaths of children younger than five, about 3.1 million deaths annually. Far larger numbers of malnourished children will suffer a lifelong intellectual deficit. Liu Jianghong, a professor at the University of Pennsylvania, found that if a child has three indicators of malnutrition, his or her IQ drops fifteen points. One problem is lack of cheap protein, and a second is a lack of micronutrients such as iron, zinc, vitamin A, iodine, and folic acid. To make yogurt, Danone usually builds giant factories, but in Bangladesh this would have produced far more yogurt than the market could bear. Grameen Danone ended up building a much smaller factory and running it on a "no loss, no dividend" basis. Danone did not want to subsidize the operation, but it would waive a financial return; any profits would go toward expanding the business in Bangladesh.

To oversee the project, Grameen and Danone turned to a rising star in the Grameen network, Khandoker Mohammad Abu Sohel, who had served as a branch manager at three different Grameen locations. Sohel's friends thought he was crazy to try to become a yogurt salesman, leaving a promising microfinance career to peddle a product that no one wanted. Since Bangladeshis had no concept of Western-style yogurt, Sohel had to create demand from scratch. The obvious marketing approach was that fortified yogurt creates strong, healthy children who will do better in school. But nutrition is not taught in Bangladesh's schools, and it's not a concept that plays a major role in buying decisions.

Sohel created campaigns to explain the concept of nutrition, selling protein and micronutrients as much as yogurt. "If the kids are not developed in the ability of the brain, how can our nation stand?" he asked. He also struggled to find the right price point and right portions and packaging. He tested the yogurt with children, getting their reactions on taste, flavors, portion size, and labeling. He created tiny cups of yogurt, in packages that people seemed to like. The result was Shokti Doi, "strength yogurt." The label has a cartoon lion character on it, connoting strength, and it was priced at just 7 U.S. cents. The yogurt would be sold in 300 shops in Bogra that had refrigeration; in rural areas, it would be sold by village women who would function as a Bangladeshi version of Avon ladies carrying around great blue cooler packs.

Production began. The initial results were disappointing. Neither sales channel was meeting its goals, and the yogurt certainly wasn't making a dent in child malnutrition in Bangladesh. The husbands of the Grameen saleswomen didn't want their wives going door-to-door making sales. Sohel realized he had to train the husbands as well as the wives, and Grameen Danone conducted an education campaign to explain the promise of yogurt in improving the nutrition of Bangladeshi children. More saleswomen joined, and business improved slightly.

In 2008, the worldwide financial crisis hit and a devastating monsoon season destroyed crops and land in Bangladesh. Milk prices rose steeply across Bangladesh, and costs for Shokti Doi skyrocketed. The factory, losing money on every cup of yogurt sold, raised the price of Shokti Doi to 10 cents. That proved too much. Sales fell 80 percent in the rural areas and 40 percent in the city of Bogra. Many of the saleswomen quit their jobs.

Sohel and his colleagues created a smaller-size yogurt cup with the same quantity of micronutrients and lowered the price to 7 cents. Business began to pick up, some of the saleswomen resumed work, and the factory began recovering. Two months later, the company raised prices by a penny a cup and also offered the larger cup in cities for 10 cents. By 2013, when we visited, the factory was selling about 80,000 cups each day, or about 150 tons each month, and operating at about 68 percent capacity. This may not solve malnutrition among all Bangladeshi children. But Sohel felt he was making more impact at the helm of a business than he would have in a straightforward aid organization. Part of the impact comes from the jobs given to 600 women who sell in the villages.

These are often the poorest of the poor, single moms such as Tahera Begum, a thirty-five-year-old woman who lives in Milkypur and walks around nearby villages calling on homes and meeting mothers to explain to them the benefits of nutrition in the yogurt. Such women are called *shokti* ladies. Every morning Tahera receives a delivery of yogurt cups and little wooden stick spoons from a man pedaling a three-wheel rickshaw with a giant cooling box. Most saleswomen are part-time and sell about 65 yogurt cups each day, with a "professional" selling about 80 to 100 cups. Tahera is an outlier: she sells 200 to 300 cups every day and earns $3 to $5 a day.

Tahera has just a fifth-grade education and was previously a housemaid. Formerly she often was paid in clothing or food, which she would then sell in the marketplace to get enough money to raise her son, now twelve years old. One day, her son asked if he could buy a Shokti Doi. She didn't know anything about the yogurt, so she found a *shokti* lady and asked the woman about the product. The *shokti* lady was actually a poor saleswoman and couldn't really explain it, but Begum found a small card explaining that the yogurt was fortified with vitamins and that it could help children grow strong and help pregnant women have healthy babies. She explained this to the *shokti* lady and accompanied the saleswoman that afternoon and helped her sell five or six cups. The next morning, she accompanied the *shokti* lady, met the rickshaw delivery man, and signed up to be a *shokti* lady. Her first day Begum sold fifty cups and quit her job as a maid.

"I know 5,000 people now," says Begum. She enjoys meeting people, building relationships, and earning money by herself. "There are a lot of good things that have come from this. It all makes me very happy."

*Tahera Begum,
who used to work
as a housemaid
in exchange
for food or old
clothes, picking up
her daily reserve
of Shokti Doi
yogurt from a
Grameen Danone
distributor
to sell in the
local villages
of Milkypur*

SHERYL WUDUNN

Previously, she told us, "my life was very sad," but selling Shokti Doi turned it around. Tahera at seventeen entered into an arranged marriage with a man who already had a wife. After five years, her son was born, but her husband, who had a small business selling vegetables, said he couldn't afford to keep two families, so he left her and her son. She has used her yogurt money to buy her own house, and she has goals for her son. "I dream he will graduate from high school and get a good, honorable job. My son is a good student and graduated seventh out of 200 students in his seventh-grade class."

Danone and Grameen are partnering with 400 dairy farmers who produce milk for the yogurt. These are people such as Mohammed Dablu Mondal, a scrawny thirty-five-year-old man who lives in the village of Ramchandrapur in northern Bangladesh with his wife and their two daughters, ages eleven and four. Before beginning the partnership with Grameen Danone, Mondal had five head of cattle, who shared the family home. Only one or two of the cows were milking at a time, producing preposterously low amounts. He or his father would take the milk to market, but the price varied; some days they couldn't sell the milk at all and would have to bring it home. The family was struggling to survive. Then someone from Grameen Danone came to his home and said he was interested in buying all his milk every single day at a fixed price — and he would pay cash for every transaction. Mondal agreed on the spot.

That's when Dr. Abdul Mannan, a thirty-one-year-old veterinarian at Grameen Danone, stepped in. He and his fellow vets train the farmers, visiting them on a regular basis on a three-wheeled vehicle. Dr. Mannan coaches them on how to feed the cows (green grass and good-quality feed rather than the rice husks that native cows are usually fed) and how to breed them. He tells them what medicines to buy when the cows are sick. Since farmers often don't have their own land on which to grow grass, Dr. Mannan tells them they have to buy bundles of it from the market to feed their cows or rent a plot with grass. Dr. Mannan was also instrumental in helping Mondal artificially inseminate his cows to develop a more productive milking cow. By the time he started selling milk to Grameen Danone, Mondal was steadily improving production. With the money from the milk, he bought another cow, then another, and another. And they began to have calves.

Mondal, a gregarious farmer who often passes along advice to his neighbors, and his wife, Pramanik, an outspoken woman full of enthusiasm, soon had fifteen head of cattle. A sturdy woman with a

Mohammed Dablu Mondal, a farmer, with his wife, Pramanik,
and family standing in front of their large cowshed in northern
Bangladesh, where he learned how to improve his family's life
by helping Grameen Danone make its Shokti Doi yogurt

determined demeanor, Pramanik washes and feeds the cows every day. "They are like my kids," she says. Mondal milks the cows twice a day and takes the milk in the morning and evenings to the local collection center. Once there, it is tested and, if accepted, poured into a local cooling unit that is then transported after each collection to a refrigeration center for onward transport to the factory.

Mondal and Pramanik were netting $14 a day in profits, and the money started piling up. Since the cows couldn't fit inside their home anymore, they built a cowshed that is the biggest structure on the farm. They also built a new home, bought a three-wheel vehicle, and, since Mondal is by nature a risk taker, built a workshop to make window grilles as a secondary business. Mondal also sold enough cows to send his younger brother to Dubai to work. "I don't know if he'll pay me back," says Mondal. "But he's happy and that's enough for me."

When we visited, the window grille business wasn't doing well; Mondal acknowledged that it had been a misstep and that he needed to refocus on the dairy business. "It's my life," he said. "I cannot live without cows. I tried that." So Mondal and Pramanik are working on building up a herd of twenty good milk cows. "I want to fill this cowshed with cows," Pramanik said. She also has dreams for their daughters, so she gives them Shokti Doi to make them strong and hopes they'll be doctors or engineers.

S ome multinational corporations—Nestlé, Unilever, Mars—have worked with farmers around the world to improve crop quality and yields or to boost harvesting efficiency. Other corporations focus on the environment. Clean water has become a social challenge that several major corporations—including Coca-Cola, Nestlé, and Unilever—have supported.* Organic food sourcing and fair-wage products have also grown in popularity, as consumers have started demanding more accountability up the value chain, from "bloodless" diamonds to cell phone parts not made with exploited labor. Some

---

* For Nestlé, these efforts don't mitigate the anger among public health experts that its aggressive marketing of infant formula in poor countries leads to less breast-feeding and thus ultimately to increased infant deaths in those countries. Nestlé has been quite cooperative on issues such as child labor in harvesting cocoa, but it has been inconsistent with infant formula and too aggressive in some countries. This is a problem for many manufacturers of infant formula, however, and Nestlé isn't worse than the others and is better than some.

companies are trying to bring about change by imposing require-ments for their suppliers around the world.

Gary Erickson and Kit Crawford, a husband-and-wife team, founded Clif Bar, which says it has five bottom lines: economic sus-tainability, brand integrity, giving back, employee well-being, and environmental sustainability. Clif Bar says that 71 percent of the raw materials it buys are certified organic. Similarly, Chipotle, founded by chef Steve Ells, says it buys no pork from factory farms and since 2001 has used pork only from ranchers who raise pigs outdoors or in deeply bedded pens. Chipotle says that its chickens are all raised without growth hormones or antibiotics, and that all meat comes from farms within 350 miles of the restaurant. (It has been criticized for not allowing third-party verification of these claims.)

There's a long-standing debate about whether corporations should even be in the business of trying to do good. In 1970, Milton Friedman wrote a prominent article in *The New York Times Magazine* in which he called corporate social responsibility programs "hypocritical window-dressing" and almost "fraud." He argued that as firms engage in socially responsible activities, they have lower net financial per-formance as a result, harming shareholders. Other critics on the left see corporate social responsibility as a feel-good promotional spin to distract consumers from unpleasant things corporations do. There is something to the criticisms—sometimes these initiatives are inef fectual window dressing—but usually it's more complicated. Danone, for example, is doing real good with yogurt in Bangladesh. But the venture may also help defuse criticism for its aggressive marketing of infant formula worldwide.

In any case, large corporations have a huge footprint, and when they move a bit, that can have an enormous impact on the ground. If the aim is to address social problems, nonprofits will accomplish far more if they can bring for-profit corporations with them into bat-tle. That's the thinking behind a partnership between the nonprofit CARE and Danone in Bangladesh. CARE was starting to build its own door-to-door sales network of women selling household neces-sities, such as soap, shampoo, and laundry detergent, in remote areas where there are few stores. But CARE needed an injection of $1 mil-lion (€600,000) for the project. Danone offered to make an invest-ment, partly so that CARE's saleswomen could help sell Shokti Doi. After much deliberation by CARE—it had never partnered before with a for-profit corporation in this kind of venture—the two of them joined forces in late 2011 and created JITA Bangladesh. CARE owns 67 percent of the distribution network, which has some 5,000 *aparajitas,* or "ladies who never accept defeat," and a former CARE program manager runs the operation.

Aparajitas, effectively door-to-door saleswomen, don't carry cooler packs and so can't keep yogurt cool enough to sell. But Grameen Danone is expanding its production line to make a new fortified yogurt that does not have to be refrigerated and has a shelf life of one to three months (the manufacturing process is similar to that of ultra-high-temperature milk, which does not need refrigeration and is common in Europe), which may hugely expand the market for fortified yogurt in Bangladesh. Ultimately, the plan is to have 11,000 *aparajitas.*

Westerners may think of CARE as supplying aid, but by creating JITA and providing sales jobs it lets people earn incomes to cover their own needs. One of its sellers is Rajeda Begum, a fifty-five-year-old woman whose wrinkles add ten years to her age. Married at sixteen, she had four sons, and a daughter who died, leaving a granddaughter. Rajeda's husband, a vegetable seller, became paralyzed ten years ago, so she had to find a way to make ends meet. She signed up to be a saleswoman. She was shy on her first day when the JITA rep

*Rajeda Begum, whose husband became paralyzed
and left her with no means to support four
sons, became an aparajita for JITA's local
sales network and found a secret that earned
her a warm welcome in many households.*

took her around. But on her second day, Rajeda sold $25 worth of products, and she has done extremely well ever since. She now has electricity in her home, chairs, a queen-size bed with a headboard, and plenty of saris to wear.

Rajeda has a secret weapon of sorts. She started selling sanitary napkins when she saw that women were too embarrassed to ask where to get them. That gave her the idea to sell another product that most villagers are too shy to ask about: condoms. Since then, she has added products such as BIC razors for men, who used to rely on straight blades, and she may add solar lamps and the new Shokti Doi.

The yogurt venture has been far from smooth, and the financial payback has taken longer than expected. Nutritional effects were positive but not transformative: testing showed that children who regularly ate the yogurt improved their levels of iodine and vitamin A and grew more quickly, but their zinc levels were not significantly better than those of children who did not eat yogurt. Still, Bangladeshi children benefited more from the project than if Danone had simply made a donation to an aid group. Bangladeshis got better cows, protein and micronutrients, and plenty of jobs, and the initiative is sustainable and will continue to benefit Bangladeshis indefinitely. For Danone, the project has become a valuable source of corporate pride. "I really believe social businesses can change the world," says Corinne Bazina, a French executive of Danone who took on a two-year posting in Bangladesh to look after the operation, and then extended her stay. "It's a system that can work."

Danone employees found the venture so inspiring that the company started danone.communities, an investment fund that places 10 percent of its capital in social businesses. It was from this fund that Danone invested in JITA Bangladesh for 33 percent of the venture. Danone seeded the danone.communities fund with €17 million in 2006, and the fund, run by a third party, has since grown to €70 million, with various investors including Danone employees putting in money.

For Yunus, all this is just a starting point. Social businesses, he argues, are much more effective ways to address social issues than aid, and more so than purely for-profit enterprises. Aid creates dependency, he says, while purely for-profit entities don't address important social issues. Grameen is partnering with other large corporations in various countries, including BASF, to make bed nets. Grameen

Intel Social Business Ltd. has launched several software initiatives to address the needs of impoverished farmers and their families in rural areas. Shumata is a software product used by mobile health workers who register details of pregnant women that doctors can use to identify high-risk pregnancies and then offer long-distance recommendations for the women. Since 2010, it has helped more than 1,000 women identify complications and get to a field doctor. Dolna, another piece of software produced by Grameen Intel, is a vaccine tracker and scheduler, allowing health workers to ensure that parents give their infants immunizations at the right time.

One of the most successful social enterprises is the Aravind Eye Care System, founded in India in 1976 by Govindappa Venkataswamy, who with David Green, a social entrepreneur and MacArthur "genius" award recipient, developed a network of eye care hospitals, as well as technology and products to support high-quality, low-cost eye care. Aravind charges wealthy clients to help deliver free care to the poor, and it has performed more than 4 million operations and helped 32 million patients. Though it is nonprofit, Aravind generates revenues, is self-sustaining, and is still expanding.

Because a business enterprise embodies a strong engine for growth, there is an argument that a large corporation that does no harm has the potential to create more value for the common good over the long term than a large foundation or nonprofit organization. In 2011, when both IBM and the Carnegie Corporation turned 100, *The Economist* compared the contributions of the two organizations to evaluate which one had more impact on society. Carnegie had enormous impact in its first quarter century, creating 2,500 libraries, funding the discovery of insulin, and seeding new institutions such as the Carnegie Institute of Technology, the Brookings Institution, the National Academy of Sciences, and TIAA-CREF, the pension fund for university teachers. But its influence has waned over the decades, while IBM continues to innovate and grow. *The Economist* concluded that the larger social value came from IBM, with its 434,000 employees around the world and a wide range of innovations, including enterprise software, cloud computing, and artificial intelligence.

In their desire to showcase corporate social responsibility, companies are giving more leeway to employees to give back—just as law firms have regularly done pro bono work. IBM developed a Corporate Service Corps, modeled on the Peace Corps, and has sent more than 2,400 people to provide consulting advice in more than thirty countries. In 2010, IBM also began a three-year, 100-city grant initiative in which employees donate their time to help cities launch large projects and resolve tough issues. IBM dispatched teams of five to six people for three weeks to formulate a master plan and strategies for execution. In St. Louis, IBM helped devise a citywide information technology system that tracked everyone who entered the criminal justice system and allowed different agencies access to that electronic information. That system contributed to a 50 percent decline in crime in some neighborhoods, IBM says. Toyota has taken its sophisticated production expertise and helped hospitals, schools, and other nonprofits improve efficiencies. In Harlem, for example, it trimmed the wait at a soup kitchen run by an organization called Food Bank for New York City from one and a half hours to eighteen minutes.

We would like to see more companies step into this arena, allowing employees to use their skills to take on pro bono projects. The nonprofit world is in desperate need of the corporate skill set, and our guess is that companies would be rewarded with increased morale and greater success in recruitment and retention. In the same vein, it would be good to see more corporations take on social joint ventures from time to time, in echoes of what Danone did with Grameen to make yogurt. If we insist on nonprofits and corporations being kept in separate silos, we all lose. If you work in a company, think about how it could help, or what a pro bono policy might look like, and see if there is interest among executives.

The best programs tackle a social problem that the company has the right toolbox for. That's why Danone's new yogurt with micronutrients and IBM's information technology systems make sense. In finance, one of the most interesting initiatives to tap private funding has been Social Impact Bonds, launched in the United Kingdom in 2010 with the help of the Rockefeller Foundation, and two years later in the United States. "There simply wasn't enough money in philanthropy, even with the explosion of philanthropy, and not enough money in government aid to really solve all the social ills," said Judith Rodin, president of the Rockefeller Foundation. "Not that money can solve everything, but that for those things that required money and big money at times, that unleashing private capital to do social good was going to be critical."

The idea is to use bonds to pay for government innovations that will save money later on, and then use the savings to pay back the bondholders. About £5 million in UK bonds were issued to fund a novel approach at Her Majesty's Prison Peterborough in England to cut recidivism through a program developed by nonprofits to help parolees find housing and other support. If recidivism falls below a certain threshold, investors get an annual return of up to 13 percent, paid for out of the savings from prison spending; if there's no impact on recidivism, then the investors get nothing. Interim results show that the recidivism rate fell by 21 percent relative to the national average, suggesting bondholders could earn a nice return. With those encouraging results, people are beginning to think about other areas where social impact bonds can be used to finance social programs. One possibility might be to help Cure Violence pay for more China Joes to battle crime.

The Perfect Product
Cheap, Clean Water

A id organizations around the world helping villagers get clean water traditionally have been reluctant to impose charges, feeling that poor people shouldn't have to pay for such a lifesaving basic. The problem is that this mind-set, however admirable, doesn't actually result in the delivery of clean water to people who need it, and the money needs to come from somewhere.

Unilever, the giant consumer products company, has taken a different approach. In 2000, Yuri Jain, a senior manager at Hindustan Unilever Ltd., was acutely aware of the challenges of getting clean water into the homes of people all across India. A significant share of malnutrition there is caused by dirty water, which often causes diarrhea, according to the World Health Organization. Few places in India have reliable and clean water around the clock; in New Delhi, water pipes are so poorly maintained that 40 percent of the supply fails to reach customers, so clean water is rationed and restricted.

"It doesn't require a lot of fancy consumer understanding to fig ure out" that clean water is a problem in India, said Jain, who suffered from a range of water-borne diseases as he was growing up. Jain pushed Unilever to look at enterprise solutions to provide clean water as part of its sustainability initiative, even though Unilever was not in the water business anywhere in the world. Jain and his colleagues created a stiff set of criteria. Clean water had to meet the highest standards set by the United States Environmental Protection Agency, which includes filtering out bacteria, parasites, and viruses. The system providing the water had to be portable and stand-alone, could not depend on an outside source of energy such as electricity, had to be very simple for the uneducated (water in, water out),

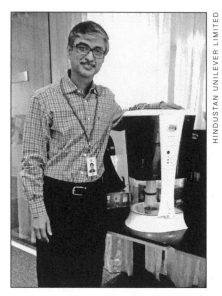

*Yuri Jain with Hindustan
Unilever's Pureit water filter*

needed its own storage unit, had to shut off automatically when the filter no longer could take any more dirty water, and had to be affordable to the masses. While it was possible to build a water filter for $200, that was far too costly for people living in poverty in India.

Jain and his team called upon a hundred Unilever experts around the world, and after five years of effort they developed an affordable product that they thought could triumph in the market. "I think only a corporation could pull this off," said Jain, whose title at Unilever is now vice president for water business. The product is called Pureit, and Unilever says it produces safe water at a cost of about half a cent per liter. Jain says that the carbon footprint of Pureit is 90 percent smaller than that of boiling water in India to purify it.

Unilever launched Pureit in 2004 and charged $35 for it. Millions were sold, and Unilever calculates that Pureit has given 45 million people access to clean water. Unilever has expanded Pureit sales to a dozen other countries in Asia, Africa, and Latin America, and now Pureit is the top-selling in-home water filter in the world, according to Verify Markets, a third-party monitor. Unilever's goal is to provide clean drinking water to hundreds of millions of people by 2020. While

Pureit will not say if it has reached profitability, it says it has a 50 percent market share for such water filters in India, and Jain has a ticker tape in his office that counts how many "lives Pureit has protected."

Unilever has since created an entire line of water filter products, including more expensive ones that sell for up to $260, alongside cheaper ones for $19. To reach the extremely poor—those at the bottom of the pyramid—Unilever has started partnering with local groups to offer microloans so poor people can afford them, but growth has been slow and by the end of 2013 they had sold only 89,000 filters this way. Critics might ask why Unilever didn't waive profits initially the way Danone did, but Unilever's approach isn't corporate philanthropy and isn't social business; rather, it is a business model that seeks to serve customers in need—and to make money doing so. "Our stake in this is very clear," says Jain. "We said the way to do this is have something scalable and sustainable, so that we need not depend on philanthropy."

PART THREE

Give, Get, Live

CHAPTER FIFTEEN

The Neuroscience of Giving

A Natural High

The happy man lives well and does well.

—ARISTOTLE, *The Nicomachean Ethics,* 350 B.C.

The high-ceilinged room, large and stark and white, was empty except for a giant tomblike white tube of a machine that weighed nearly 13,000 pounds. Sheryl lay down on the conveyer belt in front of it and put her head into a white helmet with her eyes snuggling behind frames that let her see a small computer screen. The machine's crew made adjustments and repeatedly checked that there was no metal anywhere on her body, then tightened her in the casing until she was like a mummy. After she was fully encased, the conveyer sucked her into the big white tunnel. "Don't blink," boomed a loud male voice through headphones in her ears. "And don't fall asleep."

There was a pause as the machine operators made adjustments and programmed the computers. Then the man's voice came again: "You will hear a loud noise for fourteen seconds." A high-pitched sound soon filled her ears. Then the operator said, "And now we will do an anatomical scan."

Booooooong went the machine as its components hummed into motion and an extraordinarily powerful magnet inside the tube swung into action. *Oooommmm* rang a second, longer sound. The contraption, a $2.7 million functional magnetic resonance imaging device, began to emit radio-frequency pulses, sending hydrogen atoms in

Sheryl's brain spinning. The machine spat out three-dimensional images of Sheryl's brain every two seconds, showing which areas she
was using. She was being asked a series of questions: *Do you want to
donate $20 to Red Cross? Do you want to donate $40 to United Way?
Do you want to donate $20 to Helen Keller International?* In each case,
she had the option to make a donation or move on, and the images
showed Sheryl's brain patterns as she made these decisions.

This was an fMRI scanning machine at the University of Oregon.
Normally MRI machines are used to examine sick patients or diag-
nose ailments, but this one is used for research on the brain. In our
case, we were interested in what happens in the brain when people
help others by donating to a good cause. A growing body of research
in psychology and neuroscience suggests that altruism is good not just
for the beneficiaries but also for the benefactors. The argument is that
helping others makes us happy, and even leaves us healthier and able
to live longer lives. So we were in the lab to watch brains—our own
brains, actually—as they made decisions about donating to charities.

Our guides were two of the country's pioneering investigators into
the neuroscience of altruism, Ulrich Mayr and William T. Harbaugh
of the University of Oregon. Mayr is a tall, thin professor of psychology with brown hair that seemed windswept from the sides of his
head. His eyes twinkled as he invited us into his office, a spacious,

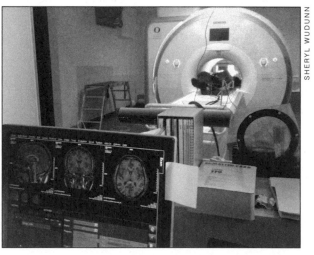

*Nick undergoing a brain scan at a University of Oregon lab to
monitor brain activity while he made donations to nonprofits*

brightly lit room that was nearly bare but for the large computer monitor on one side of the room. Harbaugh, his friendly face framed by wire-rimmed glasses and thinning gray hair, shuffled in from his office in the economics department, where he researches what motivates people to give.

"We started this about ten years ago," Mayr began, "and at that time, there were not a lot of people trying to use brain imaging to look at these big kinds of questions: What is altruism? Why do people make altruistic decisions?"

Mayr and Harbaugh were using newfangled tools of neuroimaging, but for many decades scholars have been exploring linkages between giving and happiness using other methods. Our own interest in the field goes back a decade, when we met Jonathan Haidt, who had written extensively about happiness. Haidt, now a professor at New York University's Stern School of Business, told us that most of the things we humans think make us happy don't, at least not for very long. We tend to have an individual set point for happiness, he said, making some of us pretty happy and others less so, but wherever that set point is, we tend to fluctuate around it. So if we win the lottery or get a sports car, we're overjoyed for a time, but then we drift back to our preset happiness level. One of the few things that actually will raise our set point for happiness, Haidt said, is to "connect with a cause larger than ourselves."

Our conversation with Haidt led us to explore the field further, and the first thing we found was indeed that a deluge of cash doesn't create lasting happiness. Lottery winners have been extensively studied, and typically they enjoy an exhilarating burst of happiness when they win, but it mostly wears off within a year. They get used to the Porsche and the new mansion. Sometimes the money causes rifts with friends, who tend to be more dependable sources of contentment than money.

The trajectory of Jack Whittaker, a small business owner in Scott Depot, West Virginia, shows how destructive money can be. On Christmas morning 2002, Whittaker checked a Powerball lottery number and realized he had won the grand prize with his $1 ticket. The lottery total was $314.9 million, then the largest undivided jackpot ever. Whittaker was suddenly famous. He elected to take his winnings immediately rather than in installments, which reduced the sum to $93 million after taxes.

To his credit, Whittaker shared the wealth. He bought a new vehicle and then a house for a woman who worked at the convenience store where he had bought his winning ticket. He donated 10 percent of his winnings to his church. He started the Jack Whittaker Foundation with $14 million to help feed and house the less fortunate. As a successful fifty-five-year-old businessman who knew the discipline of making payroll, he seemed a good bet to handle the challenges of sudden wealth. He was less interested in buying toys for himself than in buying things to make happier the people he loved around him: his wife of forty-two years, Jewell; his daughter, Ginger; and his granddaughter, Brandi Bragg.

Alas, things soon went sour. Seven months after winning the lottery, Whittaker called the police from a strip club to say that he had been drugged and robbed. He complained that he had brought $545,000 in cash and cashier's checks with him to the club and that it had been stolen. Soon afterward, he was arrested for drunken driving—while carrying a pistol and $117,000 in cash. "It doesn't bother me, because I can tell everyone to kiss off," he told reporters at the time. "I don't care what it costs." Then began a series of incidents and lawsuits in which Whittaker allegedly engaged in boorish and self-destructive behavior. He later calculated that he had been involved in 460 lawsuits, including litigation by a casino that said he owed it more than $1 million for checks that had bounced. He ended up in rehab to overcome alcohol addiction, and Jewell divorced him, starting a tussle between them over money. Ginger was found dead in her home, an overdose perhaps the cause of death.

Whittaker was particularly close to Brandi, his granddaughter, and he gave her four cars, along with periodic clumps of $100 bills. Her cars were strewn with cash, apparently change from her purchases, and she ended up dropping out of school. Whittaker's entire family suspected, quite correctly, that people were out to get their money, and this made them withdraw from their circles of friends. Wealth formed a barrier, because they suddenly had much less in common with old acquaintances. Extreme wealth became not liberating but isolating. Brandi found companionship instead through drugs, and her eighteen-year-old friend was found dead of an overdose in Whittaker's house. Not long after, at the age of seventeen, Brandi died of a drug overdose herself. When Whittaker learned of her death, he told reporters, sobbing, "I wish I'd torn that ticket up."

Sobered by stories such as this, we investigated how receiving (or giving) leads to happiness. One pioneering study followed 268 Harvard students through youth, midlife, and old age to determine what helped those who lived long and well. Altruists seemed disproportionately likely to age gracefully and maintain their health, the researchers found. Indeed, a willingness to help others seemed more important to longevity than cholesterol levels.

That seemed a secular manifestation of the religious and spiritual notion that "it is more blessed to give than to receive," as Jesus is quoted as saying in the Bible. Other faiths have a similar ascetic tradition or emphasize the importance of serving others. In the past few decades, evidence has mounted that these are not just religious precepts but practical observations of a self-help route to greater happiness. Researchers have repeatedly looked at large populations and found that those who donate more to charity or who volunteer more hours report that they are happier and enjoy better health. Lalin Anik and Michael Norton of Harvard Business School found that those who give away proportionally more money rank themselves happier, while there was little connection between amounts spent on oneself and happiness.

One problem with these and similar studies is that happiness may cause altruism rather than the other way around. To untangle causation from correlation, scholars randomly assigned certain students to engage in five acts of kindness a week for six weeks. These students reported being significantly happier than a control group. In another ingenious experiment, researchers randomly approached people in public places and handed them money (a $5 bill or a $20 bill). Some of the beneficiaries were instructed to spend the money that day on themselves, others on someone else (as a gift or a charitable donation). Students expected that people would derive more happiness spending the money on themselves, but that was wrong. When a researcher telephoned each participant for a follow-up, those assigned to spend money on others reported being significantly happier than those who spent it on themselves (it didn't matter if it was $5 or $20). That leads to a fascinating possibility: that we mislead ourselves into thinking that we'll be happier spending on ourselves and acquiring material objects, while actually we may be wired to gain more pleasure from giving to others. Obviously, this is not proven fact, and many of the studies involve small samples of research subjects or amounts of money that were not terribly relevant in the real world. (It's great that giving $5 or $20 away makes people happy, but what about giving away $1,000?)

Richard Easterlin, an economist, surprised the world in 1974 by arguing that rising incomes often don't lead to rising happiness. The implication was that it was pointless for people to keep struggling to earn more to achieve their dreams. His thesis, called the "Easterlin Paradox," has prompted a wave of research, with some arguing that higher income boosts happiness until basic needs are met but not much after that. Daniel Kahneman and Angus Deaton of Princeton University evaluated 450,000 survey responses and found that higher income correlates at all levels to overall life satisfaction. But in answer to questions about how happy they are or how frequently they smile or laugh, respondents' answers suggest that this kind of emotional well-being rises with incomes up to about $75,000 but not much after that.

Then came two young economists, Betsey Stevenson and Justin Wolfers, a couple, who found that higher income correlates strongly to a broad measure of happiness in all countries. They found no point of satiation, although they did find that among the wealthy it takes larger leaps in income to increase happiness. They also found that while GDP per capita has risen significantly in the United States, the level of self-reported happiness has not changed much over the past few decades.

So does money buy happiness? Yes, in that richer countries have happier populations. No, in that it's hard to verify that very rich individuals are necessarily happier than those who are merely affluent. Justin Wolfers is the first to say that money isn't everything. "One question that people send me is: 'Oh, so this proves money buys happiness and the advice I should give my daughter is she should become an investment banker rather than going out to change the world.' And my answer to that is: 'Absolutely not.'

"I think it's that broad set of choices that largely accounts for my well-being," Wolfers adds. "This is not saying that anyone is making a right or wrong choice, or that another pair of Manolo Blahniks would make you happier. It's just saying that income is a marker for people who have that broader set of choices."

G iven this uncertainty, we were intrigued by the possibility of direct study of the brain itself, using modern scanning machines. Could that offer greater rigor, improved scientific reliability? That was what brought us to the University of Oregon to peer inside our brains. Mayr and Harbaugh showed us that the pleasure zones of the brain are fairly close together and include the nucleus accumbens, the septum, the caudate, and the insula. These are the hot spots that respond to pleasure—laughter, candy, sex, and a whole lot more.

Mayr and Harbaugh, along with a third colleague, Dan Burghart, made an initial foray into brain research by showing that giving makes people happy, in ways we can see. They used fMRI scans to illuminate the brain as people received gifts of money or voluntarily donated to a good cause. Parts of the nucleus accumbens showed more activity when subjects received money, and adjacent parts lit up when subjects gave money to charity. The scans suggest that people vary significantly in the joy they derive from giving, with the pleasure centers of about half of research subjects actually lighting up more intensely when they give than when they receive. Some people strongly endorsed a general principle: *When people are less fortunate, it is important to help them, even if they are very different from us.* That's an echo of spiritual traditions in many faiths, and of Immanuel Kant's categorical imperative, and when it is internalized it has a pro-

Bill Harbaugh, left, and Ulrich Mayr
of the University of Oregon

found effect upon behavior. "People who endorse this give a lot," said Mayr. In other words, giving can become a habit.

Does that mean that when giving becomes internalized and routine, people derive less pleasure from it? Is giving like a benign drug habit, so that it takes more and more to get a high? Since the nucleus accumbens is linked to addiction, Mayr and Harbaugh presume that one can become as addicted to altruism as to cocaine or sex. Asked for an example of an altruism addict, Mayr cocked his head thoughtfully, then suggested, "Mother Teresa?"

One question that neuroscientists are attempting to answer is whether the happiness of giving comes from a pure desire to see others better off or whether it comes from basking in the respect of others for being generous. With a grin, Harbaugh cited Bernard Mandeville, a friend of Benjamin Franklin's, who wrote in 1723, "Pride and vanity have built more hospitals than all the virtues together." So far, there's some indication that the happiness from giving derives both from this kind of vanity and from selfless altruism. Men are more generous to charity when monitored by women, and the more beautiful the women the more generous the men become. The presence of men does not have a corresponding effect on the generosity of women. Yet pleasure centers of the brain show stimulation not only when research subjects make donations under observation but also when $30 is simply seized from their accounts and given to a good cause (a food bank)—something like a tax that will benefit the needy. That suggests a deeply rooted altruism, unconnected with public esteem.

While some scholars are looking at evidence that altruism may make us happier, others have been conducting research suggesting that giving may also make us healthier, perhaps by reducing stress. A 2006 study found that people who are generous have lower blood pressure than those who are not. That may be one mechanism, among several, that promotes longevity among the altruistic. "Give and you will be healthier," write Stephen Post and Jill Neimark in their book *Why Good Things Happen to Good People.* "Give, and you will even live longer." That's a bold assertion, but Post has plenty of backing and runs a research institute examining these links.

One study found that giving and generosity in high school predicted good mental and physical health even half a century later. Another study followed nearly 2,000 people—all over the age of fifty-five—for five years, examining which factors were associated with lower mortality in that time period. The researchers found that the risk of mortality dropped by 29 percent for those attending church services, by 30 percent for those exercising four times a week, and by a remarkable 44 percent for those volunteering for two or more organizations. A University of Texas study of Americans over the age of sixty-five likewise found that those who volunteer are less likely to suffer depression and are more likely to live longer.

What does all this research teach us about, as Jefferson put it, "the pursuit of happiness"? Sonja Lyubomirsky, a happiness expert, argues that the "most promising means of altering one's happiness level" is to take certain deliberate steps. These include exercise, social activities, writing down positive experiences each day, and becoming more generous. That last element confirms what we've seen. "The most selfish thing you can do is to help other people," says Brian Mullaney. "If only people could be exposed to the truth about the many joys and benefits of helping others and doing good while they are young, it would change the world."

The Most Boring Aid in the World

When Sheryl was getting her brain scanned at the University of Oregon and the question flashing at her was whether to donate $20 to Helen Keller International, she clicked yes as the image popped into her mind of Helen Keller wanting to stamp out blindness. Helen Keller International has blossomed into a global group that does far more than that, very effectively—but it also ranks as boring in most people's eyes.

Helen Keller International was founded by Helen Keller and originally addressed blindness one-on-one with clinical work, until it determined that a public health approach could be more cost effective. Vitamin A deficiency leads to some 670,000 child deaths annually and is also the most common reason for child blindness. Giving children vitamin A supplements that cost 2 cents each is a cheap solution. So is encouraging families to plant orange-fleshed sweet potatoes (which are rich in vitamin A) rather than the white sweet potatoes common in Africa. Another important approach is to fortify foods such as flour or cooking oil with micronutrients, as has been common in the United States for decades. Yet another is to breed strains of crops so that they contain more of these vitamins and minerals. Likewise, supporting moms to encourage breast-feeding improves children's nutrition and saves lives. Helen Keller International does superb work in these areas but rarely gets attention for its efforts because micronutrients are so difficult to put a human face on. There's unfortunately sometimes a mismatch between the kinds of assistance that are most effective, such as providing micronutrients or promoting breast-feeding, and those that we find most rewarding to support.

Micronutrients such as zinc, iodine, and folic acid are lifesaving, and a year's supply costs less than a hot dog. Iodine is practically a magical micronutrient. "Iodine deficiency is the most common cause

*A mother gets coaching in optimal breast-feeding
and child nutrition at a meeting at a clinic in
Niger held by Helen Keller International.*

of preventable mental impairment worldwide," says *The Lancet.*
About one-third of children worldwide don't get enough iodine as
their brains are forming, and an educated guess is that the result is a
loss of about 1 billion IQ points. One study found that if every pregnant woman had enough iodine in her body (from iodized salt or a
51-cent iodine capsule taken once every two years by women in their
reproductive years), the educational attainment of children in central
and southern Africa would increase by 7.5 percent, leading to a rise in
economic output when those children become adults.

Likewise, zinc reduces child deaths from diarrhea and infections.
The lack of iron leads to anemia, leaving people weak and lethargic
and increasing the risk that women will die in childbirth. One randomized trial in Indonesia found that men who received $7 worth of
iron-fortified fish sauce increased their earnings by $46 a year, paying
for the iron supplementation many times over. Yet, as we said, it's difficult to get attention and funding for these micronutrients.

In a similar vein, one of the United States' best programs for Africa
is a trade initiative called AGOA, the African Growth and Opportunity Act. It offers trade incentives for companies to invest in Africa
and creates hundreds of thousands of poverty-fighting jobs there. But
because it's about trade, it is dry and unappealing and thus gets little
public attention or support.

Likewise, Jimmy Carter and his Carter Center have labored for many years to combat neglected tropical diseases such as guinea worm (which causes agonizing pain and disability) and river blindness (an excruciating cause of blindness). In large part because of Carter, the number of guinea worm cases has fallen 99.99 percent — from 3.5 million in 1986 to 148 worldwide in 2013. President Carter hopes to see it eradicated soon, and he jokes about staying healthy so that he can outlive the worm. None of this is glamorous, and it's hard to sell to donors. But it's cost effective and transformative.

There's no one like Dan Pallotta championing zinc, iodine, or trade incentives with bike-a-thons, and so Helen Keller International toils in obscurity. We mention it here because it's a great organization that embraces life-saving tools even though they're not glamorous, even though our brains aren't wired to appreciate them. Sometimes essential things just aren't sexy.

CHAPTER SIXTEEN

When Social Networks Dig a Well

I do not know our destinies, but one thing I do know,
the only ones among you who will be happy are those
who have sought and found how to serve.

— DR. ALBERT SCHWEITZER,
RECIPIENT OF THE NOBEL PEACE PRIZE

Maybe you've had an email from a friend who is celebrating her birthday by raising money for a well in Ethiopia. Or maybe on social media you've seen a tweet or a video about Americans banding together to dig wells in the developing world. Neither would be surprising, because it's increasingly common to brush up against the formidable marketing power of charity:water, which we mentioned earlier, one of the fastest-growing charities in history. The growth is a tribute to a young man named Scott Harrison, who was trying to find meaning in his own life when he created the organization. He tapped into an innate truth, that giving with friends is more fun than giving alone, and he has used the power of social networks to make giving in groups easy and rewarding. His experience underscores the power of social networks to achieve change, reminding us all that helping others is much more engaging when it's seen not as a sacrifice but as a social activity. Scott, like so many others, created a channel for all the rest of us to make a difference on our birthdays and special occasions. Charity:water dates only from 2006, yet it is better known among young people than the venerable International Rescue Committee, a gold-standard aid organization that digs many of the wells that charity:water finances. The aid landscape has changed to make giving as rewarding as possible, and few people symbolize the change more than Scott Harrison.

Something happened when Harrison was four years old that changed his life forever. A gas leak in his home resulted in carbon monoxide poisoning that left his mother immune-compromised, severely disabled, and dysfunctional. Before she could read a book it would have to be baked in the oven to remove the smell of ink, and then she would hold it inside a plastic bag while wearing gloves. Through the trials of this childhood, Harrison seemed to absorb extra doses of empathy. He also came to admire his dad's patience, love, and resilience. "I admired him for sticking by her," Harrison recalls.

After growing up a devout Christian in southern New Jersey, Harrison became fashionably dissolute in his teenage years. He joined a band, wore his hair long, and lived the music scene while earning C's at New York University as a communications major. He's of modest size but exudes a larger presence, with an ebullient, outgoing personality that makes him fun to be around. Harrison was always at the center of one party or another, doing something funny, crazy, and perhaps illegal. While still in college, he produced live shows in nightclubs, and after graduation he turned to promoting nightclubs. He was a Pied Piper of the club scene, rounding up crowds of young people and getting them into high-end nightclubs so that they could drink $16 cocktails or, preferably, buy $350 bottles of Grey Goose. He was paid a share of the gross, and he built up a private database of 15,000 email addresses of "friends" to lure to nightclub events. He became so successful that he says Budweiser and Bacardi paid him to drink their products—because then others would follow. It was a wild life, full of gambling and strip clubs, and Harrison became a two-pack-a-day smoker with a fondness for cocaine and Ecstasy as well. "The story I told for ten years was: 'If you get past my velvet rope, if you get drunk, maybe laid, your life has meaning,'" Harrison remembers. It was a life that was not only decadent but also profitable, for Harrison lived the good life in a midtown Manhattan loft, wore a fancy watch, and drove a BMW.

Then, at age twenty-eight, Scott Harrison took a vacation to the beautiful beach resort town of Punta del Este in Uruguay, and amid the sun and sea breezes and beautifully tanned bodies he decided that his life was empty and he stood for nothing: "I realized I was the most selfish, sycophantic, and miserable human being. I was the worst person I knew." Harrison returned to the nightclub scene in Manhattan and began to read the Bible by day while doing drugs at night. That wasn't very satisfying, either. He kept asking himself: *What are you doing with yourself?* Then a follow-up query regularly arose: *What if I did a 180? What would that look like? What if I were to serve God and serve the poor?* That was a revolutionary thought, because in his entire adult life Harrison had never volunteered or donated to charity, and he had no idea what he could contribute to the world—except that it would have to be a part of a very different lifestyle. "I came back to my Christian faith in a different way as an adult, where it wasn't shoved down my throat, and I wanted to live it out with integrity and not hypocrisy."

Harrison applied to major aid organizations for a job—and they laughed at him. *A nightclub promoter with no development experience wants to help the needy? Look out!* Harrison's background was the kind usually associated with failed aid workers, those who are psychologically needy themselves and have no skill set useful in the developing world. Not only were aid groups unwilling to hire Scott, but it seemed that no one was willing even to take him on as an unpaid volunteer. He finally found a place with Mercy Ships, a Christian charity that sends a ship, *Africa Mercy*—really a floating hospital—to dock in poor countries to perform surgeries. It needed a ship photographer to document the surgeries, and Harrison used his charm to talk his way into the job. He would have to pay about $500 a month for the position. Harrison sold his music and DVD collection and some camera gear to help finance his stint as a volunteer.

Mercy Ships is a tribute to the power of volunteering. The doctors aboard *Africa Mercy* repair cleft palates, obstetric fistulas, and much more. The chief of surgery, Dr. Gary Parker, has lived on board for twenty-six years. He met his wife when she volunteered, and they raised their children on board as well. The staff of *Africa Mercy* is made up of doctors, nurses, and others who donate their vacation time and, like Scott Harrison, even pay for their own room and board while on the ship. They come back again and again to do so.

Harrison's first stop on the *Africa Mercy* was Cotonou, a port in the West African country of Benin. Some 5,000 people lined up desperately seeking surgeries: some had hiked for weeks, carrying a child, in hopes that a surgeon could save the child's life. The first surgery Harrison photographed was performed on Alfred Sossou, a fourteen-year-old boy who had a grotesque tumor that filled his mouth and spilled outward where his chin should have been. "He was suffocating on his own face," Harrison remembers. "I wasn't prepared for what I was seeing. I was crying in the corner." Alfred's parents had spent money on traditional witch doctors, who cut into the tumor but accomplished nothing other than injuring the boy. The tumor grew, filling his mouth so that he could barely eat. By the time Alfred arrived at Mercy Ships, he weighed only forty-four pounds, and five of those pounds were in the tumor. The staff accepted Alfred as a patient. A pathologist on the ship tested the tumor and found it to be benign. Then Dr. Parker removed it in a three-hour surgery. Alfred had his life back and quickly began to gain weight in the recovery ward.

"I took Alfred home a few weeks later to his village with a whole new face," Harrison adds. "I'd seen a kid who was near death, who was scared and angry, and then I got to take him home and see everybody celebrating, because a few doctors had given up their vacation time." (The photos that Harrison took are still on a website he set up, OnAMercyShip.com.) The encounter with the ship turned out to be life-changing not only for Alfred but also for Scott Harrison. He was overwhelmed as he watched doctors save one life after another, creating unimaginable happiness—and he was pained by how many patients had to be turned away because there weren't enough doctors or surgery slots available. Mercy Ships could only tell them: *We'll try to get to you when we come back to this port in a few years.*

After eight months, the ship went to dry dock for repairs, and Harrison flew back to New York for a break. Two hours after he arrived, he went out with some old friends, and one bought him a $16 margarita. "My worlds collided," Scott said. "My previous paradigm had been $16 bags of rice that would feed a family for a month. And here was a $16 drink, before tip." Harrison cajoled his friends into donating a gallery to host an exhibition of his photos from Mercy Ships, and he sent out invitations to the 15,000 people on his email list. New Yorkers from the nightclub scene drifted through the gallery, peering in disbelief at the images and sharing in the triumph of the successful surgeries. Afterward, they wrote checks. Harrison also worked through friends of friends and cold calls to place news of Mercy Ships' work in twenty different publications; all this raised

Scott Harrison at a charity:water well in Rwanda

$96,000 for the organization. That was a stunning sum for a Christian aid organization to bring in from nightclub denizens in Manhattan. Harrison began to wonder if he might be a Pied Piper for something grander than nightclubs.

After the ship repairs, Harrison returned to his post as ship photographer for another eight months to track how the donated money was spent, take photographs, and report back to donors. Mercy Ships also periodically drilled wells, because clean water can avert so many health problems, and Harrison began to coax friends into paying for wells. He had also stumbled upon a basic problem in the humanitarian world: people who do amazingly good work in the field are often abysmal at telling their stories, or they think that the important work is limited to the scalpel or well-drilling rig, not realizing that this kind of work can be funded only if it moves ordinary people half a world away. Just as Apple sells products not only because they are well designed but also because a sophisticated marketing team convinces the world that they are cool, good global health and development organizations need to make you appreciate that you can get more satisfaction, even happiness, from a donation than you can from a $16 cocktail.

Harrison became a virtuoso at convincing well-meaning middle-class people that they would feel great if they helped address overwhelming needs in poor countries. After his time with Mercy Ships, Harrison returned to Manhattan dreaming of starting a new kind of aid organization that would excel at making donors happy by showing them exactly what their contributions could accomplish. He wanted to build a brand that would be cool, nonprofit, and alluring. Harrison decided to focus on water projects because wells are tangible and because more than a billion people still don't have clean water.

Getting started, as Harrison remembers it, was pretty daunting: "How do you start a charity with no money, while staying on a friend's couch?" Harrison again made use of his 15,000 contacts and held a birthday party for himself—he was turning thirty-one—at a nightclub to launch his new venture, which he called charity:water. The date was September 7, 2006. He found a few wealthy donors who agreed to cover administrative expenses so that he could pledge that every penny raised at the party would go to build wells. Some 700 people showed up, each donating a bit more than $20, and Harrison had his first $15,000 to spend. He flew to northern Uganda and hired someone to build three new wells and fix three broken-down wells. Volunteers documented everything with photographs and video, and Harrison returned to his laptop: "We emailed photos to all 700 people who went to the party: 'You paid $20, and this is the impact you had in northern Uganda.'"

This was a seminal moment for Harrison. He realized that he had raised a substantial sum for good by tapping his circle of acquaintances and holding a party, where everyone who came would see who else was giving to help bring clean water to poor people in Africa. Harrison had turned a birthday from a festive occasion into a festival of giving; he had turned a drinking community into a giving community. That was the seed of his marketing strategy: offering groups of people an effective way to have fun together while also accomplishing something meaningful. Harrison has built a worldwide "water empire" based on facilitating these giving communities. He persuades people to register their birthdays online and, through pledges, very visibly help villagers get clean water.

Why are people donating birthdays? What is prompting them to help? Research on the brain shows certain chemicals are released in varying degrees when we see something that may trigger a desire to help. Paul Zak, at Claremont Graduate University, has found that watching a simple video about a child with cancer leads to the release of two brain chemicals. One is cortisol, a stress hormone reflecting the distress one feels about a sick child. It helps focus attention on a challenge. The other is oxytocin, the so-called trust molecule, which makes people want to help others. Viewers were given the chance to donate to charity after seeing the video, and those who produced more oxytocin gave more; indeed, the level of oxytocin in the blood was a strong predictor of the sum donated. Zak calls this "changing our behavior by changing our brain chemistry." It seems as though Scott Harrison's documentary style use of videos and photographs helps trigger the release of a great deal of oxytocin.

Oxytocin is most often encountered in the health care system to accelerate labor, but it's a reproductive hormone found naturally in men and women alike. It emerges in social interactions other than storytelling, including when we have sex, when we're hugged, or when we're full of good vibes. Professor Zak once drew blood before and after a wedding, and he found that the ceremony sent everybody's oxytocin levels through the roof. Higher oxytocin levels correspond to people showing greater generosity to others and donating more to the needy. When Zak and his team sprayed oxytocin into people's noses—a pathway to the brain—they found greater generosity at once. "We could turn the behavioral response on and off like a garden hose," he writes. He has found that prayer and singing release oxytocin, and so does engaging on social media—where charity:water excels at finding new supporters.

Back in Africa, the challenge for Harrison is that digging good wells is harder than it looks. One study in Tanzania found that only 54 percent of existing rural wells were still functioning. Data published by the Rural Water Supply Network suggest that more than three-quarters of wells in Guinea and Uganda function properly, but only one-third of the wells in Congo are operating as they should. In the Menaka region of Mali, only 20 percent of wells are said to work. Overall, the Rural Water Supply Network estimated that 35 percent of wells, many built with aid money, do not function properly. In Africa, some 50,000 foreign-funded wells are said to be no longer working, with $300 million in well-drilling investment squandered. Once we took a family vacation to Zimbabwe and saw an expensive water project that an American religious charity had built at great cost just two years earlier; it was no longer working, and villagers had gone back to drinking from the creek.

A pump has a few cheap rubber parts, sort of like overgrown rubber washers, that often wear out after a few years, so if no one is servicing the well, those parts break down and the whole pump stops working. In the private sector, everybody knows that there's not much point in drilling a well that won't work in a couple of years, but in the aid world, there's often a focus on delivering something tangible and glamorous, without much attention paid to sustaining it for years to come. That's why some aid groups work just on repairing wells (it's sometimes cheaper to repair an old one than to build a new one). And what's true of wells is true of all kinds of assistance at home and abroad: implementation is extremely hard. Helping people is a fraught, uncertain process that is never as easy as fund-raising appeals suggest.

That doesn't mean, of course, that aid can't be harnessed effectively. We've seen poorly planned wells that wasted donor money, but we've also seen well-designed, well-maintained water projects that sharply reduced child deaths from diarrhea. A 2004 World Health Organization study carefully examined the costs and benefits of water and sanitation projects and found that each $1 invested typically led to between $5 and $11 in benefits—a very nice return. Dirty water and other public health threats don't just kill people; they also impose a kind of tax on everyone. Children suffer from diarrhea and miss school, or they pick up intestinal parasites that leave them anemic and struggling to concentrate. Women in Africa sometimes spend many hours a day fetching water from distant wells (collecting water is invariably women's work in the developing world), so they have less time to breast-feed and care for children, let alone to start small businesses. Or parents tell their daughters to drop out of school so that they can fetch water for the family. Providing clean water doesn't just sate thirst; it also sprinkles opportunity.

Given the challenges, Scott Harrison decided that charity:water wouldn't itself drill wells or manage them. Instead, he works with partners that already own well-drilling rigs, such as the International Rescue Committee or local organizations, and gives them money to do the work. Some of the first wells Harrison arranged to be dug were in Kenya, in an area that turned out to have high amounts of fluoride in the groundwater. So he spent a fortune drilling wells—and then the water wasn't potable. "We screwed up," Harrison remembers. "We just didn't know what we were doing." A donor tied to the wells sued, alleging mismanagement. Harrison was devastated. He wondered if he would ever overcome the humiliation of a lawsuit. In the end, he wrote a blog post for the charity:water site, recounting what had happened and not sparing himself accountability for his own mistakes. Eventually the dispute was resolved.

Harrison is committed to transparency, but this can be embarrassing. In 2010, charity:water marked its anniversary by drilling a well for Bayaka pygmies in a remote part of Central African Republic, announcing that it would post a video that evening so that donors could see what their contributions had wrought. It was the equivalent of a great big drumroll across the Internet — and then the drilling led to a dry well. Donors had just invested thousands of dollars in a failure. That evening the charity:water team dutifully used a satellite unit to broadcast video of the fiasco to the world. Eventually, on the fifth attempt, the drilling team succeeded — but that was six months later. Harrison believes that donors are sometimes willing to accept failure as a reminder of the difficulty of the task at hand, as long as the organization discloses everything. Indeed, one time when we visited Harrison in charity:water's headquarters in the SoHo district of Manhattan he was happy to acknowledge the organization's latest failure. Charity:water had raised $1.2 million from 14,000 donors to buy a drilling rig for an Ethiopian partner organization, painting it a bright yellow and equipping it with a GPS locator. A Twitter account was set up to tweet each time a well was drilled — and the rig toppled over while being transported to a village. It was now on its side and out of commission.

"They were trying to reach a village that was really marginalized," Scott said, noting that the villagers had helped construct a road so that the rig could reach it. "We'll get the thing back up and we'll be drilling a couple of weeks from now. But I think that's a great opportunity to tell people, 'Look, there's determination here. This isn't easy. This isn't like drilling in your backyard, or installing a pool.'"

Harrison steadily refined his model for charity:water, ensuring that plans included a maintenance component. The maintenance varies with the local partner, but it may include training local repair crews and financing their work, or charging small sums for water so that repairs in the future can be funded. There's usually a local water committee responsible for the well (or borehole, as they are more properly called; in Africa, a well is usually hand-dug, while a borehole is machine-drilled and runs much deeper). In the Central African Republic, for example, each of charity:water's wells is visited by a crew twice a year for preventive maintenance, and local communities contribute 40 percent of that maintenance cost (sometimes in chickens and goats rather than in cash) to guarantee local buy-in. Local communities must also contribute labor for the project, so that it is their well rather than just a gift from outsiders.

Charity:water became one of America's fastest-growing charities because of several key strategies. First, Harrison found a core group of donors to pay for all administrative expenses, so every cent donated to charity:water actually goes to wells. These donors (who include tech legends such as Jack Dorsey of Twitter and Sean Parker of Facebook) even cover the bank fees charged for credit card contributions.

The second principle is to document everything with photographs and videos, and tie every gift to a particular project. If you raise enough to pay for an entire well (about $6,000 for a hand-dug well, or $10,000 for a borehole), a sign, sticker, or plaque goes on it with your name on it. In effect, charity:water sells naming rights to wells. But even if you donate only $5, you still get a thank-you for helping finance a particular well, with GPS coordinates and a link to a photo of it in action. You can look it up on Google Earth or keep an eye on it through the charity:water website. Through a $5 million grant from Google, charity:water is also developing remote water sensors for wells to deliver water flow results to donors through a smartphone app, or to alert managers if it stops working.

The third principle is to use creative and irreverent marketing, including social media, to go viral. Charity:water has 1.4 million followers on Twitter and a very popular Instagram account, and it has dazzled with advertising campaigns using donated time and space. One popular video shows prosperous American families in Manhattan stepping out of their luxury buildings and lining up to fill jerry cans with dirty water from a lake in Central Park. A mother then offers the murky water to her kids. For the most part, though, the message is upbeat: *We have the power to prevent this from happening everywhere. If you give a tiny amount of money, some Ethiopians won't have to drink dirty water, either.* Harrison rarely guilt-trips people into writing checks. "Guilt has never been part of it," he says. "It's excitement instead, presenting people with an opportunity: you have an amazing chance to build a well!"

One of Harrison's most successful innovations has been the concept of pledging a birthday. It's an echo of Harrison's birthday bash that helped launch charity:water. You sign up on the charity:water website, set a fund-raising target, and then send an email to your friends with the link saying that instead of presents you're encouraging donations to help build a well in a village that doesn't have one. (This of course is what little Rachel Beckwith did before her fateful accident.) Asking your friends is potentially a powerful mechanism. Generosity is contagious, according to Yale University sociologist Nicholas A. Christakis and his colleague, James H. Fowler, who pioneered experiments examining the social contagion effect on behaviors such as happiness, obesity, optimism, loneliness and selfishness. Christakis and Fowler primarily used a framework based on the prisoner's dilemma, in which players must decide whether to cooperate with their rival (in which case both players win a modest amount) or not to cooperate (in which case the player either wins or loses all). Christakis and Fowler found that when players cooperate, their cooperation is passed on to other players. The result was a domino effect, or cascade of cooperation, that stretched to three degrees of separation.

Scientists have also found that people are even more generous and cooperative when they are observed by others. That's why in birthday pledges, your friends can see who else is giving. The concept of giving a birthday plays to those who are deep-hearted altruists, but also to those who are trying to get out of a birthday party but want to do something useful, and few groups do birthday giving as well as charity:water. "We think it's something everybody in the world could get excited about," Harrison says. "Just with the birthday idea—everybody's got a birthday, they have one every year! About 15,000 people have raised fifteen million bucks with their birthdays. But 15,000 is a tiny number! Imagine a million people giving up birthdays—you could raise $1 billion if the $1,000 average held up."

Six years after its founding, charity:water hit a cumulative $100 million in revenues and had provided water to more than 3 million people. "Scott is an important marketing machine, lifting one of the most critical issues of our time in a way that is sexy and incredibly compelling—that's his gift," says Jacqueline Novogratz, founder of the Acumen Fund that invests in socially driven companies. Not surprisingly, Harrison is aiming ever upward. His goal is to reach a cumulative $3 billion in donations within a decade, so that charity:water can provide water to 100 million people.

Charity:water's success reflects the success of what might be called giving communities or giving circles, to mark philanthropy as a communal and social activity. Charity:water excels at uniting people and giving them all a sense that they are accomplishing something important and altruistic, maybe even life-saving, for a modest sum of money. It's an immensely social activity, and that's perhaps as it should be.

"Human beings are in some ways like bees," says Jonathan Haidt. "We evolved to live in intensely social groups, and we don't do as well when freed from hives."

S ocial networks that contribute and give together aren't new. After all, that's how churches, synagogues, and other religious congregations have operated for centuries. Likewise, America's private universities are masters of fund-raising and have turned alumni pools into giving communities because that's an effective way of eliciting alumni donations. Humanitarian organizations are newer at it.

Some of the giving communities that have sprung up are remarkably simple and effortless, rather like a church for non-churchgoers. For example, Marsha Wallace, a mother of four in Greenville, South Carolina, yearned to do something altruistic but didn't have much time. Then she had an epiphany: she would get together monthly with friends for a potluck dinner in one of their homes and then use the money they would otherwise have spent at a restaurant to donate to a charity supporting women around the world. Wallace and her cohorts had their first dinner in January 2003 and raised $750. Thus was born the first chapter of Dining for Women. Today, Dining for Women has 8,000 members in 420 chapters across the United States and abroad. It has raised millions of dollars to support 40,000 women in thirty-nine countries. Like a religious service, it provides fellowship and spiritual returns and leaves members uplifted.

A school attorney named Diana McDonough had a similar epiphany. She doted on her eight grandchildren and marveled at a new granddaughter's fragility, beauty, and promise, but she was bothered, too—by how much this child enjoyed when so many children in the world had so little. "By an accident of fate my granddaughter was born into a loving family in the world's richest country," she says, "while an equally deserving baby with loving parents was born into poverty and privation. How unfair the world seemed—and how little I was doing about it!" At that juncture, McDonough had a brainstorm. She would start an organization composed of women who would pledge that whenever they gave something to their own grandchild, they would also give to far needier children. Thus was born Global Grandmothers. As McDonough puts it: "The basic idea was simple— give to a child in need when you give to a grandchild—*linked giving*. Let the world's children benefit from the pooled generosity of caring grandmothers."

While giving communities are typically about donating money, they can also be about volunteering time or skills. One of the biggest needs in the nonprofit world is sophisticated business skills— including personnel management, marketing, customer relations, and information systems—that any good-size corporation has plenty of. Thus a skills-giving community composed of business people can be very powerful, and that's precisely the idea behind the Full Circle Fund of San Francisco. It began in 2000 when eight successful Silicon Valley entrepreneurs and venture capitalists realized they had more to offer nonprofits than just large checks. So they created a giving circle divided into three specialty sub-groups—education, environment, and global economic opportunity—and they now have about 200 members and five staff. Each year they choose a few nonprofits in each area and advise them closely on how to do a better job. The idea is to develop philanthropic skills and mind-sets among wealthy donors, and to cultivate greater efficiency in nonprofits. So far, Full Circle Fund has provided more than $10 million to more than eighty nonprofits and, more important, has provided them with 80,000 hours of consulting expertise. "Sharing my marketing and business expertise with nonprofits can have a much greater impact than just giving money," notes Robin Joy, a Full Circle member who is an executive of a tech company.

Some of the long-established aid organizations that are working day in and day out to bring clean water to far-flung villagers are resentful of charity:water's success. They see it as an interloper, an infant organization that doesn't even dig wells yet attracts celebrities and media hoopla. They worry that it oversimplifies the challenge of global health to drilling wells, reducing a vast network of problems to what can be captured with a photo op and GPS location. There's something to this concern, and it's certainly true that not every need can be photographed in this way. Yet that also misses the point. Wells are undeniably a real need, and charity:water has figured out creative ways to harness resources to drill them. Digging wells in a war zone without electricity as rebel groups attempt to kidnap your staff is one challenge. Another is winning support from uninterested people in the West. Large numbers of people in the rich world would like to help, and more than a billion people in the developing world (and many in the developed world as well) need help, yet there aren't enough bridging mechanisms to connect those groups. Charity:water has been so successful because it is an architect of these bridges.

Sometimes we hear from skeptics who complain: *Too many aid organizations are about the donor, not the beneficiaries. They need to focus on meeting needs of slum dwellers in Liberia or India, not of emotionally needy hedge fund managers in New York or London.* Our reaction is that while the needs that are most important are those of the Liberian kids, the best way of getting them help may be to please those hedge fund donors.

As for Scott Harrison himself, he's no longer living a flashy life, and his only hope of a business class seat on one of the ninety flights he takes annually is an airline upgrade. He's through with gambling, strip clubs, and drugs. He met his wife, Vik, an ad designer, when she volunteered for charity:water; she is now its creative director. The Harrisons live in a one-bedroom apartment, a fourth-floor walk-up, and they have been giving away 25 percent of their income each year—some of it right back to charity:water (in 2014, with a baby coming, they may lower the percentage to 20 percent). "We live modestly," Harrison says. "We don't have a car, but we're happy! I'm too busy to spend money."

One Girl, in Memoriam

Rachel Beckwith had a preternatural interest in helping others. Maybe this was an outgrowth of her mom's efforts to instill empathy in Rachel, by talking about people who were less fortunate and by offering an example of compassion. Or maybe Rachel was blessed with great natural empathy. In the end, the $1,265,823 raised in Rachel's campaign for charity:water was enough to provide water for 37,000 people.

The family also donated Rachel's organs, in hopes of saving the lives of others. Mark J., a fifty-three-year-old manager at a semiconductor equipment manufacturer in California, had failing kidneys and had spent six years on a waiting list to get new ones. Then he received a phone call from doctors at the hospital. In an email to Samantha Paul he explained:

> They told me that they had a kidney available that was a perfect match for my blood type, and that it was being flown by jet from Bellevue, Washington. They also indicated that it was from a nine-year-old child. I was shaking all the way to the hospital. I could not believe I was so lucky. My health had been getting worse, my body was storing so much water I was swelling and could barely put Levi pants on. The timing for me could not have been more perfect. That is why I am so emotional over this. A family lost a precious child and I benefited from it.

A year after Rachel's death, Samantha Paul traveled to Ethiopia to see the wells that her daughter had financed. In one village receiving a well, the church held a memorial service for Rachel, her photo on the altar, and the priests spent the entire night before the service praying for the girl and her mom. Another village created Rachel's

A memorial to Rachel Beckwith at a well in Ethiopia

Park to honor the girl who had brought its people their first clean water ever. Tekloini Assefa, who heads an Ethiopian well-drilling organization, declared to a group including Rachel's mom: "Samantha, your little girl is an inspiration to us all. We have heavy hearts imagining what it was like to lose Rachel due to such horrific circumstances. It is something no parent ever wants to contemplate, let alone live through. Even more remarkable is that Rachel developed such a big heart from such a young age—that she understood and felt the pain of others on the other side of the world. To give up her birthday presents so that other children can improve their lives is the most beautiful gift a person can give."

CHAPTER SEVENTEEN

Survival of the Kind

The measure of a man is the worth of the things he cares about.

— MARCUS AURELIUS

W hy are we generous? Why do we seem hardwired to be altruistic? Isn't life a Darwinian struggle, and if so, why haven't selfish genes rooted out the generous genes? Why would "survival of the fittest" nurture feelings of compassion and empathy?

Since the beginning of time, it would seem that a selfish egoist, concerned only with himself or herself, would be more likely to survive and pass on those selfish genes, while the Cro-Magnon altruist would have died trying to save a fellow being in peril or a lost child from starvation after sharing too much of the nut stockpile with neighbors.

One of the most sophisticated explanations for the evolution of generosity comes from Christopher Boehm, a distinguished biologist and anthropologist, who notes that survival of the fittest applies not just to individuals but also to social groups. If one band of hunters was better at cooperating, and each member looked out for the others, that group was more likely to flourish and spread. Thus any genetic predilection for cooperation and sharing would be transmitted, while rival bands of selfish hunters might die out. In other words, as Charles Darwin himself noted, survival of the fittest may select not just at the individual level but also at the group level. In addition, hunter-gatherers so depend upon cooperation and sharing that anyone who violates these norms is punished—sometimes even executed.

If generosity is beneficial for a group, then it can be transmitted culturally as well as biologically. Called "competitive altruism," the argument is that those who display altruism rise in the social hierarchy, so they (and their children) are in greater demand as mates. Indeed, when students in a study were asked to divide up a sum of money any way they wanted, those who took less for themselves were more admired by others and more often selected as group leaders.

Competitive altruism rings true for anyone who has attended a New York benefit dinner, where philanthropy incorporates an element of showing off, or anyone who has seen wedding and funeral festivals in Asia or Africa. Even poor families there spend vast sums on these lavish celebrations, offending outsiders. Why spend money on an extravagant village banquet instead of on school fees for your children? In the context of competitive altruism, those who throw lavish banquets may gain status, attract better mates for their children, and thus improve their children's reproductive prospects.

To understand the biochemistry of altruism, and how generosity might be transmitted from generation to generation, we watched neuroscientist Sarina R. Saturn conduct one of a series of experiments. As a student sat in front of a computer in a small room at Oregon State University in Corvallis, Saturn affixed various electrodes around his head, torso, face, and other parts of his body. She switched on an inspiring video from an Oprah Winfrey show for the student to watch, then went into another room, where monitors started picking up signals from the student's reactions to the video—his neural activity, heart rate, breathing, perspiration, and facial expressions, including disgust, happiness, and sadness. The setup looked like an electrocardiograph or a polygraph machine. Saturn wanted to see how he and others respond to an inspirational video that shows acts of altruism. Do they respond by wanting to give or help as well? Or do they smile and then forget? What is going on inside the brain and the body when people watch someone being altruistic?

As we've mentioned, one key driver in altruism is oxytocin, the "trust molecule." Saturn says, "It's almost like a social glue" that promotes "survival of the kindest." She calls it a compassion molecule that is like a "chill pill." It calms down our stress responses and makes us more interested in others; in particular, we look into their eyes more. When we look gently into someone's eyes, that person will probably release oxytocin and feel more compassion. When an owner makes eye contact with his or her dog, greater amounts of oxytocin are released in the owner; researchers suspect that the dog may be releasing oxytocin as well. "People who do have oxytocin sources in their lives tend to be less stressed and more prosocial," says Saturn. "It can be pets, lovers, kids—just love in general."

Oxytocin works alongside two other neurotransmitters, dopamine and serotonin, to make us feel good when we do good. Serotonin interacts with oxytocin and dopamine to drive the happy feeling we get as a result of an altruistic act. Dopamine helps trigger the rewarding feeling you get when you eat chocolate, and it helps to produce the rush we get when we give—what Mayr and Harbaugh measured in the nucleus accumbens using brain scans. Oxytocin, which runs near the bottom of the brain and is thus harder to image clearly, helps give us a tingle like a warm bath. "With the oxytocin system, we're hardwired to get bodily rewards from being prosocial and altruistic," says Saturn. "We kind of get those benefits very peripherally by calming down our heart and feeling warm and fuzzy."

Saturn has uncovered genetic differences in the intensity of our oxytocin responses, and therefore in the degree of altruism each of us is born with. People who are the most empathic have two copies of the G allele, one of the four basic nucleotides of the genetic code, located on the oxytocin receptor at a specific site that allows genetic variation. These GGs excel at empathy and are very good at reading

Sarina R. Saturn, an assistant professor at Oregon State University, researches the biology underlying altruism.

people's emotions. They also tend to be less stressed and more compassionate. Sometimes experts refer to GGs as having the "compassion" gene. In contrast, those with two copies of the A allele are less able to put themselves in the shoes of others and tend to get stressed out more easily. The majority of people are neither GG nor AA but somewhere in between, with a combination of AG or GA.

Evolutionary pressures may have led to a greater abundance of GG or AA genotypes in particular populations. Americans seem to have more GGs than found in some other societies, Saturn says. East Asian populations seem to have more AAs. But don't worry if you don't like your genotype. None of this is deterministic. Life experiences can also change our propensity toward altruism, and Saturn notes that our generosity may also be greatly shaped by how we were brought up, by the attitudes of our peers, by our life traumas, and by "moral exemplars or good and bad influences in your life."

Saturn has demonstrated that impact in the lab. The Oregon State University student watching the video was hooked up to a machine called an fNIRS, for functional near-infrared spectroscopy, that captures body signals and neural activity. Right after subjects watch a video, Saturn has them play a game to see if they give away more money than otherwise, a sign that the uplifting video has prompted viewers to be more altruistic. In another task, a research assistant knocks over a bunch of pens to see if the subjects offer to pick them up. She has found that the inspirational video does prompt them to be more altruistic, and those subjects who receive affection and generosity in their lives tend to be more helpful. So far, the effect of the inspirational video, called moral elevation, seems to last twenty to thirty minutes, but repetition of sources of moral elevation can keep the impact lasting longer.

None of this is to suggest that our moral behavior is shaped by our genes or environment in any simple, straightforward way. And other pieces are emerging in what is probably a giant jigsaw puzzle with different genes interacting with one another.

Some people are skeptical about possible genetic roots for altruism and morality. Philip Lieberman, an evolutionary biologist at Brown University, argues that it's often exaggerated into "simplistic genetic determinism." He warns against looking too deeply for a biological basis for moral behavior:

A properly dressed family strolling in one of [Germany's] many parks in 1932 would have been met with courtesy by a policeman if they had any reason to request assistance or report any untoward occurrence—even if they were Jewish. Eight years later, that same policeman might have been positioning a three-year-old Jewish girl, who had been stripped of her clothes, on a board positioned over the pit in which the bodies of her mother, father, brother, and older sisters lay in pools of blood. He then would have placed his police-issued pistol against her head and pulled the trigger.... No selective sweep replaced any German moral genes in the short Nazi era, nor did the moral gene return in 1945.

He further argues that a higher level of altruism—the kind that goes beyond a parental instinct, for instance—must be learned and nurtured to build on any "genetically transmitted" base we inherit. Lieberman's skepticism is a useful reminder that the study of altruism is in its infancy, and that we should be wary of early hypotheses and dogmatic conclusions. Human behavior and reward systems are immensely complex, but it seems that with the appropriate nature and nurture, we can cultivate more altruistic habits in individuals and in society.

These days, there is an emerging infrastructure of altruism, a support network for those who want to help others. It encompasses such things as community service requirements for high school students, matching gift offers for corporate employees, conferences such as the Clinton Global Initiative that offer tycoons advice on giving, and corporate social responsibility initiatives such as sabbaticals for employees who want to work for a nonprofit for six months. It also includes a network of institutes including the Greater Good Science Center at the University of California at Berkeley, which both studies "positive emotions" and encourages them.

The founder of the Greater Good Science Center is Dacher Keltner, a professor of psychology who has devoted his career to studying what makes life meaningful to people and thinks he knows the crux of the answer. Keltner beams from behind a halo of long hair and has

Dacher Keltner, a professor of psychology at the University of California, Berkeley, founded the Greater Good Science Center, which explores the neuroscience of compassion.

NATALIE KELTNER-MCNEIL

a hint of hippie in him, but he bolsters his touchy-feely side with a modern scientific panoply of experiments, neuroscience, and statistical analyses.

Keltner grew up in Laurel Canyon in the Hollywood Hills, the heart of a rock-and-roll counterculture and bohemian esprit in the 1960s. Frank Zappa, Jim Morrison, and Jackson Browne blossomed there. "I think part of my love of evidence and proof and measurement is because my parents were wild, and I had to assess their claims," he says. Later, at Stanford University, Keltner dabbled in psychology and became a devotee of Professor Paul Ekman, who had spent seven years studying movement of muscles in the face as a way to measure emotions. Keltner went off to study with Ekman in his Human Interaction Laboratory at the University of California at San Francisco. The magnitude of a startle response, he learned, is an indicator of a person's temperament and reflects how anxious, reactive, or vigilant a person is.

"Sneak up on your beloved as he is settling into a glass of wine, and drop a heavy book on the counter next to him," Keltner writes. "If he shrieks, with arms flailing and wine glass flying, you have just witnessed a few telling seconds of his behavior that speak volumes to how he will handle the daily stresses and tribulations of life."

Keltner argues that humans are a hodgepodge of competing

impulses, perhaps 40 percent benevolent and 60 percent selfish. "We're totally altruistic, and we will kill infants to survive," he says. "We're genocidal, and we are charitable. We have this bundle of propensities." Keltner says that this wide spectrum explains how there are saints of the world, the Mother Teresas renowned for their generosity, who perhaps have particularly high oxytocin and dopamine levels, a nucleus accumbens on overdrive. Then there are those at the other end. "I've been studying Machiavellians who just screw people over," says Keltner. "Machiavellians will say things like, 'It's okay to hurt people to get ahead,' or 'Ultimately, everybody is only after their own self-interest,' or 'I don't trust anybody, and most people are criminals and are masquerading as good people.'" Luckily, the Machiavellians don't wipe out the Mother Teresas. One explanation may be that compassion, generosity, and cooperation are contagious.

"When people are around the Dalai Lama, people are like, 'I feel different. I feel like giving away stuff,'" Keltner says. He says that experiments have shown that simply watching a GG person's generosity makes others more generous.

While Saturn and others show we can be "inspired by other people's goodness," as Keltner puts it, greater wealth, conversely, seems to curb the instinct for helpfulness and prosocial behavior; it seems to put people on their guard. In one fascinating experiment, research subjects were exposed to either a screensaver showing money or one showing fish. Those who saw the money were afterward more likely to prefer solitary activities and less likely to share. And when someone else entered the room, the subjects preferred to sit farther away from that person.

In another experiment, research subjects were randomly assigned either to think through their plans for the next day or to look at a pile of Monopoly money and imagine a fantastically wealthy future. Then a person walked by and tripped, "accidentally" spilling a bunch of pencils. Those who had been looking at the Monopoly money picked up fewer pencils.

Likewise, when participants in another experiment were unobtrusively reminded of money, they donated 39 percent of $2 given to them, compared to a neutral control group, who donated 67 percent. Maybe this research helps explains why the most affluent 20 percent of Americans give a smaller share of their income to charity than the bottom 20 percent.

Yet, as Mayr and Harbaugh suggested, habits can be formed, and they can even start through a contagion of compassion. One of America's founding fathers had a similar concept, as Saturn points out. Thomas Jefferson once noted the power of generosity: "When any original act of charity or of gratitude, for instance, is presented either to our sight or imagination, we are deeply impressed with its beauty and feel a strong desire in ourselves of doing charitable and grateful acts also."

Philanthropy by the Poor

If evolution has indeed left us hardwired to be social and derive satisfaction from altruism, then it's obviously not just the affluent who have these needs. Indeed, some interesting initiatives give the poor the rewards that come with helping others, and one of the most intriguing is the Restore Leadership Academy in Uganda. Its impoverished students raise money to help American kids.

The academy was founded by Bob Goff, an American lawyer who is a passionate believer in self-help and self-efficacy, and who exudes those same qualities. When his law school application was rejected, he camped outside the dean's office for a week until the dean surrendered and accepted him. Many years later, as a veteran traveler to Uganda, Goff started Restore in 2007 with just four students. It now has a middle school and a high school, with forty teachers and 350 coed students, including former child soldiers and orphans. They all grew up knowing only poverty and conflict. Official test scores from Restore Leadership Academy have ranked it as the second-best school in northern Uganda in academics and the best in athletics. Pupils pay partial tuition and donors cover the rest, including tuition, food, school supplies, medicine, and a sports program. Funders can support a student at the academy for $30 a month.

For fear of breeding dependency, Goff ensures that the students don't perceive themselves as charity cases. They plant, grow, and sell their own crops to pay for their education, and they engage in public service projects such as repairing wells. Then the academy proposed something that raised eyebrows: raising money to donate to needy kids in America. "We wanted to give the kids a sense of empowerment," explains Deborah Eriksson, the executive director of Restore International, which oversees the academy. "We wanted to switch the

Bob Goff and students at the Restore Leadership Academy in Uganda

idea from they are just beneficiaries of help to 'I am strong enough, I can give.'"

The academy chose as its target charity The Mentoring Project, which is based in Portland, Oregon, and supports at-risk boys who don't have dads. Such an organization resonated with the Ugandan children, for many in their community had lost fathers and they intuitively understood the need for mentors. Helping kids in a rich country was novel for the Ugandan students. "They see Westerners come over on trips and they seem insanely wealthy," Eriksson noted. "Kids probably think: 'They could help me so much, they have so much money.' We like the idea of switching that thinking because we don't want them to just think that 'people from the States are here to help me, pity me, and they have it all figured it out.' We want them to think in terms of friendship, and all around the world there are folks who need help."

John Sowers, president of The Mentoring Project, was stunned when he received an email explaining that a group of impoverished Ugandan children recovering from war planned a donation. "How can these kids give to us?" he wondered. "I was thinking, 'Wait a second. I've been giving money to Africa, and I can't take money from Africa.'"

He recalls telling Goff, *Bob, I don't know if we can take money from you guys.*

Empowering these kids to give, Goff replied, *is the best thing we can do for them.*

Samuel Oboma, a Restore academy graduate now at university and aiming to become a lawyer, says that the students were eager to help their American counterparts. His own father was killed in the war in northern Uganda a week before he was born, and his mother was jobless, so he never had much to share—and that made the chance to help needy American kids even more special. "It's something wonderful," Samuel said. "It's not only people within Africa or a specific part of the world who need help.... It's good to give a hand to whoever needs it. In any part of the world you're responsible, irrespective of race or color."

In Oregon, Sowers gradually came around to the idea of accepting money from Ugandan students: "I want to see the kids as victims, and they have been victimized, but Bob is all about empowering them. So Bob's idea was for them to give to us. And what an amazing idea for them to give to this country—and you're impacting America and Uganda and everyone else. That blew me away." So far, the Ugandan youngsters have raised $830, which goes to training, supporting, and recruiting mentors for the American youngsters. Every month, the Ugandan students raise another $25 or so.

CHAPTER EIGHTEEN

Healing Through Helping

Healing is a matter of time,
but it is sometimes also
a matter of opportunity.

— HIPPOCRATES

Catalina Escobar seemed to be one of those exceedingly lucky women who had it all. Her father had started a successful steel business in her native Colombia, making the family enormously wealthy. Catalina went to college in Boston, earned an M.B.A. in Bogotá, worked as an international banker, and soon was running her own international trading company. She married the scion of another of Colombia's wealthiest families, and they made a stunning couple, squired around in a bulletproof limousine through the ancient streets of Cartagena—a walled waterfront city that is one of the most beautiful in the Americas—with their two equally lovely children.

They decided to move from Cartagena to Bogotá, and in the middle of packing, their eighth-floor apartment was stacked with boxes. A maid was looking after Juan Felipe, their youngest son, seventeen months old, at home one morning. Catalina was at work when at 10:30 a.m. she received a shattering telephone call. Juan Felipe had climbed onto a pile of boxes and tumbled over the eighth-floor balcony. He was dead.

In the next few days of inconsolable grief, Catalina tried to find meaning in the tragedy. But instead, her mind kept directing her to another episode just a week earlier, one that left her racked by guilt of a different kind. Catalina volunteered two days a week at a public hospital maternity ward, and she had become close to some of the patients and staff. One day she met a teenage mother who had just lost a baby and was crying because she had been unable to afford a $30 medicine that would have saved his life. The mother's grief had seared Catalina, who kept thinking: *I have that money in my pocket.* Now in her own sorrow, she felt bonded with that teen mom.

Soon afterward Catalina and her family were dining in a fine restaurant when, halfway through the meal, she broke down and began sobbing. She said that each person's meal was costing considerably more than the medicine that would have saved the child of that teenage mom. "We're eating a baby's life," Catalina wailed. There in the restaurant, she and her husband began to sketch out on a piece of paper an idea for a foundation to memorialize Juan Felipe and reduce the number of other mothers who would have to suffer the loss of a child.

That was the origin of the Juan Felipe Foundation, which works with impoverished teen moms in Cartagena to reduce child mortality, improve child care, and teach job skills. The foundation, launched in 2002, has grown rapidly, providing support for thousands of women in Cartagena. There is talk of expanding soon to Medellín and then to other cities.

Catalina's initiative is an example of philanthropy as an exercise in healing and recovery. As the evidence has grown that, quite aside from its ability to empower others, giving is self-empowering, more people and organizations are embracing this as a strategy. Sometimes it has been a way of overcoming abuse one suffered as a child, or a

*Catalina Escobar comforting a teenage mother in
her program in Cartagena, Colombia*

way to chip away at depression or other mental health issues. Sometimes it is a crisis, the loss of a loved one or a career dead end, that makes people think more deeply about what they want their legacy to be. Paradoxically, it's when people are feeling hurt and sad that they often benefit the most from turning outward and trying to help others. Here, we want to explore how engaging in a larger cause can be a path to personal growth and recovery.

Catalina and her foundation work in some of the toughest slums of Cartagena, dominated by gangs and largely avoided by police. During a visit we made to one such slum, gang members surged onto a nearby highway, set up a barricade, and robbed a vehicle. We asked whether the police would intervene, and one resident said sourly, "I've never seen police come to someone's aid here. They only come when someone is already dead."

We were in the slum to visit a teen mom who was under consideration for sponsorship by the Juan Felipe Foundation. Each January and July, the foundation sponsors more than 200 troubled teenage girls—typically pregnant girls or new teen moms—bringing them in for an initial six-month phase of support, medical care, counseling, and job training. It's a bit like the Nurse-Family Partnership in its focus on at-risk moms, but the interactions mostly take place not in the home but at a lovely foundation campus with a cafeteria, meeting rooms, clinic, and nursery. The moms get transportation money to come each day.

"Here, I learned how to smile," said Roxana, a seventeen-year-old girl who endured a brutal rape and years of violence in the slums. "Here, I learned to value myself."

"Female empowerment" is one of those slogans that is repeated so much in the aid community that it has lost much of its meaning. But Roxana is an example of what "female empowerment" actually can mean. While in the Juan Felipe Foundation program, Roxana heard discussions about how sexual violence is always unacceptable, about how women have to stand up for each other. One day she was going home when she passed a vacant lot and heard a girl sobbing. Roxana stopped and listened. She could hear the girl saying, "No! No!" It was a gang area, and almost anybody else would have hurried off. But Roxana, who herself had been abused as a girl, grabbed a stick and charged into the vacant lot. She found a man who was abusing a six-year-old girl.

"You can't do this!" Roxana yelled at him. "This isn't right! You're a disgrace!" As she yelled, she kept whacking the man with the stick. He began running, and Roxana chased after him, thrashing him with the stick. Then she went back to the little girl, calmed her down, and helped her return to her family.

Catalina Escobar will never, of course, fully recover from the loss of Juan Felipe. Perhaps no parent ever entirely rebounds from the shock of surviving one's child. For Catalina, it was at first difficult to work through her own grief while surrounded by hundreds of other moms all proudly clutching their infants. "It was a tough time," she recalls. "At the beginning, it was lots of anxiety. Every baby looked like Juan Felipe." But Catalina threw herself into her campaign to transform the lives of slum girls like Roxana, and so she has seen sadness and misfortune far greater than her own. She has also found that when they are given an opportunity, many of these girls leap for it and turn their lives around. Now the Roxanas of Cartagena are sending forth their own ripples and transforming other people's lives. Some of the girls have found good jobs in Cartagena's booming tourism industry, working in fine hotels and restaurants, and can now give their own children the kind of upbringing they never had. Catalina still cries when she talks about Juan Felipe—and about the mother who lost her child for want of $30—but she has found a new life full of purpose.

You see an almost maternal pride in Catalina's face as she sits on the floor of a counseling room, listening to the story of a girl named Yurleidys Peñaloza (Yurleidys's name is a Spanish rendition of the English "your ladies," apparently derived from encounters with American navy sailors). Yurleidys is an oval-faced young woman with light brown skin, black hair, and a poise and calm that seem at odds with the brutality she is recounting.

"My life changed when I was seven years old, when my mom's brother raped me," Yurleidys began. The rapes continued for almost three years. At the age of nine, she said, "I got tired of being abused. I got tired of being raped so many times." She went to her grandmother and confided what was happening. The grandmother confronted the uncle, who denied the rapes; the family doubted anything so repulsive could be true, and the matter was dropped. The next time the uncle was home alone with Yurleidys, he took his revenge. "There was a big tank of water, and he tried to drown me in it," she recalled. "He was saying, 'I'm going to kill you! I'm going to drown you!'" Yurleidys begged for her life, repeating over and over, "I won't tell! I won't tell." Finally the uncle stopped dunking her head in the water tank and let her stumble off.

Three days later, Yurleidys walked by herself to the local police station. She marched up to a police officer, who smiled at the nine-year-old girl and asked her what was wrong. "I have this uncle who has been raping me for three years," Yurleidys replied. The police officer immediately summoned the senior officer, a lieutenant, who listened to Yurleidys and then called his wife to come and talk to the girl. The lieutenant's wife was warm and comforting; she took Yurleidys to a hospital, which confirmed the rapes. The uncle was arrested.

Yurleidys pulled a faded piece of newspaper from her purse. "I always carry this around with me," she said, and she carefully unfurled it. It was a slightly yellowed, fragile clipping about the arrest of her uncle on charges of abusing a minor.

After a few months with a social services unit, Yurleidys returned to her mother, a single mom, and tried to put her life back together. It didn't work. When Yurleidys was twelve, her mother was hospitalized and needed $400 to pay the medical bill. "We didn't have the money, so I went to the streets," Yurleidys recalled softly. "I thought, 'I already lost the battle, I've been through this, it doesn't matter as long as I get my mom through this.' So I served ten clients."

When Yurleidys was fourteen, her pimp introduced her to the more lucrative practice of drug smuggling around Colombia. For every trip she made carrying marijuana or cocaine from one city to another she earned $300. That worked well for a time, until she and a nineteen-year-old friend, Katerina, were transporting a ten-kilogram bag of cocaine and caught the attention of police. With the police chasing them, they dumped the bag and managed to escape. Feeling relieved and happy with their narrow escape, they went on to the town of Santa Marta to explain to the drug traffickers. The drug lords, though, were fuming.

"They started beating us with iron rods," Yurleidys recalls, and then they stripped the girls naked and began torturing them with iron bars heated until they were red hot.

"Why are you doing this?" Yurleidys screamed.

You ruined everything because you dropped the bag of drugs, one replied as he tortured her. Yurleidys showed us the scars on her legs from the torture, but the worst was yet to come: one of the men pulled out a gun and fatally shot Katerina in the head. Yurleidys pretended to pass out and just lay there as the men beat her. When the men walked away, Yurleidys jumped up and ran away, stark naked and bleeding profusely, through a field to a road. A passing truck driver slowed for the raving fourteen-year-old girl, let her jump into the cab, and gave her a jacket to cover herself.

Yurleidys returned to Cartagena, lay low, and returned to school. "I wanted a new life," she said. Through the Juan Felipe Foundation she studied to be a waitress and then interned at a fine hotel coffee shop. When we visited during her internship, she proudly showed us that she knew how to make a cappuccino and could distinguish a dessert fork from a dinner fork, a champagne flute from a wineglass. "I love to study hotel work," she said simply.

Catalina, who was with us, was bursting with pride. When Yurleidys stepped away, Catalina whispered to us, "These are my mentors. They teach me so much. They have given me so much."

We spent a week with Catalina and were awed by her devotion to these girls from the slums and by the difference she was making in their lives. Colombia is a country where traditionally the wealthy elites showed no interest or compassion for the poor, and that's one reason for the rise of the guerrilla movements and subsequent civil war in that country. That does seem to be changing, and Catalina is emblematic of the change. In Colombia, the wealthy have seen through bitter experience that not even the highest walls or the best security guards can fully protect them from the upheavals resulting from poverty and hopelessness. So Colombian elites have begun, albeit too slowly, to take steps to address inequality, poverty, and lack of educational opportunity. Most strikingly, Colombia's affluent agreed to shoulder a tax to finance improved security for the masses. Colombia still has many problems, including gang violence in the slums and very high rates of teen pregnancy, but there has been considerable progress.

Recent scholarship endorses the idea that helping can be healing. Volunteering has been associated with lower mortality, better physical function, higher self-rated health, fewer depressive symptoms, diminished pain, and greater life satisfaction. In one large data survey, Nancy Morrow-Howell of Washington University in St. Louis looked at people over sixty and found that those volunteering more hours reported higher levels of well-being, although gains tapered after about 3 hours of volunteering a week. Other research shows that 40 to 100 hours of volunteering a year is associated with health benefits and lower mortality. Some American veterans suffering from post-traumatic stress disorder and other maladies are also discovering that social engagement is a particularly effective way to heal.

Timothy Smith still has trouble talking about April 29, 2004, when eight of his buddies were blown up and killed by an improvised explosive device in Iraq. He had been hanging out the day before with one of the victims, a dad who was talking to his two daughters by phone. Smith still can't stand the smell of sulfur or the sound of explosives, even on the Fourth of July. He still wakes at night and instinctively gropes for his weapon under the bed.

When Smith was discharged from the military in February 2007, he couldn't find a job for six months. That was the hardest time for him, the period when memories of war threatened to capsize him. "I had too much time to think," he says. The only work he could find was part-time at the post office. He took a few courses to get his bachelor's degree. He struggled to relate to his wife, Terri, and young son. "I was aggravated, I was irritated," he said. "If Terri said something, I'd shut down." So he sought help, and he was diagnosed with post-traumatic stress disorder. Someone told him about a new fellowship offered by a group called The Mission Continues, offering veterans a stipend as long as they work in public service. Smith coveted the fellowship money, which would help him feed his family and pay bills, so he applied for it and was accepted.

The Mission Continues was founded in 2007 by Eric Greitens, a Rhodes scholar and Navy SEAL. Greitens is a lean former boxer who stands very straight and strong, his blue eyes focusing like lasers as he speaks intensely, then softening as he breaks into an easy grin. His staff of thirty-eight has designed a rigorous six-month program that attracts interest from ten times as many veterans as it can accept. The essence of the fellowship program is a philosophy that Greitens shaped beginning with visits he made as a college student to refugee camps in Bosnia and Rwanda in the 1990s. In the Bosnian camps, Greitens noticed that the parents and grandparents fared best because they had children to look after. The worst off were the teenagers. "They didn't feel they had a social purpose," he says. When camp leaders started challenging the refugees, those who responded by organizing activities or teaching children tended to find traction and do better. "For the teenagers who accepted that call to service and started to get engaged, it actually helped them in their own adjustment, transition, and recovery."

After Greitens earned his doctorate with a dissertation on humanitarian aid and community strategies for healing, he signed up to join the Navy SEALs. He was posted in Afghanistan, Southeast Asia, Kenya, and Iraq and soon encountered violence. One morning in Fallujah, Iraq, at 6:00 a.m., as he and his teammates were waking, his barracks was blown up by an explosion and hit with mortar fire. A close friend was wounded in the head, and his blood spattered Greitens. He understood how difficult it would be for soldiers to return from this kind of wartime environment and fit back into American life. He says that reintegration depends in part on finding a sense of purpose. Soldiers have that sense of mission in combat, and then risk feeling a sudden loss of purpose upon returning to civilian life. Greitens argues that there are ways of boosting this sense of post-service mission so that veterans adjust better.

Greitens begins his program for new fellows at The Mission Continues with an extreme physical challenge that they tackle together as a group to create a bond. They eat together, study together, and serve together. At the end of the orientation, they take an oath to serve. Then they begin a six-month fellowship in public service at an organization of their choosing. Each month, they're setting and reaching personal goals in the office and at home, and they're making career plans, too. By the end of the program, they are expected to be moving toward a job, an educational program, or a position in a service organization. Eighty-four percent of fellowship recipients in 2011 and 2012 have achieved that goal six months after finishing the program; they are on the road to recovery by turning their focus to others.

One of those successes is Timothy Smith, the struggling Iraq vet. He started his fellowship in March 2008 and chose to work as a peer counselor at the local veterans hospital, where he advised other veterans on how to navigate the bureaucracy of the Veterans Administration. At first he was nervous, fearful of giving out incorrect information. But he says that during the fellowship he "grew as a person." Smith saw others with the same challenges or worse, leading him to face his own problems more squarely; helping them gave him a sense of mission, a feeling of purpose.

After the fellowship ended, Smith wrote a twenty-seven-page business plan for a new enterprise—a cleaning company that would employ veterans at night so that they could go to school by day. At the end of 2010, as he was finishing a master's in social work, he applied for a business license. He won his first customer contract in January 2011 from a Vietnam veteran who wanted to help. As soon as Smith won the contract, he withdrew his life savings of $5,300 from his military retirement fund. He received an additional small grant from a local organization, Work Vessels for Veterans. His company was launched. "Life is short, so you've got to go for your dreams, as long as you have a plan," he says.

Smith now recruits veterans through networking. His fifteen employees work from 3:30 p.m. until 11:30 p.m., often at schools, where they strip the floors and put on new layers of finish, clean halls, bathrooms, and classrooms, and perform other janitorial duties. Because they are all veterans, there's an unwritten bond among them that's reinforced by a common language that Smith still uses: workers belong to a unit, and there's a chain of command within the company.

In a sense, Smith treats his company almost as a mini version of The Mission Continues, and he's focused on helping his employees with their return home from war, too. As Greitens explains, "Tim won't say this about himself, but he's not only providing them a job

Eric Greitens, left, with Tim Smith and his wife, Terri

with this work, but he's also providing them a model with his own life and counseling about how to take these next steps in your life, which is really powerful."

Smith's trajectory reflects a truth that social scientists are still exploring: that the act of supporting others somehow seems to be a step toward overcoming one's own injuries. When we are hurt physically or psychically, we often feel we want to curl up and hide. Yet that's a time when it can be particularly important to reach out and, paradoxically, try to help others. It's also worth wondering: since so many people would benefit from a little more engagement with others, why wait for a crisis or tragedy to serve as the catalyst?

Encore Careers

L ester Strong, whom we met earlier, had had a long and successful career as a television executive and journalist, culminating in a role as a news anchor at a station in Boston. It was a far cry from his childhood in Braddock, Pennsylvania, where his third-grade teacher had moved his desk into the hallway, pronounced him incapable of learning, and suggested that he was unfit for anything but manual labor. Strong was a major presence in Boston and had been feted at the White House, yet at the age of fifty he was ready for something new that would allow him to give back.

So Strong left the television anchor seat and started working in the nonprofit world. By 2009 he had become chief executive of Experience Corps, presiding over an organization that brings volunteers over the age of fifty-five into classrooms at low-income schools to coach children on reading and other subjects. Strong also oversaw a merger with AARP, which he hopes will supply many more volunteers.

Experience Corps volunteers, who receive training and a small stipend, generally work fifteen hours a week in a classroom, typically kindergarten through third grade. The volunteers work with specific children, aiming to create an emotional bond so that they can provide the children with guidance and mentoring as well as instruction in reading or using a library.

Studies have shown that Experience Corps helps the children with reading, but researchers are also finding that it helps the volunteers. Volunteers get exercise, if only walking up and down stairs at school, that they might not normally get. They gain a strong sense of purpose. They are more socially engaged, working with students, teachers, and other volunteers.

Michelle C. Carlson, a professor at Johns Hopkins University, conducted randomized controlled trials that found that Experience Corps volunteers improved their mental sharpness relative to controls. The elderly often see a waning of executive function, which refers to the mental processes for planning and organization, a bit like an airport's air traffic control system. But Carlson found that after only six months the volunteers who started out with impaired executive function showed a 44 to 51 percent improvement compared to declines in the control group.

A second trial found that 63 percent of Experience Corps participants reported they were more active than before, compared to only 43 percent of the controls. Forty-four percent of Experience Corps participants reported feeling stronger, compared with 18 percent of the controls. And the volunteers reported fewer than half as many falls as before, while in the control group falls increased slightly. Carlson scanned the brains of Experience Corps volunteers and nonparticipants and found improvements in neuroplasticity in the volunteers. "What's exciting is that even in an aging and older adult brain we could expose them to this enriched environment, and we could see that we were doing something that was improving the function of their prefrontal cortex," Carlson said. "What that suggests to us is that we may be able to help them age better." One benefit of such experiences that improve executive control and memory, she said, might be the delayed onset of dementia.

One of the subjects in Carlson's brain-scanning experiments was Rhodi Hill, sixty-six years old. In quick succession, her mother, sister, and brother all died, and she fell into a deep depression. By volunteering with Experience Corps, she says, she was able to manage her grief and reintegrate into a community. "The children, I love them," she said. "I'm giving back and I'm getting."

The result is a symbiotic relationship. "Public schools need help; older adults have the experience, the time, the desire," notes Professor Morrow-Howell, whose work on older volunteers we cited earlier. "The primary reason is so they can help—so they can teach kids to read. . . . But guess what, good news, there's a secondary gain: it's good for them. It's also possibly one of the best health promotion programs."

So it's not surprising that senior citizens are joining the social entrepreneurship revolution, embarking on "encore careers" the way Strong has. These can be paid or unpaid but typically include a heavy element of personal fulfillment.

The theorist of encore careers, Marc Freedman, runs an organization, Encore.org, that gives an annual $100,000 Purpose Prize to a handful of men and women making a difference in a second career. Freedman suggests that a new life stage is emerging. This new stage, as he sees it, is the ten, twenty, even thirty years after a person's main career but before infirmity has set in. In this period, a person can still work full- or part-time, and often is more concerned about a job's meaning than with its salary. Such people have a lifetime of business skills that are invaluable to the nonprofit sector. If more people follow Lester Strong into encore careers rather than just fussing over their golf game, then we baby boomers could in our dodderdom have consequences for society as profound as we did in our youth.

CHAPTER NINETEEN

A Hundred Flowers Bloom

If you don't like someone's story, write your own.

—CHINUA ACHEBE

Elizabeth Scharpf was pursuing joint degrees at Harvard Business School and Harvard's Kennedy School of Government when she began working one summer in Maputo, the balmy capital of Mozambique, in southern Africa. A female boss there happened to gripe to Scharpf about female employees missing work during their menstrual periods. Sanitary pads were unaffordable, so the women and girls just stayed home, out of sight. In the fall, Scharpf returned to Harvard and asked friends from Bangladesh, Nicaragua, and other countries if they had ever heard of this problem. Of course, they said. One explained the reasoning behind schoolgirls staying home: *What if I get called to the blackboard and I have a stain on the back of my skirt?*

The more Scharpf investigated, the more indignant she became. Girls were missing school because they couldn't afford sanitary pads? Women couldn't go to work for lack of pads? And all this was taboo to discuss? So Scharpf joined the change-maker revolution, the wave of social entrepreneurs trying to craft a better world through their own efforts, and taking risks in doing so.

If helping others can be restorative and healing, why not make it a regular part of your lifestyle? And unlike so many entrepreneurs, who want to make it big, why not try to add value to society at the base of the pyramid? This approach is gaining appeal for younger and older people who are simply looking for some more happiness and purpose.

The traditional model of making a difference was conservative, passive, and risk-averse. In December, a little before the holidays, you pulled out your checkbook and made a donation to a charitable organization that you liked, and that was that. These days, a growing number of people like Scharpf want to experiment, dive in more fully, engage in what might be called do-it-yourself philanthropy or social entrepreneurship, and try to drag their friends and families along with them. This is a high-wire act that is both maddening and exhilarating. Gary Slutkin started Cure Violence because he had a vision that nobody else was putting into practice. The same is true of Dr. Hawa Abdi in Somalia. What has struck us over and over is how often the drivers of change are not those who are the wealthiest or best-connected but those at the grassroots who are most persistent. Yes, Earl Warren, as chief justice of the Supreme Court, had a huge impact on ending segregation. But so did Rosa Parks.

There are many change makers who have led the way, people such as Muhammad Yunus of Grameen Bank, or his Bangladeshi compatriot, Sir Fazle Hasan Abed, founder of BRAC. Or Jennifer Staple-Clark, who as a college sophomore founded Unite for Sight, which has now provided eye care to 1.7 million people around the world. Or Dr. Paul Farmer, whose Partners in Health is widely regarded as the gold standard of aid groups working in health care. Or Ela Bhatt, who founded India's Self Employed Women's Association, one of the world's largest grassroots organizations. These organizations are all reminders that social entrepreneurs can become large and influential enough to achieve remarkable results and global respect. Just as the economy needs large corporations and also entrepreneurs working out of their garages, the humanitarian sphere needs the professionalism of major organizations such as CARE, Save the Children, the International Rescue Committee, and Mercy Corps, but it also needs humanitarian start-ups.

As soon as Scharpf finished her graduate programs at Harvard she began to design a company that would manufacture cut-price sanitary pads for Africa and Asia, distributed by local women themselves on a franchise system. Scharpf visited Rwanda, where the cheapest pads commercially available were Chinese-made and cost $1.10 for a pack of ten. Scharpf recruited a team of wonks who consulted villagers,

HANNAH BRICE

*Elizabeth Scharpf with raw materials for
a banana fiber sanitary pad in Rwanda*

agriculture experts, and professors of textile engineering. They asked: *What is there that is really absorbent, widely available, and cheap?* The team narrowed the choices to cassava leaves, banana leaves, banana trunk fibers, potato roots, foam mattresses, and textile scraps. "We brought a blender to Rwanda and started blending things, boiling leaves from potato and cassava, things like that," Scharpf says. "We would drop Coke on it to measure absorbency." That was when they noticed: "Hey, those banana fibers really slurp up the Coke!"

While her fellow Harvard Business School graduates were taking six-figure jobs in finance, Scharpf accepted a $30,000 grant from Echoing Green, which helps finance social entrepreneurs with great ideas. Her team engineered a biodegradable, inexpensive sanitary pad out of banana tree fibers; a pack of ten could eventually retail for just 60 cents. Scharpf's organization, Sustainable Health Enterprises (SHE), began manufacturing banana fiber sanitary pads on a trial basis in Rwanda. Scharpf's team developed a supply chain made up of 600 small-scale banana farmers, mostly women; aid groups will help fund the distribution of the pads at orphanages, schools, and refugee camps.

Still, banana fiber sanitary pads have a hard road ahead, particularly in a country where industrial manufacturing expertise is practically nonexistent and it's not clear that there is even a market for the pads. Just as most venture capital start-ups fail, so do many social entrepreneur start-ups—and SHE may end up among them. Families may consider a 60-cent pack just as unaffordable as a \$1.10 pack. Or suppose for a moment that everything goes perfectly: pad franchises spread, and families buy packets of pads for girls who are now dropping out of school because of difficulties managing menstruation. Will those girls now stay in school? We can't be sure of that. One study in Nepal found that while girls appreciated help with menstrual hygiene, they weren't significantly more likely to attend school as a result. Research in Malawi by the Population Council suggests that bicycles would get more kids to go to school than sanitary pads would. On the other hand, a study in Ghana suggests that supplying pads to rural girls there might reduce girls' absenteeism significantly. Other people think that menstrual cramps are as much of an impediment as lack of pads, so aspirin would deal with absenteeism more effectively and cheaply than pads. In short, it's complicated. Scharpf is engaged in a noble experiment—but entrepreneurs often fail. Anybody wrestling with poverty at home or abroad learns that good intentions and hard work aren't enough. Our view is that the pads won't eliminate the problem but may mitigate it. In the real world, that's how progress usually arrives—as incremental improvements.

The rise of social entrepreneurs starting their own ventures has caused some consternation among large antipoverty organizations. The latter feel that they have the professionalism, the experience, the accounting standards, and the scale to make a difference most effectively—and yet the public embraces social entrepreneurs who have no proven record whatsoever. There's something to that. Do-it-yourself ventures often have a charming backstory and an appealing simplicity, yet they are hobbled by the social entrepreneur's lack of hardheaded business experience. Starting something yourself seems romantic and heroic, a view that fades when you've caught malaria or been mugged by the people you're trying to help. The truth is that start-ups very often fail and rarely scale up. When they collapse, they can leave in the lurch the very people they are trying to help.

PlayPump, an ingenious design for a water pump powered by playing children, is an example of all that can go wrong. Trevor Field, an advertising executive, left his job to back it. He formed a company and started making these pumps with dreams of revolutionizing access to water across rural Africa. A PlayPump looks a bit like a small merry-go-round and is meant to be built on top of a well in an African village; children are meant to push it around and around and in their fun pump the water. As the marketing materials put it, "the village women no longer have to walk far and work hard to get water, and their children are overjoyed with their new toy." The World Bank was sufficiently impressed that it gave PlayPumps its Development Marketplace Award in 2000, and the United States government announced a public-private partnership worth $60 million to build PlayPumps across Africa.

The engineering and business plan were impressive. But to make the scheme work, children had to play with the pump nearly around the clock, which didn't happen. So the women who normally fetched water were forced to turn the merry-go-round themselves, which was hard work and much less efficient than just operating a hand pump. The PlayPumps were also several times more expensive than conventional pumps, and repairs were complicated. The partnership quickly collapsed.

To be harnessed effectively, idealism needs to be grounded in a practical sense of how to get results and a grassroots understanding of the lay of the land. In recent years the explosion in social entrepreneurship has resulted in an outpouring of new initiatives and assistance: everyone wants to start something new, not join an existing program. There is almost no barrier to setting up a public charity—the Internal Revenue Service approves 99.5 percent of applications—and almost no scrutiny over the small ones. Today there are simply too many charities, most of them tiny, inefficient, and inconsequential. We have deliberately not started our own foundation or aid group to gather contributions for causes we believe in. Instead, we point readers and viewers to the many existing ones doing great work. The last thing the world needs, we believe, is one more aid group on top of the 1.4 million already operating in America.

On a visit to Swarthmore College in Pennsylvania, we were hugely impressed by student social entrepreneurs who had started organizations working on problems in China, Peru, Sierra Leone, Ghana, Ecuador, and other countries. Yet every single organization turned out to have been founded within the previous three years. If we had visited six years earlier, we would have learned of equally amazing organizations, most of which would have disappeared when the students involved graduated.

"It's a nightmare," says Cheryl Dorsey, the head of Echoing Green, a nonprofit we mentioned earlier that supports social entrepreneurs. "I start every talk I give at a university saying, 'Please don't start another social enterprise!' Young people have equated success with being a founder. That's the Achilles' heel of our movement. We're heading in the wrong direction if we let a million flowers bloom. It's not enough to have these tiny centers for excellence that never amount to anything. They're too fragmented, too balkanized to ever move the needle." Dorsey tells young people that the biggest need now is for the "intrapreneur," the person who can move into an existing enterprise or institution, shake it up, and boost its productivity.

Some humanitarians note that pursuing a career in the social sector isn't always the most effective way to contribute to society. If you have a talent for numbers, some argue, you should go work on Wall Street, earn millions, gain a skill set, and then contribute financially to a proven charity while coaching a favored aid group on financial management. Bill Gates and Warren Buffett both went into business, succeeded beyond anyone's dreams, and now are able to do far more good for society than the average person who has devoted a lifetime to an aid group.

All that said, social entrepreneurs do periodically have ingenious ideas that contribute substantially to dealing with the world's problems; we want to be cautionary but not discouraging. Shannon May is among those pouring her soul into a new venture, one that had its origins when she was teaching primary school in a poor rural village in northeastern China. Shannon was undertaking ecological research for her Ph.D. dissertation and was told that the only way she and her boyfriend, Jay Kimmelman, would be permitted to live in the village was if she agreed to teach at the school. Teaching would pull her away from her research, she fretted, and she bristled when students started calling her "Teacher May." But as the year unfolded, Shannon con-

Shannon May, cofounder of Bridge International
Academy, with a five-year-old student in Kenya

cluded that her dissertation focused on the wrong topic. The experience taught her that education mattered more than anything.

"It definitely shaped my understanding of poverty and how poverty moves through generations," she said. The school also underscored everything that can go wrong with education in a village. The principal drank at lunchtime, and he and two other tipsy teachers rarely showed up in the afternoons. Nine of the ten teachers were not qualified to teach. Some were regularly absent. The most qualified teacher refused to teach more than one class. The only computer in the school was taken home by the principal. Most villagers were barely literate—few had graduated from high school—but the small number who were educated were by far the most successful economically, because they could read up on changing agricultural rules and take advantage of techniques open to them (such as raising fur animals for their pelts).

"If you don't do something drastic for children in education, essentially before they hit puberty," May concluded, "everything else is just catch-up."

Kimmelman and May puzzled over the challenge of bringing high-quality basic education to poor countries. This was of special interest to Kimmelman, who had previously started and sold an education technology company. After marrying in China, May and Kimmelman took a six-week honeymoon to Malawi, Tanzania, Kenya, Uganda,

Rwanda, and Nigeria to investigate other failures in basic education in poor rural areas. They then began outlining a for-profit business model for private schools in poor countries, targeting low-income families.

It may seem odd to envision for-profit private schools as a solution to education in poor countries; in the West, private schools are a refuge for the wealthy. But in many nations in Africa and Asia, government schools are regarded as almost irredeemably bad. Teachers don't show up because they are paid by a central ministry, whether or not they do anything. Some "ghost schools" exist only on paper, the funds allocated to those institutions pocketed by bureaucrats. Even when a school exists and teachers show up, there may be more than a hundred students in a class and only one textbook for every ten students. Sometimes teachers are interested in students primarily to extort sex from them. The public schools are so bleak that it is common for even poor families to send their kids to private schools. In India, a government survey found that 30 percent of children in grades one through eight attend private schools, some at a cost of a few dollars each month. In Hyderabad, where three-quarters of students attend private schools, those in private education score 22 percentage points higher on math exams than students in public schools.

So May and Kimmelman founded what became Bridge International Academies, a chain of private schools targeting families earning less than $2 a person daily. They launched it in Kenya with a third cofounder, Phil Frei. This was a leap of faith. May had built up experience in China and had worked in finance for Morgan Stanley; now she was attempting something much riskier. Friends tried to dissuade her, saying she wouldn't make a dent in the problem in Kenya and might well fail altogether. May had her doubts but forged ahead. "There are so many kids not learning and being abandoned," she said, "it was worth trying."

Bridge spent about $50 million to start up—on technology, research, operations systems, curricula, teacher training materials, land acquisition, and construction—raising it from New Enterprise Associates, Learn Capital (closely linked to Pearson Education), Khosla Ventures, and Omidyar Network. Bridge developed a "school-in-a-box" strategy with standardized content, teacher training materials, and lesson plans delivered wirelessly via computer tablets that can also track instruction. Students attend school for fifty-five hours each week and families are charged on average $6 a month. Bridge now has classes from pre-kindergarten to seventh grade, with plans to add an eighth-grade class in 2015, and to expand to Nigeria and Uganda and beyond.

The pace of growth is blistering. Bridge acquires one new plot of land every two and a half days, and allocates five and a half months to open a fully staffed school. Bridge researchers use mobile survey technology, satellite imaging, and local demographic data to determine a good location for a school, and then an acquisition team moves in. When land is acquired, Bridge begins recruiting teachers and administrators who go through two months of training, particularly in how to use the software technology, which tracks attendance, lesson completion, and assessment of student progress. There is even a "customer care" center for teachers, administrators, parents, and students to call in with questions. Most schools launch with ten teachers, a principal, and two staff workers, but each school needs more than 300 students to break even.

Ramping up has entailed many challenges for May and her cofounders. When walls of a school started crumbling after a year, it was discovered that only half of the cement that had been purchased had been used; the rest had been sold off. Something similar happened with iron sheeting for roofing—the foreman had sold the extra iron sheets. Workers sometimes wanted to take ten tea breaks and complained of long hours (teaching hours are nearly twice those at local schools). Teachers read the newspaper in class. May found it difficult to inculcate "that kind of drive and work ethic and culture into this environment. Not that they can't do it; it's just that there hasn't been that kind of work culture."

Bridge has also tinkered with the teacher model. Instead of devising their own lesson plans, teachers use a tablet with prewritten scripted lessons, so it's possible to recruit people who lack teaching experience but who live within walking distance of a school and have credibility in the neighborhood.

The aid world has looked at Bridge with a mix of suspicion and enthusiasm. Some are skeptical of the for-profit approach, while others welcome it as creating sustainability and competitive pressure on government schools. So far the results seem promising. Bridge cites standardized exams to show that its students are distinctly ahead in math and reading compared to those at nearby government schools.

In 2013, for instance, a typical fourth grader at Bridge read 60 percent more words per minute and correctly answered 44 percent more math word problems.

It's because of brave souls like May and Scharpf that we resist the view in some circles that the first third of life can be spent studying, the middle third earning money, and the final third giving back. To adopt that approach means that you will deprive yourself for two-thirds of your life of all the satisfactions that come from engaging with a cause larger than yourself.

A Hundred Million Books

Kyle Zimmer was wired to be a leader and a self-starter. At age twelve, she was the youngest board member at her local YWCA in the conservative town of Zanesville, Ohio. In high school she was president of the student council. She was raised by parents who believed strongly in social justice, subscribed to *Mother Jones* and *Soviet Life,* and held up Cesar Chavez and Ralph Nader as role models fighting for social justice. "It was pretty deeply ingrained that there was an expectation that either professionally or in your down time you would do what you could to change the world for the better," said Zimmer. "Also there was a real deep belief in education as being the transcendent and ultimate social change vehicle."

Later Zimmer worked for the governor of Ohio and then on Walter Mondale's presidential campaign in 1984. After graduating from George Washington University Law School, she took a corporate law job at a midsize firm in Washington, D.C. Then she began tutoring children in reading.

While visiting the homes of those children, she noticed that there were few if any books. When she gave some children books, they would confide: *This is my first book.* That gave her the idea to found First Book, a nonprofit to deliver books to children living in poverty and then encourage them to read. She started the endeavor with two colleagues originally as a hobby organization, but it turned out to be impossibly tough to hire a good manager for it: "We had about $1.30 in our bank account." So she quit her corporate law job in 1995 and took on the role of chief executive.

Zimmer started raising money to buy books and donate them to literacy programs. Over the years, she has set up First Book volunteer chapters in all fifty states to raise money. First Book now distributes books to church groups, libraries in low-income neighborhoods,

Head Start programs, homeless shelters, youth outreach centers, and pediatricians' offices through Reach Out and Read. After twenty years—and significant transformation—First Book has distributed some 115 million books to 90,000 organizations. In 2013, First Book accounted for 2 percent of the children's books distributed in the United States. Not bad for a nonprofit.

Attempting to inculcate the mentality of a nimble, fast-moving start-up, Zimmer has developed business lines for First Book to generate its own revenues that offset close to half of the organization's budget. She aims to take that even further. "We are moving quickly to self-sufficiency," she said. "That has been our design from the very beginning."

She keeps tabs on the publishing market in order to move with the trends and find opportunities for First Book. In 1999, when she noted that publishers were getting many returns and sizable buildups in inventory on children's books, she started a national book bank to utilize all those books returned to the publishers by having them donated to First Book. She was allowed to store books at warehouses of the U.S. Coast Guard, where the commandant, Admiral James Loy, supported the cause and provided logistics training to Zimmer and her team so that they could ship books effectively to thousands of reading programs.

There were plenty of missteps. When First Book started asking for book donations, Zimmer arranged for a few trucks to pick them up. "I was sitting up here thinking I knew what I was doing, and started rounds of calls to get books donated," said Zimmer. "The publishers were wonderfully generous, and the fire hose of books got turned on." First Book soon was scrambling for pickups, larger trucks—any form of transport. When one employee found a distributor willing to transport the books, Zimmer was delighted. But they had some explaining to do when a truck with a beer company logo pulled up in front of the schools to unload boxes of books.

With distribution handled professionally, recipients are now charged 45 cents for each book shipped to them, and that helps First Book cover costs. "At every spot, we've pushed on efficiencies," said Jane Robinson, chief financial officer. The increasingly sophisticated ordering system now allows reading programs to select according to topics that children demand: dinosaurs, animals, rhymes. "If you run a preschool for children in Maine, you register for free with us

*Kyle Zimmer, president and CEO of First Book, with
a public school class in Washington, D.C.*

online," explained Zimmer. "You would get a notice every time there
was a donation at the Book Bank. It would say: 'Simon & Schuster
has given us a quarter of a million books; sign in on March 3 to see.'
You could log on and accept or decline any or all of that inventory
for your kids. If you happen to be close geographically, our software
gives you a date and a time, you pull up in your Subaru, and we put
the books in your Subaru. And everything is free."

First Book distributed tens of millions of new books to children
that way. Then publishers started cutting costs and reducing print
runs, leading to fewer returns. So in 2008 Zimmer added a second
business: she aggregates the buying power of thousands of small
literacy programs—screened for need by First Book—and negoti-
ates deeply discounted prices on their behalf from publishers. By
guaranteeing no returns, she often gets bulk discounts of more than
50 percent. Since some literacy programs can't afford even deeply discounted books, First Book uses its local chapters to help raise funds.

The average price for these commercial paperback books is $2.50,
including shipping. That's much more than the 45-cent-per-book cost
of those that are donated, but these are brand-name books. *Where
the Wild Things Are* (retail $8.95) sells for $2.79. *Encyclopedia Brown
and the Case of the Sleeping Dog* (retail $5.50) goes for $1.85. *To Kill
a Mockingbird* (retail $7.99) is $3.50.

First Book is hoping to expand further by venturing into content.

After its first customized bilingual edition of Eric Carle's *The Very Hungry Caterpillar* ($3.25) sold 90,000 copies, First Book set up a relationship with HarperCollins and Lee & Low publishers to work with authors from Latino and Asian communities and create new books that would have greater appeal to minority children to encourage them to read more.

First Book supplies 15 million books each year to organizations serving more than 2 million children—but Zimmer calculates that there are more than 32 million kids who need the books. So she sees plenty of room to expand, while developing the ability to self-fund and reduce the need for outside money.

"I've always been someone with a private sector head and a public sector heart," says Zimmer.

CHAPTER TWENTY

A Giving Code

Millions of people . . . are trapped in the prison of poverty.
It is time to set them free. Sometimes it falls upon a generation to be great. You can be that great generation.

— NELSON MANDELA

One Father's Day, our teenage kids banded together and got Nick the perfect gift for any dad—a rat. It was an African giant pouched rat, to be precise, and it has a wondrous sense of smell that allows it to do heroic work detecting landmines. Our kids sponsored one rat's training in Nick's name. The breed is thirty inches long including the tail, with poor eyesight but a superb sense of smell. A Belgian aid group called Apopo figured out how to train these animals to do this lifesaving work. The rats are too light to set off the mines, and they are easily trainable. With a life span of eight years, the rats have plenty of time to earn back the training costs. In a single day, one of these rats—dubbed HeroRats—can clear 400 square meters of land otherwise unusable because of landmines. The HeroRats are deployed to clear mines in Mozambique and Angola, and in twenty minutes they can help clear as much land as a human could in two days.

Our children's donation made a difference to some very needy people, so we were thrilled that Nick received so meaningful a gift.[*] And that's one of the basic points that we've been trying to make

---

[*] If you want to sponsor a HeroRat in someone's honor, visit www.apopo.org. The cost is $84 a year, or €60, and you get an "adoption certificate."

throughout this book: there are ways to incorporate giving into our daily lives so that they constitute not a sacrifice but an opportunity and a heady pleasure.

One of the fastest growing aid groups in the world has been Room to Read, founded by a Microsoft executive named John Wood. Wood faced a midlife crisis and, rather than buying a sports car or having an affair, started an organization that has opened more than 15,000 libraries and 1,600 schools in poor countries, while handing out more than 10 million books. Room to Read has attracted more than 10,000 volunteers because it makes it exciting to finance a school or library for kids who want to learn. One couple decided to forgo an engagement ring and use the money to build a school. Another supporter started an offshoot, Beers for Books, in 2009. The idea is to find a bar that will donate $1 to Room to Read for each drink sold on a particular night, and then invite all your friends to party there.

One of Wood's friends told him what he considered the secret of life: *Think early on what you want your legacy to be, what you would like to be able to say on your deathbed. Then work backward from there.* That's a useful framework for thinking about the impact we hope to have in our lives.

We started by talking about expanding opportunity, about the aphorism that "talent is universal, but opportunity is not." We're optimistic because we see what happens when that hidden talent meets opportunity. Paul Lorem is an orphan from a South Sudan village with no electricity, school, or clinic. His homeland was torn apart by civil war, so he spent most of his childhood without adult supervision in a refugee camp, Kakuma, just across the border in Kenya. He was raised by other Sudanese war refugee boys just a few years older than himself. War and impoverishment somehow led those older boys to don a mantle of responsibility. They knew they would never get a decent education, but they forced Paul to get the schooling they were too old for. They would wake him up each morning and make him trudge to a refugee camp school run by the United Nations, where his "class" sometimes consisted of 300 pupils meeting under the shade of a tree. The children lacked pencils and notebooks, so they practiced writing letters in the dust. Gradually, with the help of teachers and the older boys, Paul found that he had a natural talent for letters and numbers.

"It dawned on me that this school can really take me somewhere," he recalls. He devoured books in a tiny camp library set up by a Lutheran aid group. Teachers noted his prodigious intellectual gifts, and they went out of their way to arrange for him to transfer to a Kenyan school in the seventh grade. That way he could attend Kenyan classes for two years and sit for Kenyan high school examinations, giving him some hope of going to high school. There was one challenge: instruction was in Swahili, which Paul did not speak. He studied hard, with crucial help from classmates, and then scored second-highest in that entire region of Kenya on the high school entrance exams. It won him admittance to Alliance, a top boarding school in Nairobi.

Paul struggled financially in Nairobi and was lonely, but a German Catholic nun, Sister Luise Radlmeier, enveloped him in love and paid his school fees; Sister Luise has mothered countless South Sudanese children like Paul. With her support and his own hard work, Paul climbed the ranks of the student body. By his third year, he won a scholarship to finish high school at the African Leadership Academy, created in South Africa in 2004 with strong support from American donors to rear a new generation of African leaders.

Paul was grateful for the chance to attend, but on a vacation break at the academy he terrified his teachers by undertaking an odyssey across much of Africa to return to his native village. There he found his younger brother and sister unschooled, and he insisted that they go to the Kakuma refugee camp to get an education. Their grandparents resisted, and for three weeks Paul argued and browbeat them. Finally they consented. After enrolling his brother and sister in the refugee camp school, Paul returned to the African Leadership Academy, where a counselor who was a Yale University graduate nurtured his talents and ushered him through the application process to Yale. When Yale accepted him, the Hotchkiss School in Connecticut agreed to give him a year of prep school to prepare him for the Ivy League.

So now an orphan from a refugee camp is a student at Yale, studying in his fifth language. We spoke to him in the book-lined study of Jeffrey Brenzel, a former Yale admissions director who has become his mentor. Paul recounted his story, sometimes fighting tears as he thought of all those whose help had been indispensable. What sets him apart from other South Sudanese, he says, is not the disadvantages he faced but the extraordinary opportunities he enjoyed from a chain of generous people: workers at the United Nations, staff of the Lutheran aid group, the Catholic nun, the counselor at the African Leadership Academy, teachers at Hotchkiss, and admissions officers and professors at Yale. Each helping hand made it possible for him to reach the next level. What strikes him, looking back, is that there were so many other kids pretty much like him who never had a chance.

Although neuroscience suggests that humans are hardwired to care and to help, many of us don't, at least not very often. If we're reasonably well-off, we're often insulated from people in need. If you're a middle-class American, you would probably gladly reach out and help someone like Khadijah, the homeless girl who attended Harvard—but there may be no one like her in your suburb, your car pool, your health club, your church congregation. Some people when traveling abroad interact only with the bellman at their hotel or their taxi driver—not with a child like Paul Lorem seeking an education. This insulation from the needy seems to be why more affluent Americans give a smaller share of their income than the middle class or poor. It's not that the rich are intrinsically less compassionate; rather, they encounter fewer needy people than the poor, who are surrounded by those in need of a helping hand. For similar reasons, wealthy households in economically diverse neighborhoods give more than the wealthy in areas that are uniformly affluent.

In this vein, it's humbling for us to travel to some of the most impoverished places on earth and see how much more generous people are there than they are in the United States. In war-torn Darfur, those who still have homes shelter some of those whose huts have been burned down. In Congo, survivors of the brutal war take in orphans even when there is not enough food for their own children. In Somali refugee camps, even children instinctively share their scarce water with others who are thirsty. The crowd-sourced book *Random Acts of Kindness Then and Now* includes this wonderful vignette of intuitive, automatic giving:

> A friend who was working in the Dominican Republic with Habitat for Humanity had befriended a small boy named Etin. He noticed

that when Etin wore a shirt at all, it was always the same dirty, tattered one. A box of used clothes had been left at the camp, and my friend found two shirts in it that were in reasonably good shape and about Etin's size, so he gave them to the grateful boy. A few days later he saw another boy wearing one of the shirts. When he next met up with Etin he explained that the shirts were meant for him. Etin just looked at him and said, "But you gave me two!"

One reason we in the West are sometimes less generous is that we learn to "otherize" people who aren't like us. Perhaps it's a defense mechanism in a world of immense needs, an adaptation to mass suffering in distant lands that reaches us on our television screens. Or we anesthetize ourselves with the mistaken notion that problems are so vast and intractable that there is nothing to be done.

We perhaps bought into that notion a bit ourselves, and then we were walking through the Cambodian jungle and heard an eerie, unreal screaming ahead. We didn't know if it was human or animal, and we approached cautiously. We came upon a clearing with a wooden shack, where a gaunt man named Yok Yorn was wailing over

One Somali refugee child shares scarce water with another at the Dadaab refugee camp in Kenya.

the body of his small son. The boy, Kaiset, had just died of malaria, and Yok Yorn was beside himself. He sobbed, he beat himself on the chest, he screamed.

"This was the smartest boy in my family," Yok Yorn whispered inconsolably, "and I couldn't save him." No one encountering that raw grief could ever think that people in poor countries become inured to suffering.

Over time, we came to believe that it's not the people in poor countries or poor neighborhoods who are numbed by suffering, it's we who are better off. For them, it's a part of daily life, unavoidable, and so they respond and do what they can. But those of us in safe and comfortable communities, we're the ones who do little to help despite our vastly greater resources. The problem isn't that we're hard-hearted but that we don't directly encounter need and don't know quite how to address those more distant needs we're aware of only intellectually. We also tend to be skeptical that a modest sum can actually make a difference. Yet one of the clearest lessons in our long journey is that it is indeed possible to have an impact with a modest sum.

In our travels, one of the most wrenching diseases we've seen is trachoma, which is caused by repeated eye infections. Gradually the eyelid turns inward, and the eyelashes begin to scrape the cornea. This is excruciatingly painful and feels like grains of sand constantly abrading the eye.

"It's like the pain of childbirth, but it goes on for year after year," said Yagare Traoré, an elderly woman in Mali who endured this agony for six years. She is a widow who spent the time sitting in her hut, blinded and in pain, unable to farm or to care for her eleven children; perhaps as a result, six of them died. Trachoma used to be common in America as well but now is found only in poor countries and is on its way out—in part because it is simple to prevent and to treat. Training villagers in hygiene, such as face washing, is a big help, and in areas where it is endemic, an annual dose of an antibiotic called azithromycin (Zithromax) given to everyone in the community usually causes trachoma to disappear after three years. The Zithromax is donated by Pfizer, and the cost of distributing it is just 25 cents per person annually. This means that a three-year program to eliminate blindness due to trachoma typically costs just 75 cents per person through an aid group like Helen Keller International.

Is there a better use for 75 cents?

*Yagare Traoré celebrates her successful surgery to end
the excruciating pain of trachoma, together with the
nurse in rural Mali who performed the operation.*

For those like Yagare who already have advanced stages of trachoma and turned-in eyelids (a condition called trichiasis), surgery is still needed. But this is a simple procedure performed by a single specialized nurse who can undertake twenty such operations a day. Trichiasis surgery takes about fifteen minutes under local anesthetic and costs less than $40 per person. When Yagare had her surgery and the bandages were removed, a boy stepped forward to guide her home.

"Get out of my way!" she told him. "I can see! I can walk by myself!"

Is there a better use for $40?

We sometimes paralyze ourselves with the conviction that global problems are hopeless, but in fact this should be a remarkably hopeful time to be alive. Crippling diseases such as leprosy, guinea worm, and polio are on their way out, and in the next twenty or thirty years malaria and AIDS are also likely to be eliminated as public health threats (although cases will still be reported here and there). The number of children dying before the age of five has almost halved since 1990, even though the number of children has risen. As recently as 1980, half the population of the developing world lived in extreme poverty, defined by the World Bank as less than $1.25 per person per day in today's money. That share is now down to 20 percent, and the World Bank aims to lower it to near zero by 2030. At that time, just about every boy and girl around the world will go to primary school and learn to read. For all of human history until about 1950, a majority of human adults were illiterate; in one lifetime the adult illiteracy rate worldwide has dropped to about 16 percent. On our watch in the next few decades, we have a chance to eliminate the conditions—illiteracy, famine, parasitic disease, and the most abject poverty—that have shaped the majority of human existence since our ancestors began to walk upright.

Throughout history, only a tiny fraction of human talent has been nurtured so as to have the chance to learn, create, and contribute. Virginia Woolf famously imagined that if Shakespeare had had a sister who was a brilliant writer, she never would have been able to produce great plays because of her gender. Likewise, so many potential Shakespeares and Einsteins have died in childhood or ended up as illiterate laborers. That is changing.

Aside from improvements in education and literacy around the world, another reason for optimism is the emergence of new technological solutions to old problems. Granted, technology brings new problems, such as climate change and security and privacy violations. But on balance, the spread of mobile phones, the Internet, and other innovations gives us reason for measured hope. One interesting effort is the Soccket, a soccer ball that doubles as an electric generator. Kick the ball around for a bit and the kinetic energy generates electricity that can be used to charge a mobile telephone or power a small light. Behind one of the panels on the Soccket is a plug receptacle. The Soccket was invented by a group of college students, and now a couple of them have formed a social enterprise, Uncharted Play, to mass-produce it. We don't know whether that initiative will succeed, but it is representative of a wave of devices being tested that might ameliorate extreme poverty.

There are far more causes, organizations, and ways to give than we could possibly describe here. We have barely mentioned climate change, and we haven't said enough about job creation, homelessness, substance abuse, mental illness, and the need for a more equitable mechanism to fund public education in the United States. We have offered little about human rights campaigns, even though we deeply believe that they are a way to promote more just societies. We have only touched on conflict and peacekeeping, which are central issues in some of the world's poorest countries.

So while we hope we've given you a taste of some of the options for making a difference, and an introduction to some of the people on the front lines, this is only a tiny sampling. We also want to remind you that a good deal of charity isn't particularly effective and avoid the rah-rah cheerleading that is too common about nonprofits, while emphasizing that increasingly there is good evidence about what kinds of interventions make a difference—and that at its best, assistance works extraordinarily well. We believe in this so much that a portion of our royalties for this book will go to some of these causes.

If you want to take the next step, we have a few suggestions.

1. *Find an issue that draws you in and research it.* There's no single humanitarian topic that is paramount; there's no answer to the question "What is the most important issue?" Just choose one that speaks to you.

If you're looking for a cause or an organization, you'll come in a few pages to an appendix listing organizations trying to create opportunity around the world. You can also find ideas at the websites for GiveWell and Focusing Philanthropy. There are good suggestions on the website for the Coalition for Evidence-Based Policy, which pays rigorous attention to what works. Likewise, we regularly cite great organizations on Twitter (Twitter.com/NickKristof and Twitter.com/WuDunn) and Facebook (Facebook.com/Kristof and Facebook.com/SherylWuDunn).

Once you have found an organization that you like, check the Internet for ratings, reviews, and critiques of its work. Treat making a gift as seriously as you would making a big purchase, like a new sofa, a TV, or even a car. Just as you wouldn't buy shares in a company simply because a marketing firm called to tout it, be careful of making blind donations. To be generous does not mean being gullible or a pushover.

Narrow your giving. It's more efficient, for you and for the causes you support, if you donate to five organizations each year rather than seventy-five. Your time and money will go further, you're more likely to understand what those five groups do, and they may become long-term relationships.

Look for verifiable impact. How many people does the charity help? Does it cite metrics of success? Does it cite outside evaluations (maybe even randomized trials, though that is not essential), or comments by scholars or journalists that can be verified on the Web? When an organization doesn't back up its claims and relies on vague feel-good anecdotes, it's probably because that's all it has to offer.

One basic question is whether to focus on problems in the poorest countries or in neighborhoods closer to home. We believe both are reasonable options. We push back at the idea that we should "solve our own problems first" before tackling global challenges. The needs abroad are unquestionably greater. There is malnutrition in America and Europe, but there are incomparably more children in Mali or Ethiopia whose bodies (and brains) are being stunted because they're not getting enough breast milk, food, or micronutrients in the first couple of years of life. Your donation also goes much further abroad, and if all lives have equal value, then it is certainly cheaper to save a child's life or educate a student in Uganda or Pakistan than it is in New York.

That said, Americans sometimes find it glamorous to rush off to faraway countries to start schools or fight sex trafficking, while needs at home are seen as banal. That is a misguided view. Neither is more "cool," neither is more "right," and they are too important to be pitted against each other. Our counsel is simply to go where your heart directs you, but don't forget to bring your head, too.

2. *Volunteer, get involved, or do something more than just writing checks.* Think about the skills and passions you have and how they could be put to good use. Following the model of people such as Khandoker Mohammad Abu Sohel or his French boss, Corinne Bazina, at Grameen Danone, one way to give is to pinpoint your skills and influence, and identify groups that could benefit from them. If you're a great teacher, mentoring is an outlet; if you're a talented business manager, try creating a team of colleagues like Full Circle Fund to donate consulting services to nearby nonprofits.

Browse the volunteering opportunities at www.idealist.org and www.omprakash.org and get inspired. Maybe you can start an informal giving club to get together with friends and make donations or volunteer together. Maybe form a Dining for Women chapter and get together with others for an occasional potluck dinner, or a Poker for Men club—and then donate the money that would have been spent at a restaurant or the winnings on the poker table. Or if you're in a book club, maybe it can include a giving dimension as well.

Ideally, try to see the fruits of your efforts. Many organizations will help donors arrange a visit. Does it make sense to visit a literacy project in India to see it for yourself when the money spent on travel could send dozens of Indian children to school for a year? Our answer is yes, as long as the money comes from your entertainment budget and not your giving budget. Indeed, research by Michael Norton and Elizabeth Dunn, scholars whose work on happiness we've already cited, suggests that money spent on such experiences is more effective at fostering happiness than money spent on purchases.

You can also look for equally inspiring experiences closer to home, such as mentoring an underprivileged student in your neighborhood or nearby, much like the local barber and minister did for Lester Strong. You can mentor through Big Brothers Big Sisters or iMentor, teach English to immigrants, or tutor reading in a prison. There's a special need for men to mentor boys, with long waiting lists of boys whose moms have signed them up. Several other organizations have also sprouted to help people address social needs. VolunteerMatch, Catchafire, and MovingWorlds connect people with expertise to initiatives that can benefit from their skills. MicroMentor, run by Mercy Corps, targets businesspeople who are willing to help guide entrepreneurs just starting out, including those running social enterprises.

3. Use your voice to spread the word or advocate for those who are voiceless. Not all problems can be solved by donations to aid groups or by volunteers, however courageous and passionate. We also need to hold governments—our own and others—accountable for doing their share. We can't build a highway network or a sanitation system with private donors, and we can't build an early childhood education program or crack down on child traffickers unless our elected officials do a better job. We can make a difference by speaking up. For some, that will mean speaking with friends or family about issues that might otherwise be ignored. For others, it will mean joining a Facebook or Twitter campaign, writing letters, or making phone calls. One way to help the people of Ethiopia is to build wells, as supporters did to honor Rachel Beckwith's birthday goal. Another way is to join campaigns by Human Rights Watch, Amnesty International, or the Committee to Protect Journalists in support of dissidents there such as Eskinder Nega, a journalist serving an eighteen-year sentence on

cooked-up terrorism charges. Human rights advocates and trouble-
some journalists help keep governments accountable and honest in
ways that benefit the entire society, and they need our support.

There is a deep human yearning for "the answer," but it should
be clear by now that there is no single answer. Rather, there
are thousands of ways to the mountaintop, and the right route for
you depends on your interests and background. More broadly, the
approaches we've explored are not so much discrete alternatives
as they are synergistic tools. Each makes an incremental gain that
allows others to be more effective as well. We yearn for the alchemy
of an overnight success, but that's not the usual paradigm; even the
most important transformations are often plodding. One of the great
American public health successes has been the nearly century-long
campaign to save lives in traffic accidents. If the United States had
the same auto fatality rate today that we had in 1921, some 715,000
Americans would now perish annually in crashes. Instead, we've
reduced the number of fatalities per 100 million miles driven by more
than 95 percent, so today the toll is a bit more than 30,000 lives per
year. That's still too many but reflects a saving of more than one life
every minute, well over half a million lives a year—not through any
single dramatic game changer but rather through a painstaking process of research and innovation. We introduced seat belts, air bags,
prominent brake lights, padded dashboards, and better bumpers. We
improved road design, lane markings, and traffic lights; built clover-
leafs; and erected barriers to prevent cars from shooting over cliffs.
We cracked down on drunk drivers and introduced graduated licenses
for young drivers. No single step was "the answer," but collectively an
iterative process of evidence-driven improvements had a transforma-
tional effect. In the same way, we need to stop our quest for silver
bullets to create opportunity, and instead turn to silver buckshot.

The broader need is not just for technical answers—a better childhood program, more micronutrients—but also for greater empathy.
As long as society sees misfortune as the just deserts of those who
are lazy or immoral, we're not going to solve these problems. The
flip side is that those who are successful need to understand that the
root cause of their achievements isn't just hard work and innate intel-

ligence but also often luck in the lottery of birth followed by a supportive middle-class upbringing. "Society is responsible for a very significant percentage of what I have earned," notes Warren Buffett. "If you stick me down in the middle of Bangladesh or Peru or someplace, you'll find out how much this talent is going to produce in the wrong kind of soil. I will be struggling thirty years later."

How much you walk the walk is up to you. For our part, we don't spend every moment struggling to make a difference, nor do we think that everybody should devote themselves full-time to creating a better world. As we've said, we believe there is a great deal to be said for a regular career in which you build skills that can then be leveraged to help others in your spare time. Some of you might go a step further to try to fold altruistic motives into your work, like Yuri Jain at Unilever, through a new service, a new technology, or a product extension that serves a real need among the less fortunate and brings in revenue at the same time. Who is going to be the next Scott Harrison or Kyle Zimmer? Which ventures will be the next Revolution Foods or Better World Books?

Of course, there are wonderful people out there who scrimp by in their daily lives and donate half their incomes, and they belong in a hall of heroes. A young Oxford philosopher, Toby Ord, has become the leader of this camp. Ord, lean and gangly with chaotic dark hair that is beginning to recede, recalls: "As an undergraduate, I often argued with my friends about political and ethical matters. I regularly received the retort 'If you believe that, why don't you just give most of your money to people starving in Africa?' This was meant to show that my position was absurd, but as time passed and I thought more about ethics, I found the conclusion increasingly sensible: if my money could help others much more than it helps me, then why not?" Ord became increasingly committed to applying his moral ideals to daily life. He figured that his total future earnings would be around £1.5 million and pledged to give away £1 million over the course of his career. As he puts it: "Since I already had most of the things I value in life on my student stipend, I realized that my money would do vastly more good for others than it could for me and decided to make a commitment to donating to the most effective charities I could find."

Ord set up an organization, Giving What We Can, for people who pledge that for the rest of their lives they will contribute at least

10 percent of their earnings to those who need it more. The hope, Ord says, is that living abstemiously and giving large sums to charity will become a lifestyle, a bit like vegetarianism—and he insists it's not as much of a sacrifice as people assume. "The project of making the world a better place," he said, "is worth far more to me than some new gadgets or a slightly larger house."

We're in awe of supergivers like Toby Ord, but not everyone can take such steps. Society has many needs, and as we've shown, the humanitarian world itself benefits from people with diverse skill sets built up over a career in, say, accounting, finance, engineering, or marketing, who can then volunteer occasionally with a nonprofit. We can splurge on a dinner or play without chastising ourselves with the thought that the money could have been better spent on schistosomiasis. Our struggles to do the right thing are a part of life but not the whole of it. A life with meaning isn't a destination but a journey.

O ur efforts at altruism have a mixed record of success at helping others, but they have an almost perfect record of helping ourselves. They can also be a way of asserting our values, or responding to pain or horror by reaffirming a higher standard of humanity. Ann Curry of NBC News was upset and frustrated when she was covering the horrifying Newtown, Connecticut, school shooting of December 2012, in which twenty children were killed. Seeking some way to build something positive from that nightmare, she tweeted a proposal to her million-plus Twitter followers: *Imagine if all of us committed to 20 mitzvahs/acts of kindness to honor each child lost in Newtown. I'm in. If you are, RT #20Acts.* The result was an outpouring of enthusiasm, and her tweet went viral. Americans wanted to respond to evil by doing something good, and they tweeted their small acts of goodness: giving a colleague a ride home, buying a cup of coffee for a homeless person, inviting a surly neighbor to a party, ordering toys for children in a homeless shelter, bringing hot drinks to construction workers on a cold and rainy day. By popular demand, the movement expanded from twenty acts of kindness, honoring each child, to twenty-six acts to symbolically include the adults who were murdered while trying to save the children. Some proposed raising it to twenty-seven acts, to include the murdered mother of the gunman. A few wanted to raise it one more, to include the gunman himself, so that kindness could trump killing.

After the Boston Marathon bombing, Curry proposed another round of twenty-six acts of kindness, one to mark each mile of the race. Again the proposal went viral. One woman named Kirsten tweeted: *I have a day care in my home, and for the rest of this week, my fee for parents is free. . . . :-)* A man named Nick tweeted: *just picked up every table's check at Waffle House "7" tables all together/24 people.* And Jillian said: *Just bought coffee for our custodians at work. Most under appreciated people ever.*

What struck Ann was the eagerness to participate in acts of kindness as an antidote to the poison and hatred represented by the school shooting and the marathon bombing. "It made people feel better," she said. "If you do good, you feel good. It's the most selfish thing you can do." People wanted to heal after the tragedy, and one way to do so was to take the initiative and help somebody else. When terror and murder dominated the news, kindness was a way of asserting our humanity, our connections to others, our basic decency and integrity. Participating in a cause larger than yourself builds up our social networks, creates a sense of fulfillment, gets us out of bed in the morning with a bounce in our step, and helps make a difference in the lives of others—even as it affirms a purpose for our own lives on earth.

Six Steps You Can Take in the Next Six Minutes

1. Write an email to friends and ask if they'd be interested in creating an informal giving circle that meets once every month to explore powerful ways of making a difference—perhaps over drinks or a meal to keep it fun. Or see whether your book club can incorporate a giving component.

2. Consider supporting an early childhood program. That might mean giving to Reach Out and Read, which for a $20 donation can take on a new child and introduce him or her to the joys of reading. Or it might mean sponsoring a young child, in the United States or abroad, through Save the Children or another program for around $30 a month.

3. Go to www.againstmalaria.com and think about a donation to buy antimalarial bed nets for needy families. A single net costs about $5 and offers solid protection from malaria. How's that for value?

4. Explore the website of GlobalGiving, which lets you browse projects all over the world, including many mentioned in this book. You can support a girl going to Kennedy Odede's school in Kenya, the HeroRats detecting landmines in Africa, or any of a thousand other causes. DonorsChoose.org lets you help teachers with classroom projects.

5. Become an advocate. On www.results.org, sign up to join the public lobbying efforts to get Congress to pay more attention to poverty at home and abroad. Or, on www.one.org, you can join petitions backing evidence-based spending on global health.

6. Register so that your organs can be donated to others upon your death, saving the lives of up to eight other people. You can register as a donor at www.organdonor.gov or when you renew your driver's license. On Facebook, you can share your organ donor status with online friends to encourage them to register too. Tell family members so that they will be aware of your wishes and can share them with doctors if necessary.

You certainly don't have to do everything on this list. These are not endorsements for any organizations but just starting points for research. Consider this an invitation. We offer these six steps as a gateway that opens onto a path to greater engagement that will be good for the world—and for you.

A Gift List

For holidays and birthdays, we sometimes inflict on each other neckties and scarves that do little more than fill up a closet. One of the problems of affluence is that when we have money to give presents, we often have little to give that is meaningful. So instead of getting Aunt Mildred a box of chocolates, or your brother a little tool kit that he will roll his eyes at, think about these suggestions for gifts of meaning. Here you can get a gift in someone's name that will truly have a transformative impact.

$25 at www.care.org
Supply a village savings and loan group with a lockbox, ledger, and other start-up tools to help them save and manage loans.

$25 at store.thistlefarms.org
Buy a spa kit of lotions and balms made by survivors of U.S. sex trafficking.

$25 at www.greyston.com
Buy a brownie gift box from Greyston Bakery, which employs and supports the homeless and formerly incarcerated in Yonkers, New York.

$50 at www.evidenceaction.org
Deworm 100 students and increase their chances of staying in school.

$50 at www.stopteenpregnancy.com
Fund a student's savings account in the financial literacy component of the Carrera Adolescent Pregnancy Prevention Program in the United States.

$50 at www.firstbook.org
Give one child in need twenty books for a year of bedtime stories.

$100 at www.aarp.org/experience-corps
Provide one year of books and supplies for Experience Corps volunteers to use in K–3 classrooms.

$120 at hki.org
Provide micronutrient powders to enrich the food of ten children in Cambodia for one year, preventing the detrimental effects of anemia on their health and education.

$125 at www.givetonfp.org
Provide a week of support for a team of Nurse-Family Partnership nurse home visitors, or browse their website (www.nursefamilypartnership.org) to find and support a local NFP agency.

$125 at www.cureviolence.org
Fund one inner-city community workshop that engages ten high-risk youth in addressing neighborhood conflicts nonviolently.

$250 at www.youthvillages.org
Provide five at-risk young adults with life skills training in personal budgeting, writing résumés, and interviewing for jobs.

$300 at www.springboardcollaborative.org
Sponsor a needy child in Springboard Collaborative summer school in Philadelphia.

List of Useful Organizations

Here are some groups that do strong work in education, crime and violence prevention, family planning, public health, and quite a bit more. This is not a screened list based on a set of criteria. For evaluations, please check Charity Navigator, CharityWatch, Philanthropedia, or the Better Business Bureau's Wise Giving Alliance. There are many more organizations doing impressive work. This is a list of the groups we have seen in action or taken the time to learn about, and it is meant to be only a launching pad for your own personal research.

Abdul Latif Jameel Poverty Action Lab, www.povertyactionlab.org, conducts rigorous randomized controlled trials to determine the most cost-effective interventions in fighting poverty.

Acumen Fund, www.acumen.org, raises charitable donations to invest in companies that are tackling poverty.

African Leadership Academy, www.africanleadershipacademy.org, is a high-quality secondary school with strong American connections.

Against Malaria Foundation, www.againstmalaria.com, is a cost-effective intervention that provides bed nets to populations with a high risk of malaria. A single net costs about $5.

Amnesty International, www.amnesty.org, is a global network of supporters, members, and activists in over 150 countries and territories who campaign to end human rights abuses.

Apopo, www.apopo.org, uses mine-detection rats (and existing demining technology) to help clearing teams detect mines.

Aravind Eye Care System, www.aravind.org, is a network of hospitals, clinics, community outreach programs, and research and training institutes in India that provides eye care.

Bead for Life, www.beadforlife.org, supports Ugandan artisans by selling their jewelry in America and helping the artists set up savings accounts and launch businesses.

Becoming a Man, www.youth-guidance.org, is a school-based counseling, violence prevention, and educational enrichment program for at-risk male youth.

Beers for Books, www.beersforbooks.org, helps individuals organize and attend events at bars that agree to donate $1 to the literacy organization Room to Read for every beer consumed on a specific night.

Better World Books, www.betterworldbooks.com, sells new and used books and accepts donations of used books for resale, giving a portion of revenues to literacy programs.

Big Brothers Big Sisters, www.bbbs.org, matches adult volunteers with children between the ages of six and eighteen to provide mentorship in communities around the United States.

Bill & Melinda Gates Foundation, www.gatesfoundation.org, works on global health, global development, and education issues to improve the quality of life for individuals around the world.

BRAC, www.brac.net, is a terrific Bangladesh-based aid group that works in Africa and Asia. It has an office in New York City and accepts interns.

Bridge International Academies, www.bridgeinternationalacademies .com, is a large chain of high-quality private schools serving families living on less than $2 a day per person.

CARE, www.care.org, an international humanitarian organization, sets up microsavings programs in developing countries.

Carrera Adolescent Pregnancy Prevention Program, www .stopteenpregnancy.com, uses a holistic approach to help low-income students learn about pregnancy prevention, health and sexuality, jobs, and financial literacy.

The Carter Center, www.cartercenter.org, seeks to prevent and resolve conflicts, advance democracy and human rights, and improve health around the world.

Catchafire, www.catchafire.org, matches professionally skilled volunteers with nonprofits and social enterprises that can use their help.

Catholic Relief Services, www.crs.org, is an international humanitarian organization that has reached more than 100 million disadvantaged people in ninety-one countries.

Center on the Developing Child, www.developingchild.harvard.edu, led by Jack Shonkoff at Harvard University, conducts research on early childhood development and evaluates innovative programs.

charity:water, www.charitywater.org, funds the construction and maintenance of wells in developing countries. You can pledge your birthday at www.charitywater.org/birthdays.

Chess in the Schools, www.chessintheschools.org, sends part-time chess tutors into underprivileged public schools. Or donate directly to the IS 318 chess program at www.is318chessteam.com.

Child First, www.childfirst.com, provides home visitation to low-income families with at-risk children.

Cincinnati Early Learning Centers, www.celcinc.org, runs seven early childhood centers in Ohio that support needy children.

Citizen Schools, www.citizenschools.org, partners with low-income public high schools to provide a second shift in the school day with the help of AmeriCorps fellows and volunteer teachers.

Coalition for Evidence-Based Policy, www.coalition4evidence.org, seeks to increase government effectiveness by identifying programs in education, poverty reduction, and crime prevention that have scientifically rigorous evidence of success.

College Advising Corps, www.advisingcorps.org, places recent college graduates as college advisers in underserved schools to increase the number of low-income, first-generation students who complete higher education.

Committee to Protect Journalists, www.cpj.org, promotes press freedom worldwide.

Compassion International, www.compassion.com, provides a platform for donors to sponsor individual children around the world. Sponsored children receive special tutoring and counseling, retreats, and coaching in goal setting.

Cure Violence, www.cureviolence.org, trains ex-convicts and former gang members to prevent the spread of gun violence in rough inner-city neighborhoods.

Dining for Women, www.diningforwomen.org, runs chapters of women who meet for monthly potlucks and donate the saved "dining out" dollars to carefully selected organizations that empower women worldwide.

DonorsChoose, www.donorschoose.org, allows donors to sponsor specific projects in schools around the United States.

DoSomething.org, www.dosomething.org, helps motivate young people to take action around social change through grant-making and national campaigns.

Echoing Green, www.echoinggreen.org, supports early-stage social entrepreneurs.

Eden House, www.edenhousenola.org, is a two-year residential program with counseling, education, and job training for women who have been commercially and sexually exploited.

Educare, www.educareschools.org, is a research-based program that prepares young, at-risk children for school.

Encore, www.encore.org, helps older adults realize a productive "encore career" that provides personal fulfillment, social impact, and ongoing income.

Evidence Action, www.evidenceaction.org, invests in programs that have been proven in randomized controlled trials to effectively address poverty.

Experience Corps, www.aarp.org/experience-corps, run by AARP, engages older adults as reading tutors for struggling students in public schools. A $100 donation can help provide books and supplies for volunteers to use in the classroom throughout the school year.

FAIR Girls, www.fairgirls.org, uses prevention education, care for survivors, and advocacy to combat and prevent the sexual exploitation of girls in Washington, D.C.

Family Check-Up, www.thefamilycheckup.com, assesses high-risk families and tailors interventions to meet the specific needs of the family and child.

First Book, www.firstbook.org, a nonprofit organization, connects book publishers and community organizations to provide access to new books for children in need.

First Five Years Fund, www.ffyf.org, provides data, knowledge, and advocacy to help encourage federal policymakers to invest in the first five years of a child's life.

FirstStep, www.1ststep.org, finances clubfoot treatment in developing countries where medical care is unaffordable for many.

Focusing Philanthropy, www.focusingphilanthropy.org, identifies nonprofit organizations for personal philanthropy to help assure donors that contributed funds and time are achieving great impact.

Full Circle Fund, www.fullcirclefund.org, a group of Silicon Valley professionals, provides funding and consulting to high-impact, early-stage Bay Area nonprofits working on education, economic empowerment, and environmental issues.

GEMS Girls, www.gems-girls.org, provides support for young female trafficking survivors in New York City.

George Kaiser Family Foundation, www.gkff.org, invests in proof-of-concept initiatives against poverty in Oklahoma.

Girls2Women, www.girls2women.org, teaches Ethiopian students how to make their own sanitary pads in order to increase school attendance.

GiveDirectly, www.givedirectly.org, gives cash directly to extremely poor families to allow them to pursue their goals.

GiveWell, www.givewell.org, conducts thorough research to find cost-effective charities with evidence-based models that are in need of funding.

Giving What We Can, www.givingwhatwecan.org, evaluates charities that are fighting against extreme poverty and encourages people to pledge 10 percent of their income to those that are most cost effective.

Givology, www.givology.org, allows donors to give directly to students and grassroots projects around the world.

GlobalGiving, www.globalgiving.org, connects donors with social entrepreneurs and nonprofits around the world that are raising money to improve their communities.

Global Grandmothers, www.globalgrandmothers.org, organizes grandmothers to give to those in need each time they give to their own grandchildren.

Grameen Bank, www.grameen.com, founded by Muhammad Yunus, is a microfinance organization and community development bank in Bangladesh.

Greater Good Science Center, www.greatergood.berkeley.edu, conducts research on the psychology, sociology, and neuroscience of well-being and compassion.

Greyston Bakery, www.greyston.com, a social enterprise in Yonkers, New York, provides jobs in a bakery to formerly incarcerated and homeless people. Greyston brownies are available at Whole Foods and on Greyston's website.

Haitian Education and Leadership Program (HELP), www.uhelp.net, offers university scholarships to outstanding high school graduates from across Haiti.

Head Start, www.nhsa.org, along with Early Head Start, offers educational programs for children through age five and a variety of support services for their parents. Go to www.nhsa.org/find_a_head _start_program to find your local Head Start program and donate or volunteer there.

Healthy Families America, www.healthyfamiliesamerica.org, is a national evidence-based home visiting program that works with children at risk for adverse childhood experiences.

Healthy Steps, www.healthysteps.org, builds close relationships between health care professionals and parents to address the physical, emotional, and intellectual growth of children from birth to age three.

Helen Keller International, www.hki.org, works to reduce malnutrition and prevent blindness through highly effective food fortification and vitamin A supplementation programs.

Human Rights Watch, www.hrw.org, is an international organization that conducts research and advocacy on human rights.

Idealist.org, www.idealist.org, aggregates volunteer opportunities, nonprofit jobs, internships, and organizations that are focused on social change.

iMentor, www.imentor.org, matches college graduates with low-income high school students to serve as in-person and online mentors for several years.

International Justice Mission, www.ijm.org, rescues victims of violence and slavery, and works with police around the world to hold human traffickers to account.

International Rescue Committee, www.rescue.org, responds to the world's worst humanitarian crises in more than forty countries.

JITA, www.jitabangladesh.com, a Bangladesh-based social business, employs rural women to sell socially responsible products such as soaps, seeds, and solar lamps to underprivileged consumers.

Juan Felipe Gómez Escobar Foundation, www.juanfe.org/en, a residential program in Cartagena, Colombia, supports impoverished teen moms, provides counseling and health care, and teaches improved child care and job skills.

Kiva, www.kiva.org, lets individuals lend as little as $25 to help entrepreneurs launch small businesses around the globe. Learn about an individual's story, lend to her new business, and watch it grow as your loan gets paid back.

Landesa, www.landesa.org, gains secure property rights for the world's poor, especially women.

Magdalene, www.thistlefarms.org, offers trafficking survivors therapy, job training, and help staying off drugs and away from dangerous social networks in a two-year residential program.

MDRC, www.mdrc.org, conducts rigorous experiments on how best to address problems of poverty in the United States.

Mercy Corps, www.mercycorps.org, is an international development organization that helps people around the world survive after conflicts, crises, and natural disasters.

Mercy Ships, www.mercyships.org, sends professionally trained and highly qualified volunteers to provide free medical care on a hospital ship that travels to port cities around the world.

MicroMentor, www.micromentor.org, carefully connects mentors with specific business skills to individual entrepreneurs in need of their expertise.

Mothers Against Drunk Driving, www.madd.org, works to prevent families from drunk driving and underage drinking and supports drunk driving victims.

MovingWorlds, www.movingworlds.org, is a paid subscription community that matches members based on their skills and interests to a verified social impact organization abroad. It's like Match.com meets the Peace Corps.

Nurse-Family Partnership, www.nursefamilypartnership.org, provides important nurse home visits to first-time mothers from pregnancy until the child turns two years old.

Omprakash, www.omprakash.org, connects volunteers and donors with grassroots social impact organizations in more than thirty countries around the world.

ONE, www.one.org, a campaigning and advocacy organization, raises public awareness and works with political leaders to back evidence-based spending on global health.

Opportunity International, www.opportunity.org, provides small business loans, savings, insurance, and training to millions of people working their way out of poverty in developing countries.

Options for Youth, www.options4youth.org, a Chicago-based organization, helps adolescent mothers return to the education system and delay a second pregnancy.

Oxfam International, www.oxfam.org, is a global development organization that identifies innovative and practical ways for people to lift themselves out of poverty.

Partners in Health, www.pih.org, is a global health organization committed to improving the health of poor and marginalized people around the world.

Plan, www.planusa.org, connects donors to sponsor children in developing countries.

Planned Parenthood, www.plannedparenthood.org, works to improve women's health and safety, prevent unintended pregnancies, and advance the right and ability of individuals to make informed choices about parenthood.

Polaris Project, www.polarisproject.org, combats and prevents U.S. human trafficking through a national human trafficking hotline, services for survivors, and efforts to pass antitrafficking legislation around the country.

Population Institute, www.populationinstitute.org, promotes universal access to family planning information, education, and services around the world.

Reach Out and Read, www.reachoutandread.org, runs a network of pediatricians who provide books to young patients and their parents to promote early literacy. A $40 donation supports a child for two years, and a $100 donation ensures that a child graduates after five years with at least ten books.

ReadyNation, www.readynation.org, is a network of business leaders, organizations, and other individuals who advocate for greater federal investment in early childhood development programs.

Red Cloud Indian School, www.redcloudschool.org, provides an excellent education to young people who live on the Pine Ridge Indian Reservation.

Restore Leadership Academy, www.restoreinternational.org/uganda, is a top-tier school in Northern Uganda for students who grew up during the civil war there.

RESULTS, www.results.org, recruits and trains volunteer citizen lobbyists on global and domestic poverty issues.

Revolution Foods, www.revolutionfoods.com, makes and sells nutritious school meals and snack packs at affordable prices for underprivileged children.

Robin Hood Foundation, www.robinhood.org, takes a results-driven approach to ending poverty in New York City.

Room to Read, www.roomtoread.org, led by former Microsoft executive John Wood, builds schools and libraries in Asia and Africa to promote literacy and gender equality in education.

Rotary International, www.rotary.org, is a membership organization that provides humanitarian services worldwide.

Save the Children, www.savethechildren.org, in its U.S. Early Steps to School Success program, provides at-home early education services to at-risk children from birth to age five.

Schistosomiasis Control Initiative, www3.imperial.ac.uk/schisto, works with governments in sub-Saharan Africa to scale up deworming programs.

Self Employed Women's Association, www.sewa.org, is a huge union for poor, self-employed women in India. It accepts volunteers.

Shining Hope for Communities, www.shininghopeforcommunities.org, in the Kibera slum in Kenya, provides health services, a school for young girls, microsavings initiatives, a gender violence program, and job training to residents. You can sponsor a female student for $1,200 a year.

Smoking Cessation and Reduction in Pregnancy Treatment (SCRIPT), www.sophe.org/SCRIPT.cfm, is an evidence-based program that helps pregnant women quit smoking.

SOPUDEP, www.sopudep.org, a Haitian grassroots organization, provides free education to kids and adults and supports women's rights and economic empowerment for underserved Haitians.

South Central Scholars Foundation, www.southcentralscholars.org, helps high-achieving, low-income Los Angeles high school students become successful college students.

Springboard Collaborative, www.springboardcollaborative.org, offers attendance at a summer program to help low-income students replace typical summer reading losses with reading gains.

Sustainable Health Enterprises (SHE), www.sheinnovates.com, designs affordable banana fiber sanitary pads in Rwanda to improve feminine hygiene and increase school attendance.

TAMTAM, www.tamtamafrica.org, distributes bed nets to underserved areas through cost-effective methods.

The Mission Continues, www.missioncontinues.org, provides public service fellowships and mentorship for returning post-9/11 veterans.

Thirty Million Words Initiative, www.tmw.org, coaches parents to engage their children in conversation, interact with them, and ask them questions.

Thistle Farms, www.thistlefarms.org, a social enterprise, provides jobs to trafficking survivors who run a café and make and sell candles, soap, and fragrances.

Tinogona Foundation, www.tinogona.org, founded by Dr. Tererai Trent, rebuilds schools in rural Zimbabwe.

Uncharted Play, www.unchartedplay.com, creates products that harness the energy of play into electricity. For each purchase of a Soccket soccer ball, Uncharted Play donates one to a child living without reliable electricity.

Unite for Sight, www.uniteforsight.org, supports eye clinics worldwide by investing in social ventures to eliminate barriers to eye care for underserved patients.

Valentino Achak Deng Foundation, www.vadfoundation.org, increases access to education in postconflict South Sudan by building schools, libraries, teacher-training institutes, and community centers. A $300 donation supports a girl for a year of high school.

VisionSpring, www.visionspring.org, hires and trains local "vision entrepreneurs" to sell eyeglasses in remote parts of developing countries to keep children in school and support productivity in the workplace.

Vital Voices, www.vitalvoices.org, identifies, invests in, and brings visibility to extraordinary women around the world.

VolunteerMatch, www.volunteermatch.org, provides volunteer information and listings in your local community.

WonderWork, www.wonderwork.org, supports life-changing surgeries and treatments for underserved populations in need of medical care for clubfoot, burns, and blindness.

World Assistance for Cambodia, www.cambodiaschools.com, provides educational opportunities for children and medical care for the rural poor in Cambodia.

World Vision, www.worldvision.org, allows donors to sponsor a child for $1 a day to provide clean water, nutritious food, health care, and education.

Youth Villages, www.youthvillages.org, provides highly successful mentorship, home visitation, and evidence-based therapy to troubled children, young adults, and their families.

Acknowledgments

We've had the remarkable good fortune to be associated with two companies that pursue profits by embracing quality. The New York Times Company may publish news, while Knopf publishes books, but they have similar corporate values—above all, an insistence on being the best. We're lucky and proud to be a part of the *Times* and Knopf.

At the *Times,* credit goes to Arthur Sulzberger and the entire Ochs/Sulzberger family for their stewardship. Andrew Rosenthal, the editorial page editor, gave Nick a leave of absence to work on this book, and so many colleagues have been supportive. Natalie Kitroeff read the manuscript—twice!—and Alison Leigh Cowan, a dear friend, stayed up very late nights reading. Stephanie Strom and David and Sherill Sanger read it as well, all offering excellent suggestions.

At Knopf, Sonny Mehta ensures that it's not just a publishing house but a home for so many people who care about great books. Credit also to the über-boss, Markus Dohle, chief executive of Penguin Random House, who is a friend as well as a great steward of one of the world's leading publishing companies. Our editor at Knopf, Jonathan Segal, is renowned in publishing circles both for his tolerance of bullheaded journalists and for his ability to coax the best from them. From the conceptual stages to the line editing, Jon edited every page of this book several times in a way that is very rare in the publishing world these days; we're utterly in his debt, and if you've gotten this far, then you are, too. Jon's assistant, Meghan Houser, helped get everything in order. Paul Bogaards is masterful at overseeing all promotion, and Chip Kidd designed the cover. We are grateful to them both. The foreign rights team, Serena Lehman and Suzanne Smith, help turn the books into Español, 中文, and other languages.

Sheryl has been working in recent years as a banker with start-ups, especially those with a social mission. She owes thanks to many colleagues including Stephen Bodurtha, Edward Eisert, Norman Friedland, Larry Ikard, Stephen Leist, Subhash Marineni, John Park, Ralph Veerman, and Bob Wien.

We've been so lucky to work with an extraordinarily committed team of filmmakers, led by the indomitable Maro Chermayeff of Show of Force, to make our previous book, *Half the Sky,* and now this one into PBS documentaries and multimedia platforms. PBS and Independent Television Service (ITVS) were ideal hosts for the project, and Mikaela Beardsley, Josh Bennett, Mira Chang, Jessica Chermayeff, Jeff Dupre, Jamie Gordon, and Rachel Koteen became passionate and sensitive advocates of the projects. They have been great companions as we haggled over the price of a camel in Somaliland and battled a mob of brothel owners in India.

The documentaries have included a number of prominent actors to try to direct the attention that naturally follows them to highlight those who need it rather more. Special thanks to George Clooney, America Ferrera, Diane Lane, Eva Mendes, Meg Ryan, Gabrielle Union, and Olivia Wilde for the *Half the Sky* documentary. Those involved in the *A Path Appears* documentary include Malin Akerman, Mia Farrow, Ronan Farrow, Jennifer Garner, Regina Hall, Ashley Judd, Blake Lively, Eva Longoria, and Alfre Woodard. They all gave up time to travel around the world and try to make a difference; they deserve Oscars for moral leadership. Their participation was possible because of the stewardship of Pat Harrison at the Corporation for Public Broadcasting, and Sally Jo Fifer and Tamara Gould of Independent Television Service. A second special dollop of thanks goes to Olivia Wilde for reading this entire manuscript aloud in a studio for the audiobook version—and for her own efforts to build opportunity in Haiti.

We want to thank everyone involved in the multimedia project for *A Path Appears,* and this includes a remarkable team of videographers, on-the-ground crew, film editors, producers, researchers, and graphic designers. Many of these folks also worked on our previous multimedia project, which included an online game, overseen by Asi Burak and Michelle Byrd of Games for Change; the game attracted more than a million players through Facebook. Particular thanks to Richard Fleming, Bob Hanna, Wolfgang Held, François Huyghe, Jenni Morello, Mark Roy, David Smoler—and especially photographer Audrey Hall, who supplied some of the images in this book. An extra-special thanks to Liriel Higa, known on Twitter as @half and @iDiplomacy, who tutored us on social media and led the campaign to make a difference with our books on Facebook, Twitter, Google+, and Instagram.

We owe an enormous debt to Lizzie Presser, who started as a director of the *Half the Sky* campus ambassador program and then became the researcher for this book. Lizzie poured her soul into these pages and these ideas, correcting facts, improving writing, and nailing down photos—always with a smile. Whatever the hour of the day, she was always energetic, thorough, and devoted to these issues, making her a superb companion for this journey. You also see a few photos she has taken in these pages. We look forward to reading her books in a few years.

Lizzie's help, in turn, was made possible by a generous grant from the Ford Foundation, which also gave us a spacious office to work in. Tremendous thanks to Luis Ubiñas, the former president of the Ford Foundation, and to Darren Walker, his successor, who has been encouraging and supportive from the very beginning. Grace Anonuevo, Lori Matia, Ken Monteiro, and Brian Polk were also very helpful during the entire process. The Ford Foundation is a model of an organization seeking evidence-based solutions to the challenges of the twenty-first century.

We have been so lucky all these years to have the best literary agents around, Mort Janklow and Anne Sibbald, introduced to us by the late Bill Safire when we were young reporters in China thinking about writing a book. Mort, Anne, and their colleagues, including Stefanie Lieberman, have been so helpful as we have waded into unusual areas such as gaming and museum exhibits.

We've also been fortunate and grateful to have the formidable legal talents of Marty Schwimmer on our side. Marty was a classmate of Nick's many years ago and now practices copyright law while also blogging about it. He is always a voice of reason and good judgment, with a dry wit to boot.

Others who read part or all of this manuscript include Shawn Baker, Lisa Belkin, David Bornstein, and Ken Levit. They offered sage advice that we repeatedly seized. The "Fixes" column that David writes in *The New York Times* with Tina Rosenberg is an invaluable source of great journalism on what works in addressing social problems.

One of the things we learned in our reporting for the book is the importance of strong families. That has made us extra grateful for our own: Alice and David WuDunn, Darrell and Sondra WuDunn, and Jane Kristof, who also read this manuscript several times. After learning about the importance of early childhood, we belatedly appreciate all that our parents did for us! And thanks so much to our kids—Gregory, Geoffrey, and Caroline—for putting up with our occasional negligence as we fussed over this manuscript.

It's difficult to overstate how much we owe the sources who spoke to us and enliven these pages. These include scholars who walked us through brain chemistry and neuroscience, helping us translate journal articles into layman's English. Above all, there were many other people who spoke openly and on the record about their personal histories, their challenges, and their vulnerabilities so that readers could appreciate the issues more deeply. It's an extraordinarily difficult thing to talk so publicly about being poor, about fighting addictions, about being raped or prostituted, about falling short in raising one's children. Yet many did so because they understand the need for public understanding as the first step toward making a difference. Thank you—all of you—for we have learned so much from you, and this book would not have been possible without your candor.

It's customary to conclude such acknowledgments by saying something to the effect that despite all the help, any remaining errors are the author's alone. Rubbish! In this case, we each disclaim any mistakes. Any lingering errors are entirely the fault of our spouse.

Notes

Most of the quotations and reporting in this book derive from our own interviews. All names in this book are real, unless otherwise noted. Where we use quotation marks, that typically means the comment came in an interview with us or at least was written down soon after the event (as in a police report in the case of Anthony Brown's killing). Where people are recalling dialogue and it may not be so reliable, we use italics, but not quotation marks, to signify that it may not be quite right. We use the royal "we" even if only one of us was present at the scene.

What follows is an attempt to provide documentation for quotations or information that came from sources other than interviews. It's an attempt to provide further resources for those who want to dig further.

TITLE AND EPIGRAPH

vii   "Hope is like a path": Lu Xun's quotation comes from his essay "Guxiang." The translation is our own, although it borrows from the approach of Simon Leys in *The Burning Forest: Essays on Chinese Culture and Politics* (New York: Holt, Rinehart, and Winston, 1986), p. 223. Our translation is not a literal one, since the first part is difficult to express in idiomatic English. It reflects the idea that hope can't be said fundamentally to exist or not exist in any metaphysical sense; rather, it is created by our actions, just as we create a path in the countryside. Hope, he is saying, depends on us.

CHAPTER ONE *Introduction*

5   Rachel's campaign raised $1,265,823: You can see Rachel's birthday campaign and watch a video of her mother, Samantha, visiting a well site in Ethiopia in honor of Rachel at www.charitywater.org/rachel.

7   But he had burned out: Slutkin had burned out working in refugee camps in Somalia, not camps for internally displaced people.

10   Strikingly, those in the bottom 20 percent: Ken Stern, "Why the Rich Don't Give to Charity," *The Atlantic,* March 20, 2013. Stern's figures come from the Bureau of Labor Statistics' 2011 Consumer Expenditure Survey. The figures account for the share of income before tax that is contributed to charities, religious organizations, educational institutions, and political organizations. According to our tabulations, the middle-income bracket gave 1.4 percent of their income to charity. In 2012, those in the bottom 20 percent gave 3.5 percent of their income before taxes to charity, while those in the top 20 percent gave 1.4 percent and the middle quintile gave 1.5 percent. *The Chronicle of Philanthropy* shows different figures based on IRS data from taxpayers who itemize on their tax returns. In that analysis, researchers found households that earned $50,000 to $75,000 in 2008 gave an average of 7.6 percent of their discretionary income to charity, whereas those that made $100,000 or more gave an average of 4.2 percent. The survey also found that red states are more generous than blue states. See Emily Gipple and Ben Gose, "America's Generosity Divide," *Chronicle of Philanthropy,* August 19, 2012.

10   About two-thirds of Americans donate: Giving USA provides some of the most thorough data on charitable giving in the United States. For the most recent report, see *Giving USA 2014: The Annual Report on Philanthropy for the Year of 2013, 59th Annual Issue* (Indianapolis: Lilly Family School of Philanthropy, Indiana University, 2014).

11   earn 20 percent more: See Sarah Baird, Joan Hamory Hicks, Michael Kremer, and Edward Miguel, "Worms at Work: Long-Run Impacts of Child Health Gains," working paper, Harvard University, March 2012. For more information on deworming, see www .dewormtheworld.org or www.evidenceaction.org.

14   Successful people often scorn: For more on this, see Susan T. Fiske and Shelley E. Taylor, *Social Cognition: From Brains to Culture* (New York: McGraw-Hill, 2007).

15   An American boy in the bottom 20 percent: Markus Jäntti et al., "American Exceptionalism in a New Light: A Comparison of Intergenerational Earnings Mobility in the Nordic Countries, the United Kingdom and the United States," discussion paper 1938, *IZA,* January 2006. A 2012 report found that children born in the bottom 20 percent in income in the United States had a one-in-twenty-five chance of reaching the top 20 percent. See *Pursuing the American Dream: Economic Mobility Across Generations* (Washington, DC: The Pew Charitable Trusts, 2012).

16   Queen Victoria asked the sultan of the Ottoman Empire: Turkey

also sent five shiploads of assistance to the Irish during the potato famine. The British denied the ships permission to dock, so the Turkish ships secretly unloaded their cargoes. In Queen Victoria's defense, it should be noted that the £2,000 she donated was from her private account and would be worth more than $100,000 today.

16   Peter Singer is the philosopher of this growing humanitarianism: Singer pairs recent economic analysis of charity impact with philosophical advice on why we should make charitable donations to maximize lives saved. See, for example, Peter Singer, "Good Charity, Bad Charity," *New York Times,* August 10, 2013.

17   One study on mortality following 7,000 people: Lisa F. Berkman and S. Leonard Syme, "Social Networks, Host Resistance, and Mortality: A Nine-Year Follow-Up Study of Alameda County Residents," *American Journal of Epidemiology* 109, no. 2 (1979): 186–204.

CHAPTER TWO *A Drop in the Bucket*

19   About one baby in a thousand: This statistic is for the United States. The prevalence of clubfoot varies around the world and is as high as 6.8 per 1,000 births in Hawaii. See Fred Dietz, "The Genetics of Idiopathic Clubfoot," *Clinical Orthopaedics and Related Research* 401 (August 2002): 39–48.

21   save a life for a couple of thousand dollars: Estimates of the cost of saving a life vary by order of magnitude, and most public health experts don't focus on the cost of a life saved (or cost per death averted) but on the "disability-adjusted life year," or DALY. That measures how many extra years of human life are gained by a treatment. If you extend the life of an octogenarian by two years, that may be worth two DALYs. Saving a child's life may be worth sixty DALYs or more. One relatively low set of estimates for the "best buys" in global health, based on DALYs, can be found in Ramanan Laxminarayan and Lori Ashford, *Using Evidence About "Best Buys" to Advance Global Health* (Washington, DC: Disease Control Priorities Project, 2008).

24   one-third of overall charitable giving: *Patterns of Household Charitable Giving by Income Group, 2005* (Indianapolis: The Center on Philanthropy at Indiana University, 2007), p. 30.

27   "I got involved in tuberculosis work": Ohio senator Sherrod Brown's quotation and the information on the increase of federal support for child survival and tuberculosis come from David Bornstein, "Lobbying for the Greater Good," *New York Times,* May 29, 2013.

28   RESULTS has volunteer chapters: New members can sign up individually to join a nearby chapter or sign up with a group to start a new chapter; each member commits about five hours each month. Groups meet and take action once a month, and RESULTS schedules a monthly national call with all 1,000 members as well. For those who can't make that much of a commitment, sign up for the email list only and commit to about ten minutes of volunteer work a month—a quick call to a representative or an email to a senator, for example.

CHAPTER THREE   *From Anecdote to Evidence*

33   household air pollution: Stephen S. Lim et al., "A Comparative Risk Assessment of Burden of Disease and Injury Attributable to 67 Risk Factors and Risk Factor Clusters in 21 Regions, 1990–2010: A Systematic Analysis for the Global Burden of Disease Study 2010," *The Lancet* 380, no. 9859 (December 2012): 2224–60. This is one paper from an extensive series, the Global Burden of Disease Study 2010. To see the complete study, visit www.thelancet.com/themed/global-burden-of-disease.

34   clean cookstoves were an utter failure: For more on Duflo's findings, see Rema Hanna, Esther Duflo, and Michael Greenstone, "Up in Smoke: The Influence of Household Behavior on the Long-Run Impact of Improved Cooking Stoves," working paper 12-10, Massachusetts Institute of Technology Department of Economics, April 2012.

37   Rockefeller Foundation dewormed children: Results from this trial can be found in Hoyt Bleakley, "Disease and Development: Evidence from Hookworm Eradication in the American South," *Quarterly Journal of Economics* 122, no. 1 (January 2007): 73–117.

37   Kremer and Miguel found that the cost: They have done many deworming studies, but one of the early influential ones was Edward Miguel and Michael Kremer, "Worms: Identifying Impacts on Education and Health in the Presence of Treatment Externalities," *Econometrica* 72, no. 1 (January 2004): 159–217.

37   follow-up randomized trials in Kenya: A bibliography of deworming studies and publications can be found at the website of Deworm the World, an organization that helps finance deworming initiatives. The organization Evidence Action now manages and helps grow Deworm the World.

38   an Indian microfinance institution, Spandana: Esther Duflo, Abhijit Banerjee, Rachel Glennerster, and Cynthia G. Kinnan, "The Mir-

acle of Microfinance? Evidence from a Randomized Evaluation," working paper no. 18950, National Bureau of Economic Research, May 2013.

38 "We were quite pleased with these results": Abhijit V. Banerjee and Esther Duflo, *Poor Economics: A Radical Rethinking of the Way to Fight Global Poverty* (New York: Public Affairs, 2011), p. 171; more information on the Spandana study can be found in chapter 7.

39 40 percent annual interest: "Smooth Operators," *The Economist,* May 14, 2009.

39 In a 2013 study conceived by Pascaline Dupas: Pascaline Dupas and Jonathan Robinson, "Savings Constraints and Microenterprise Development: Evidence from a Field Experiment in Kenya," *American Economic Journal: Applied Economics* 5, no. 1 (2013): 163–92.

40 "not so much to increasing rigor": Sanjay Reddy, "Randomise This! On Poor Economics," *Review of Agrarian Studies* 2, no. 2 (July–December 2012): 63.

40 it is helpful to get guidance: One of the most important questions randomized controlled trials have helped answer is how best to distribute bed nets to curb malaria. There used to be a vigorous debate, with evidence on each side, about whether to give nets away free to save lives, or to charge modest sums so that they would be valued. There were reasonable arguments made that when nets were given away free, villagers misused them (as curtains, for example). A series of randomized controlled trials tested these propositions and settled the matter: it's much better to give the nets away free. Even charging tiny sums for the nets reduces use overwhelmingly. And the long term benefits of their use are enormous. See Pascaline Dupas, "Short-Run Subsidies and Long-Run Adoption of New Health Products: Evidence from a Field Experiment," *Econometrica* 82, no. 1 (January 2014): 197–228.

CHAPTER FOUR *The Land of Opportunity—If You Catch Them Early*

49 two-thirds of adults may be alcoholics: For more of Nick's reporting on Pine Ridge, see Nicholas D. Kristof, "A Battle with the Brewers," *New York Times,* May 5, 2012, and Nicholas D. Kristof, "Poverty's Poster Child," *New York Times,* May 9, 2012.

49 one-quarter of children on the reservation: This statistic comes from a lawsuit the Oglala Sioux Tribe brought against some of the world's largest beer makers.

50 life expectancy is more like that of a developing country: Figures

for longevity on the Pine Ridge Indian Reservation come from correspondence with Michael McCurry, the South Dakota state demographer. Other figures come from tribe officials and others interviewed in our reporting on Pine Ridge. Life expectancy on Pine Ridge reservation is variously estimated: the Centers for Disease Control say it's fifty-eight, shorter than in Haiti or Sudan; the Indian Health Service puts the number at sixty-six, shorter than Bangladesh; and the most recent figure is from WorldLife Expectancy.com, which pegs life expectancy at seventy-one, less than in Honduras.

51　　A study by Ann Streissguth: Ann Streissguth, Helen Barr, Julia Kogan, and Fred Bookstein, *Understanding the Occurrence of Secondary Disabilities in Clients with Fetal Alcohol Syndrome (FAS) and Fetal Alcohol Effects (FAE): Final Report* (Seattle: University of Washington School of Medicine, Department of Psychiatry and Behavioral Sciences, Fetal Alcohol and Drug Unit, 1996).

52　　Patricia A. Brennan of Emory University found: Patricia A. Brennan, Emily R. Grekin, and Sarnoff A. Mednick, "Maternal Smoking During Pregnancy and Adult Male Criminal Outcomes," *Archives of General Psychiatry* 56, no. 3 (March 1999): 215–19.

52　　14 percent of the women: Smoking Cessation and Reduction in Pregnancy Treatment (SCRIPT) Program has been evaluated in six well-conducted randomized controlled trials. The program is currently run by the Society for Public Health Education. These data represent the average quit rates across the six trials. For more on the intervention and the related randomized controlled trials, see *A Pregnant Woman's Self-Help Guide to Quit Smoking* (Washington, DC: Coalition for Evidence-Based Policy, 2012).

52　　one study examined Muslims in Uganda and Iraq: See Douglas Almond and Bhashkar Mazumder, "Health Capital and the Prenatal Environment: The Effect of Ramadan Observance During Pregnancy," *American Economic Journal: Applied Economics* 3, no. 4 (October 2011): 56–85.

53　　Meaney mixed up the rat pups: Darlene Francis, Josie Diorio, Dong Liu, and Michael J. Meaney, "Nongenomic Transmission Across Generations of Maternal Behavior and Stress Responses in the Rat," *Science* 286, no. 5442 (November 1999): 1155–58.

53　　Genes mattered less: For more on how maternal behavior had an epigenetic effect, see Ian C. G. Weaver et al., "Epigenetic Programming by Maternal Behavior," *Nature Neuroscience* 7, no. 8 (August 2004): 847–54.

53　　But the attentive mothers: More on how attentive mothers shaped the behavior and brains of their pups can be found in Frances A. Champagne, Darlene D. Francis, Adam Mar, and Michael J. Meaney, "Variations in Maternal Care in the Rat as a Mediating Influence for the Effects of Environment on Development," *Physiology & Behavior* 79, no. 3 (August 2003): 359–71, and Frances A. Champagne and Michael Meaney, "Transgenerational Effects of Social Environment on Variations in Maternal Care and Behavioral Response to Novelty," *Behavioral Neuroscience* 121, no. 6 (2007): 1353–63.

54 Shonkoff calls this "toxic stress": For more on toxic stress and its lifelong implications, see Jack P. Shonkoff, Andrew S. Garner, Committee on Psychological Aspects of Child and Family Health, Committee on Early Childhood, Adoption, and Dependent Care, Section on Developmental and Behavioral Pediatrics, "The Lifelong Effects of Childhood Adversity and Toxic Stress," *Pediatrics* 129, no. 1 (January 2012): e232–e246. The Center on the Developing Child's website, www.developingchild.harvard.edu, is another great resource for information on toxic stress and early childhood development.

54 Kids from poor families had less brain specialization: Rajeev D. S. Raizada, Todd L. Richards, Andrew Meltzoff, and Patricia K. Kuhl, "Socioeconomic Status Predicts Hemispheric Specialization of the Left Inferior Frontal Gyrus in Young Children," *NeuroImage* 40, no. 3 (April 2008): 1392–401.

55 "Growing up poor is bad for your brain": This quotation came from Martha Farah at the American Association for the Advancement of Science's annual meeting in 2008. See Richard Monastersky, "Researchers Gain Understanding of How Poverty Alters the Brain," *Chronicle of Higher Education*, February 18, 2008.

56 The first big ACEs study: Vincent J. Felitti et al., "Relationship of Childhood Abuse and Household Dysfunction to Many of the Leading Causes of Death in Adults: The Adverse Childhood Experiences (ACE) Study," *American Journal of Preventative Medicine* 14, no. 4 (1998): 245–58.

57 scanned the brains of many murderers: To get a better sense of the brain scans, see Adrian Raine, *The Anatomy of Violence: The Biological Roots of Crime* (New York: Vintage Books, 2013), pp. 67–78.

57 "Traumatic and chronic stress during childhood": Charles A. Nelson III and Margaret A. Sheridan, "Lessons from Neuroscience Research for Understanding Causal Links Between Family and Neighborhood Characteristics and Educational Outcomes," in *Whither Opportunity? Rising Inequality, Schools, and Children's*

Life Chances, ed. Greg J. Duncan and Richard J. Murnane (New York: Russell Sage Foundation Press, 2011), p. 36. See this paper for more on the hippocampus and amygdala and how different developmental patterns can affect mental health.

58   Bucharest Early Intervention Project: For an excellent account of the Bucharest project, and more broadly of the toll of institutionalization on child development, see Charles A. Nelson, Nathan A. Fox, and Charles H. Zeanah, *Romania's Abandoned Children: Deprivation, Brain Development, and the Struggle for Recovery* (Cambridge, MA: Harvard University Press, 2014).

58   The majority of human mothers: For more on how children of same-sex couples do not face setbacks, see *The Australian Study of Child Health in Same-Sex Families (ACHESS)* (Melbourne: University of Melbourne, School of Population and Global Health, 2013).

59   A University of Minnesota research team: For more, see L. Alan Stroufe, Byron Egeland, Elizabeth A. Carlson, and W. Andrew Collins, *The Development of the Person: The Minnesota Study of Risk and Adaptation from Birth to Adulthood* (New York: Guilford Press, 2005). For details on high school graduation correlation, see pp. 76–77; for the psychosocial measures as a better predictor than IQ, see p. 228; for more on Serena and Ellis, see p. 287.

62   Olds took a job evaluating a children's program: Some of the background on David Olds comes from Andy Goodman, *The Story of David Olds and the Nurse Home Visiting Program* (Chicago: Robert Wood Johnson Foundation, 2006).

63   the results of Olds's intervention were impressive: For more on Olds's early study in Elmira, see David L. Olds, Charles R. Henderson Jr., Robert Tatelbaum, and Robert Chamberlin, "Preventing Child Abuse and Neglect: A Randomized Trial of Nurse Home Visitation," *Pediatrics* 78 (1986): 65–78.

64   Women in that category: See David L. Olds et al., "Long-Term Effects of Home Visitation on Maternal Life Course and Child Abuse and Neglect: Fifteen-Year Follow-up of a Randomized Trial," *Journal of the American Medical Association* 278, no. 8 (August 27, 1997): 637–43.

64   The results were very similar: You can see a full list of publications and randomized controlled trials on the Nurse-Family Partnership on its website, www.nursefamilypartnership.org.

64   The Nurse-Family Partnership has now grown: In 2010, the Patient Protection and Affordable Care Act established the Maternal, Infant, and Early Childhood Home Visiting Program (MIECHV),

which provides $1.5 billion over five years to states to establish home visiting program models for at-risk pregnant women and children from birth to age five. Seventy-five percent of these funds must go to rigorously tested, evidence-based programs, of which Nurse-Family Partnership is one.

Save the Children, in the USA

70   The Nurse-Family Partnership has data: David Olds has conducted studies showing that paraprofessionals—employees without bachelor degrees—are not as effective in the home visiting role as professional nurses, in part because they lack some credibility. See David L. Olds et al., "Effects of Home Visits by Paraprofessionals and by Nurses on Children: Follow-up of a Randomized Trial at Ages 6 and 9 Years," *Journal of American Medical Association Pediatrics* 168, no. 2 (February 2014): 114–21.

70   Rival research suggests: For example, studies on Early Head Start home visiting programs, which employ both nonprofessionals and professionals, found that children in a well-implemented program for 36 months had fewer social behavior problems, higher cognitive development scores, and were more likely to attend a formal early childhood program at age 3 and 4 when compared to a control group. See Brenda Jones Harden, Rachel Chazan-Cohen, Helen Raikes, and Cheri Vogel, "Early Head Start Home Visitation: The Role of Implementation in Bolstering Program Benefits," *Journal of Community Psychology* 40, no. 4 (2012): 438–55. For a study on paraprofessionals' impact on development and health outcomes of children, see Shelley Peacock et al., "Effectiveness of Home Visiting Programs on Child Outcomes: A Systematic Review," *BMC Public Health* 13, no. 17 (2013): 1–14.

70   The Coalition for Evidence-Based Policy: See *HHS's Maternal, Infant, and Early Childhood Home Visiting Program: Which Program Models Identified by HHS as "Evidence-Based" Are Most Likely to Produce Important Improvements in the Lives of Children and Parents?* (Washington, DC: Coalition for Evidence-Based Policy, 2011).

70   Deborah Daro of the University of Chicago: Daro has written a helpful overview of the evolution and recent progress of home visitation programs in the United States. Deborah Daro, *Home Visitation: Assessing Progress, Managing Expectations* (Chicago: Chapin Hall Center for Children, 2006).

CHAPTER FIVE *A Thirty-Million-Word Gap*

72   "With few exceptions": See Betty Hart and Todd R. Risley, *Meaningful Differences in the Everyday Experience of Young American Children* (Baltimore: Paul H. Brookes, 1995).

75   Many low-income parents weren't read to themselves: When Nick was in third grade, he had a close friend, Deano, a Native American who struggled with reading. One afternoon, Deano accompanied Nick to the local library, where Nick's mother helped Deano get his first library card. The next day, Deano's grandmother made him give it up, for fear that he would incur a fine.

75   One randomized controlled trial in Rhode Island: Pamela C. High et al., "Literacy Promotion in Primary Care Pediatrics: Can We Make a Difference?" *Pediatrics* 105, no. 4 (April 2000): 927–34.

75   focused on low-income Hispanic children: Natalia Golova et al., "Literacy Promotion for Hispanic Families in a Primary Care Setting: A Randomized, Controlled Trial," *Pediatrics* 103, no. 5 (May 1999): 993–97.

76   helps kids in a crucial window of development: Another interesting approach to reduce the thirty-million-word gap is being tried in Chicago, using an audio recorder called the LENA. LENA records sixteen hours of everything a child hears. Once plugged into a computer, it reports how many words the child heard and how interactive the conversation was. It is used in a twelve-week program through the Thirty Million Words Initiative that coaches parents and care providers on how to speak to children, along with feedback from the recorder, to dramatically increase the number of words spoken to a child. Learn more about LENA and the Thirty Million Words initiative at www.tmw.org.

76   Sean Reardon of Stanford University: Sean F. Reardon, "The Widening Academic Achievement Gap Between the Rich and the Poor: New Evidence and Possible Explanations," in *Whither Opportunity?: Rising Inequality and the Uncertain Life Chance of Low-Income Children,* ed. Greg J. Duncan and Richard J. Murnane (New York: Russell Sage Foundation Press, 2011).

77   families already spent four times as much: Miles Corak, "Income Inequality, Equality of Opportunity, and Intergenerational Mobility," *Journal of Economic Perspectives* 27, no. 3 (Summer 2013): 79–102.

77   Perry Preschool Project, a randomized controlled trial: You can find all results at www.highscope.org. For the study through age forty, see Lawrence J. Schweinhart et al., *Lifetime Effects: The High/*

Scope Perry Preschool Study Through Age 40 (Ypsilanti, MI: High/ Scope Press, 2005).

77 Infant Health and Development Program: Charles Murray has presented IHDP as an example of how early childhood education doesn't work, but that's not our reading of the evidence. It didn't have lasting effects for the extremely low-birthweight babies (although there was an impact on them as measured when the program ended at age three), but it did have long-term beneficial effects for those weighing closer to the normal range, in behavior and in math and verbal skills. See Katie Beckmann, Anne Martin, and Jeanne Brooks-Gunn, *Summary of the Infant Health and Development Program (IHDP)* (New York: Teachers College, Columbia University, 2010).

78 "Head Start simply does not work": Joe Klein, "Time to Ax Public Programs That Don't Yield Results," *Time*, July 7, 2011.

79 David Deming of Harvard University: David Deming, "Early Childhood Intervention and Life-Cycle Skill Development: Evidence from Head Start," *American Economic Journal: Applied Economics* 1, no. 3 (2009): 111–34.

79 Alexander Gelber of the University of Pennsylvania: See Alexander M. Gelber and Adam Isen, "Children's Schooling and Parents' Investment in Children: Evidence from the Head Start Impact Study," working paper 17704, National Bureau of Economic Research, December 2011.

80 It is a leader in Educare: A large portion of the support for Educare comes through the family foundation of the successful Tulsa businessman George B. Kaiser. The George Kaiser Family Foundation invests in proof-of-concept initiatives against poverty in Oklahoma, with a focus on early childhood development and education.

80 William T. Gormley Jr. at Georgetown University: Timothy J. Bartik, William Gormley, and Shirley Adelstein, "Earnings Benefits of Tulsa's Pre-K Program for Different Income Groups," *Economics of Education Review* 31, no. 6 (December 2012): 1143–61.

82 "We can invest early to close disparities": This quotation and Heckman's calculations on the yearly return of Perry Preschool come from James J. Heckman, "The Economics of Inequality: The Value of Early Childhood Education," *American Educator* (Spring 2011): 31–47.

82 "More and more business people are supporting the need": This quotation is from "More than 300 Business Leaders and Organizations from 44 States Sign Letter Asking Lawmakers to Support Early Childhood Programs," America's Promise Alliance press release, May 29, 2013.

A Summer Springboard for Kids

84   two-thirds of the achievement gap: Karl Alexander from Johns
      Hopkins has done extensive research on the summer slide in the
      Beginning School Study. See Karl L. Alexander, Doris R. Entwisle,
      and Linda Steffel Olson, "Lasting Consequences of the Summer
      Learning Gap," *American Sociological Review* 72 (April 2007):
      167–80.

CHAPTER SIX *Who Grabs the Marshmallow?*

89   "as a group, they drop out of everything they start": This quota-
      tion comes from Heckman's notes on a presentation. James J.
      Heckman, "Investing in Early Childhood: Developing Skills for a
      Better Future," presentation at the Education Writers Association
      National Seminar, Palo Alto, CA, May 3, 2013.

89   the GED gives them book learning: See James J. Heckman, John
      Eric Humphries, and Tim Kautz, eds., *The Myth of Achievement
      Tests: The GED and the Role of Character in American Life* (Chi-
      cago: University of Chicago Press, 2014).

92   Mischel conducted further research on self-control: For an exten-
      sive follow-up on the preschool children assessed between 1968
      and 1974, see Yuichi Shoda, Walter Mischel, and Philip K. Peake,
      "Predicting Adolescent Cognitive and Self-Regulatory Competen-
      cies from Preschool Delay of Gratification: Identifying Diagnostic
      Conditions," *Developmental Psychology* 26, no. 6 (1990): 978–86.
      See also Jonah Lehrer, "Don't! The Secret of Self-Control," *The
      New Yorker,* May 18, 2009.

93   Richard Nisbett, a University of Michigan psychology professor:
      Richard E. Nisbett, *Intelligence and How to Get It: Why Schools and
      Cultures Count* (New York: W. W. Norton, 2009).

94   Duckworth carried out a research program: Angela Lee Duck-
      worth, Teri A. Kirby, Anton Gollwitzer, and Gabriele Oettingen,
      "From Fantasy to Action: Mental Contrasting with Implementation
      Intentions (MCII) Improves Academic Performance in Children,"
      Social Psychological and Personality Science 4, no. 6 (2013): 745–53.
      This research is one of a number of new programs aimed at trying
      to teach grit.

95   "These demographic trends are stunning": Gregory Acs, Kenneth
      Braswell, Elaine Sorensen, and Margery Austin Turner, *The Moyni-
      han Report Revisited* (Washington, DC: Urban Institute, 2013), p. 5.

95   it's distressingly common, though often unreported: In 1962, a

landmark article in *The Journal of the American Medical Association* shocked Americans by suggesting that there were more than 749 documented cases of battered children in the country in a single year. The resulting media alarm led all fifty states to institute reporting requirements for child abuse—and once people began looking for abuse, they found it everywhere. There now are more than 900,000 confirmed cases of child abuse annually in the United States, and that is probably a significant undercount.

95 promoting marriage: It's worth noting that a traditional household benefits not just the wife and child but also the man. One Boston study found that one of the factors that had the greatest power to turn at-risk men away from crime was marriage. As Steven Pinker, the Harvard psychologist, writes: "The idea that young men are civilized by women and marriage may seem as corny as Kansas in August, but it has become a commonplace of modern criminology." See Steven Pinker, *The Better Angels of Our Nature: Why Violence Has Declined* (New York: Viking, 2011).

95 Supporting Healthy Marriage: See JoAnn Hsueh et al., *The Supporting Healthy Marriage Evaluation: Early Impacts on Low Income Families,* report 2012-11 (Washington, DC: OPRE, 2012).

96 One study found that by age twenty-three: Robert Brame, Shawn D. Bushway, Ray Paternoster, and Michael G. Turner, "Demographic Patterns of Cumulative Arrest Prevalence by Ages 18 and 23," *Crime & Delinquency,* January 2014.

97 When economists examined 35,000 juvenile offenders: Anna Aizer and Joseph J. Doyle Jr., "Juvenile Incarceration, Human Capital and Future Crime: Evidence from Randomly-Assigned Judges," working paper 19102, National Bureau of Economic Research, June 2013.

97 Among the leaders in this effort: For more on these states and other national and state incarceration trends, see *The Comeback States: Reducing Youth Incarceration in the United States* (Washington, DC: National Juvenile Justice Network and the Texas Public Policy Foundation, 2013).

CHAPTER SEVEN *Coaching Troubled Teens*

106 One study by the Guttmacher Institute: Jennifer J. Frost, Mia R. Zolna, and Lori Frohwirth, *Contraceptive Needs and Services, 2010* (New York: Guttmacher Institute, 2013).

106 Public investment in pregnancy prevention: The National Center for Health Statistics found that the rate of teen births was

roughly 31 per 1,000 women ages fifteen to nineteen in 2011. This is half of what the rate was just twenty years ago, but the U.S. teen birthrate is still higher than the rate in every other industrialized nation. For more on teen pregnancy prevention work in the United States, see Elizabeth Wildsmith, "Teenage Pregnancy Prevention: Finding Some Common Ground," April 30, 2013, Child Trends blog *Trend Lines*, http://childtrends.org/teenage -pregnancy-prevention-finding-some-common-ground.

108 A Harvard study found: See Raj Chetty, John N. Friedman, and Jonah E. Rockoff, "Measuring the Impacts of Teachers II: Teacher Value-Added and Student Outcomes in Adulthood," working paper 19424, National Bureau of Economic Research, September 2013, and Raj Chetty, John N. Friedman, and Jonah E. Rockoff, "The Long-Term Impacts of Teachers: Teacher Value-Added and Student Outcomes in Adulthood," working paper 17699, National Bureau of Economic Research, December 2011. See also Nicholas D. Kristof, "The Value of Teachers," *New York Times*, January 11, 2012.

108 one of the most dangerous times of day: See Howard N. Snyder and Melissa Sickmund, *Juvenile Offenders and Victims: 2006 National Report* (Washington, DC: U.S. Department of Justice, Office of Justice Programs, Office of Juvenile Justice and Delinquency Prevention, 2006).

109 Results are encouraging: While results for Citizen Schools have been encouraging, a Mathematica Policy Research study on afterschool programs around the United States has found that, on the whole, after-school programs show no statistically significant effect on student self-care, generally no improvements in academic outcomes, and mixed evidence on negative behavior. Students in afterschool programs, however, reported feeling safer after school than students not in such programs. See Mark Dynarski et al., *When Schools Stay Open Late: The National Evaluation of the 21st Century Learning Centers Program: New Findings*, U.S. Department of Education, National Center for Education Evaluation and Regional Assistance (Washington, DC: U.S. Government Printing Office, 2004).

111 Researchers at Harvard examined: See Jennifer Karas Montez and Anna Zajacova, "Explaining the Widening Education Gap in Mortality Among U.S. White Women," *Journal of Health and Social Behavior* 54, no. 2 (2013): 166–82.

112 "The announcement startled the journalists": These quotations come from Waldfogel's book, which offers excellent lessons for the

United States from Britain's experience. See Jane Waldfogel, *Britain's War on Poverty* (New York: Russell Sage Foundation, 2010).

CHAPTER EIGHT *The Power of Hope*

119 Esther Duflo and Abhijit Banerjee: Abhijit V. Banerjee and Esther Duflo, "The Economic Lives of the Poor," *Journal of Economic Perspectives* 21, no. 1 (Winter 2007): 141–68.

120 A 2010 Urban Institute study: Tracy Vericker, Jennifer Macomber, and Olivia Golden, *Infants of Depressed Mothers Living in Poverty: Opportunities to Identify and Serve* (Washington, DC: Urban Institute, 2010).

120 "A mom who is too sad": Donna St. George, "Study Links Poverty to Depression Among Mothers," *Washington Post,* August 26, 2010.

120 a Gallup poll in 2012: See Alyssa Brown, "With Poverty Comes Depression, More than Other Illnesses," *Gallup Well-Being,* October 30, 2012.

120 frequent markers of depression: Anne Case and Angus Deaton, "Health and Well-Being in Udaipur and South Africa," in *Developments in the Economics of Aging,* ed. David A. Wise (Chicago: University of Chicago Press, 2009): 317–49, especially p. 341, table 9.4.

121 Another study, by the University of Queensland: Alize J. Ferrari et al., "Burden of Depressive Disorders by Country, Sex, Age, and Year: Finding from the Global Burden of Disease Study 2010," *PLoS Medicine* 10, no. 11 (November 2013).

121 Sendhil Mullainathan and Eldar Shafir: For a fascinating book that looks closely at human mind-sets when struggling with scarcity—of money, food, time, or even friends—see Sendhil Mullainathan and Eldar Shafir, *Scarcity: Why Having Too Little Means So Much* (New York: Times Books, 2013).

122 Seligman launched a new series of experiments: Seligman discusses the dog experiments and more on learned helplessness in Martin E. P. Seligman, *Learned Optimism: How to Change Your Mind and Your Life* (New York: Vintage Books, 2006), especially pp. 18–28.

123 The families in the study: Abhijit Banerjee, Esther Duflo, Raghabendra Chattopadhyay, and Jeremy Shapiro, "Targeting the Hard-Core Poor: An Impact Assessment," working paper, Poverty Action Lab, Massachusetts Institute of Technology, November 2011.

125 Bruce Wydick of the University of San Francisco: Bruce Wydick, Paul Glewwe, and Laine Rutledge, "Does International Child

Sponsorship Work? A Six-Country Study of Impacts on Adult Life Outcomes," *Journal of Political Economy* 121, no. 2 (April 2013): 393–436. Wydick's quotation is from an email to the authors.

126 In his book *A Thousand Hills to Heaven:* For more on the story about alcoholism, see John Ruxin, *A Thousand Hills to Heaven* (New York: Little, Brown, 2013), p. 163. For more on the story about pomegranates, see pp. 302–3.

127 "Charity is no solution to poverty": Muhammad Yunus, *Banker to the Poor: Microlending and the Battle Against World Poverty* (New York: Public Affairs, 1999), p. 249.

128 gifts of cash reduce hunger: Johannes Haushofer and Jeremy Shapiro, "Household Response to Income Changes: Evidence from an Unconditional Cash Transfer Program in Kenya," working paper, Massachusetts Institute of Technology, November 2013.

128 This is an experiment worth watching: Rigorous evaluation organizations such as GiveWell have ranked GiveDirectly as a top-rated charity, but some are still skeptical. See, for example, Kevin Starr and Laura Hattendorf, "Give Directly? Not so Fast," *Stanford Social Innovation Review,* March 11, 2014.

CHAPTER NINE *A Doctor Who Treats Violence*

142 There he soon died: Some scenes and dialogue having to do with the stabbing of Anthony Brown come from *People of the State of Illinois v. Martavia Lambert,* Appellate Court of Illinois, First Judicial District (Ill. App. 2011), no. 1-09-2805. Through a Freedom of Information Act request, we also obtained the original twenty-nine-page police report on the killing, and some material comes from that. An interview with Linda Harris, an eyewitness to the killing, provided perspective as well, as does the original incident report filed by China Joe at the time. We also examined the indictment of Martavia Lambert and other court documents.

142 The University of Chicago Crime Lab: Roseanna Ander, Philip J. Cook, Jens Ludwig, and Harold Pollack, *Gun Violence Among School-Age Youth in Chicago* (Chicago: University of Chicago Crime Lab, 2009).

148 the program reduced shootings: See Wesley G. Skogan, Susan M. Hartnett, Natalie Bump, and Jill Dubois, *Evaluation of Ceasefire-Chicago* (Chicago: Northwestern University, 2009), pp. 7–46.

149 it reduced violent crime arrests: *B.A.M. — Sports Edition, Research and Policy Brief* (Chicago: University of Chicago Crime Lab, 2012).

CHAPTER TEN *Attacking Sex Trafficking*

156 Rachel Lloyd runs an outstanding program: Rachel Lloyd has written a terrific first-person account about how she came to be trafficked that illuminates why women who are prostituted don't always try to escape the pimps who brutalize them. Rachel Lloyd, *Girls Like Us: Fighting for a World Where Girls Are Not for Sale: A Memoir* (New York: HarperPerennial, 2011).

158 the most common victims of human trafficking: A recent State Department report found that as many as 100,000 children may be victims of domestic human trafficking in the United States, and that as many as 17,500 people may be brought into the United States by traffickers each year. See Matthew DeLuca, "'Modern-Day Slavery': State Dept. Says Millions of Human Trafficking Victims Go Unidentified," NBC News, June 19, 2013.

158 The Justice Department estimates: See Richard J. Estes and Neil Alan Weiner, *Commercial Sexual Exploitation of Children in the U.S., Canada, and Mexico* (Philadelphia: University of Pennsylvania School of Social Work, 2001).

CHAPTER ELEVEN *Charity*

168 The scare sent Pallotta into therapy: Some of the description of Pallotta's early years is drawn from interviews and from Dan Pallotta, *When Your Moment Comes: A Guide to Fulfilling Your Dreams by a Man Who Has Led Thousands to Greatness* (San Diego: Jodere Group, 2001). Some other material on Pallotta is drawn from Dan Pallotta, *Uncharitable: How Restraints on Nonprofits Undermine Their Potential* (Lebanon, NH: Tufts University Press, 2008), and Dan Pallotta, *Charity Case: How the Nonprofit Community Can Stand Up for Itself and Really Change the World* (San Francisco: Jossey-Bass, 2012).

169 fining Pallotta TeamWorks $110,000: This information comes from the Pennsylvania attorney general's opinion, *Commonwealth of Pennsylvania v. Pallotta and Associates*, Assurance of Voluntary Compliance, No. 358, 1997, dated April 14, 1997.

169 dipped to 21 percent: Pallotta TeamWorks made all their fundraising data transparent on their website, www.pallottateamworks.com.

172 The Girl Effect videos: Some of the information on the Girl Effect videos comes from personal communications with the Nike Foundation.

173   Researchers from the Bridgespan Group: To read more about the Bridgespan study, see Peter Kim and Jeffrey Bradach, "Why More Nonprofits Are Getting Bigger," *Stanford Social Innovation Review,* Spring 2012. The figures were 40 percent higher than in a former similar study that found that only 144 organizations had reached $50 million in annual revenues between 1970 and 2003. See William Foster and Gail Fine, "How Nonprofits Get Really Big," *Stanford Social Innovation Review,* Spring 2007.

176   "America's Worst Charities": See the *Tampa Bay Times* and the Center for Investigative Reporting's list of America's worst charities at "America's Worst Charities," last modified November 15, 2013, www.tampabay.com/americas-worst-charities.

177   The Crouches enjoyed thousand-dollar dinners: Erik Eckholm, "Family Battle Offers Look Inside Lavish TV Ministry," *New York Times,* May 4, 2012.

179   IRS Form 990: You can sign up for free on www.guidestar.org to search and download Form 990s from any nonprofit organization you are considering supporting to see how it allocates funds.

CHAPTER TWELVE   *Madison Avenue Helps the Needy*

186   Operation Smile was running into its own problems: In 2000, it was reported that Operation Smile conducted a review of its work after widely publicized deaths arising from its operations in developing countries. See Elisabeth Rosenthal and Reed Abelson, "Whirlwind of Facial Surgery by Foreigners Upsets China," *New York Times,* November 25, 1999, and Reed Abelson, "Charity Promises Sweeping Changes After Review," *New York Times,* April 12, 2000.

186   While continuing to expand Smile Train: Information on Smile Train and Wonderwork is drawn from interviews with Brian Mullaney and Smile Train spokesmen as well as internal documents.

187   *Smile Pinki: A Real-World Fairy Tale:* You can watch *Smile Pinki* in its entirety on Vimeo.

188   he was later required to give some back: Some of Mullaney's compensation was paid through Smile Train UK, but the UK High Court ruled in 2013 that Mullaney should repay £633,509 in unauthorized payments for his work for Smile Train UK in 2007, 2008, 2010, and 2011. See Andy Hiller, "How Smile Train UK Ended Up in Court," *Third Sector Online,* March 25, 2014. Mullaney also says he gave hundreds of thousands of dollars back to Smile Train in donations.

188 the same direct mail techniques: Economists Uri Gneezy and John List write about how carefully Brian Mullaney measures the returns of his direct mail campaigns in Uri Gneezy and John List, *The Why Axis: Hidden Motives and the Undiscovered Economics of Everyday Life* (New York: Public Affairs, 2013), chap. 10.

189 a $250 check to help Rashida with her clubfoot: The actual cost of surgery on the ground for both cleft and clubfoot is about $250, though it varies by country. As is the case with many other charities, a donor's check for $250 may also contribute to other expenses, such as doctor training and educational materials. The charity evaluator GiveWell reported that Smile Train raises more money than it can deploy directly to surgeries. Smile Train's approach, which GiveWell supports, is that it allocates some of those excess funds to education, training, and grants to other cleft programs. See Holden Karnofsky, "Smile Train," *GiveWell Blog,* November 30, 2009, http://blog.givewell.org/2009/11/30/smile-train. WonderWork and, by extension, FirstStep, use a similar approach to account for the costs of surgery in a particular country.

191 Slovic conducted a series of experiments: See Deborah A. Small, George Loewenstein, and Paul Slovic, "Sympathy and Callousness: The Impact of Deliberative Thought on Donations to Identifiable and Statistical Victims," *Organizational Behavior and Human Decision Processes* 102, no. 2 (2007): 143–53.

192 Rokia's photo accompanied the text: For more on the Rokia studies, see Paul Slovic, "'If I Look at the Mass I Will Never Act': Psychic Numbing and Genocide," *Judgment and Decision Making* 2, no. 2 (April 2007): 79–95. Other parts of this chapter draw from this paper as well.

193 Singer called his excellent book: Peter Singer, *The Life You Can Save: How to Do Your Part to End World Poverty* (New York: Random House, 2009).

193 Tehila Kogut and Ilana Ritov of Hebrew University: Tehila Kogut and Ilana Ritov, "The 'Identified Victim' Effect: An Identified Group, or Just a Single Individual?" *Journal of Behavioral Decision Making* 18 (2005): 157–67.

194 Schooler and a colleague conducted experiments: This story about the tiny sea monkeys comes from personal correspondence with Schooler.

195 "I remember going to Davos": This long quotation comes from Bill Gates's commencement speech at Harvard in 2007. See Bill Gates, "Remarks of Bill Gates, Harvard Commencement 2007," June 7,

2007, transcript, *Harvard Gazette,* http://news.harvard.edu/gazette/story/2007/06/remarks-of-bill-gates-harvard-commencement-2007.

Lessons from a Master Pastor

201 "What sickened me most": Richard Stearns, *The Hole in Our Gospel: What Does God Expect of Us? The Answer That Changed My Life and Might Just Change the World* (Nashville, TN: Thomas Nelson, 2009), p. 10.

CHAPTER THIRTEEN *Scaling Social Good*

204 socially driven companies that generate revenues: The *Stanford Social Innovation Review* is one great resource for more information on this shift. See, for example, William Landes Foster, Peter Kim, and Barbara Christiansen, "Ten Nonprofit Funding Models," *Stanford Social Innovation Review* 7, no. 2 (Spring 2009): 32–39. Also see Antony Bugg-Levine, Bruce Kogut, and Nalin Kulatilaka, "A New Approach to Funding Social Enterprises," *Harvard Business Review* 90, no. 1 (January–February 2012): 119–23.

204 Jacqueline Novogratz: For more on Novogratz's story, see her book Jacqueline Novogratz, *The Blue Sweater: Bridging the Gap Between Rich and Poor in an Interconnected World* (New York: Rodale Books, 2009).

205 folding a social mission into a for-profit business: For more on impact investing and social entrepreneurship, see Georgia Levenson Keohane, *Social Entrepreneurship for the 21st Century: Innovation Across the Nonprofit, Private, and Public Sectors* (New York: McGraw-Hill, 2013).

207 But historically it has been a challenge: For more on the difficulties of scaling up social enterprises, see Alan Hirzel, "To Grow, Social Enterprises Must Play by Business Rules," *Harvard Business Review Blog,* January 9, 2013.

208 Nearly one-third of American consumers: See "Purpose Driven Consumers Planning Sharp Increase in Socially Conscious Purchases," Good Must Grow press release, April 3, 2013.

Impossible, Possible Task

213 Revolution Foods won a $9 million contract: See "Biting Commentary," *The Economist,* May 4, 2013.

CHAPTER FOURTEEN *Doing Good While Being Big*

216 multinational companies in social responsibility: See Rosabeth Moss Kanter, "It's Time to Take Full Responsibility," *Harvard Business Review* 88, no. 10 (October 2010).

217 Undernutrition is a factor in 45 percent: Information on malnutrition comes from a series of papers in *The Lancet* in 2013. For this statistic, see Robert E. Black et al., "Maternal and Child Undernutrition and Overweight in Low-Income and Middle-Income Countries," *The Lancet* 382, no. 9890 (August 2013): 427–51.

217 Liu Jianghong: Liu Jianghong et al., "Malnutrition at Age 3 Years and Lower Cognitive Ability at Age 11 Years: Independence from Psychosocial Adversity," *Archives of Pediatric and Adolescent Medicine* 157, no. 6 (June 2003): 593–600.

223 "hypocritical window-dressing": Milton Friedman, "The Social Responsibility of Business Is to Increase Its Profits," *New York Times Magazine,* September 13, 1970.

225 Nutritional effects were positive: Sunil Sazawal et al., "Impact of Micronutrient Fortification of Yoghurt on Micronutrient Status Markers and Growth—a Randomized Double Blind Controlled Trial Among School Children in Bangladesh," *BMC Public Health* 13 (May 2013): 1–11.

227 companies would be rewarded with increased morale: Adam Grant of the University of Pennsylvania wrote a very interesting book on how people who give more to others often show greater energy, strong fund-raising and sales skills, and, in some cases, increased earnings. Adam Grant, *Give and Take: A Revolutionary Approach to Success* (New York: Viking, 2013).

228 the recidivism rate fell by 21 percent: *Annex A: Interim Reconviction Figures for the Peterborough and Doncaster Payment by Results Pilots* (London: Ministry of Justice, 2014).

The Perfect Product

229 40 percent of the supply fails to reach customers: For an excellent report on access to clean water in developing countries, see "Enough Is Not Enough," *The Economist,* May 20, 2010.

CHAPTER FIFTEEN *The Neuroscience of Giving*

237 The trajectory of Jack Whittaker: There are many accounts of Whittaker's misfortune after winning the lottery. One good one is David

Samuels, "Lottery Winner Jack Whittaker's Losing Ticket," *Bloomberg Business Week,* December 13, 2012. Also, a good eBook is Don McNay, *Life Lessons from the Lottery: Protecting Your Money in a Scary World* (Richmond, KY: RRP International, 2012).

239 One pioneering study: For a more thorough look at this study, see Joshua Wolf Shenk, "What Makes Us Happy?" *The Atlantic,* June 1, 2009.

239 Lalin Anik and Michael Norton: For more on the research showing that happier people give more and that giving more may make people happier, see Lalin Anik, Lara B. Aknin, Michael I. Norton, and Elizabeth Dunn, "Feeling Good About Giving: The Benefits (and Costs) of Self-Interested Charitable Behavior," working paper, Harvard Business School Marketing Unit, August 6, 2009.

239 To untangle causation from correlation: For more on this study, see Sonja Lyubomirsky, Kennon M. Sheldon, and David Schkade, "Pursuing Happiness: The Architecture of Sustainable Change," *Review of General Psychology* 9, no. 2 (May 2005): 111–31. In another approach, researchers asked retirees to give infants a massage three times a week for three weeks. Those who did so afterward exhibited less anxiety and depression, better overall health, and a reduced level of stress hormones. See Tiffany M. Field et al., "Elder Retired Volunteers Benefit from Giving Massage Therapy to Infants," *Journal of Applied Gerontology* 17, no. 2 (June 1998): 229–39.

239 In another ingenious experiment: Elizabeth W. Dunn, Lara B. Aknin, and Michael I. Norton, "Spending Money on Others Promotes Happiness," *Science* 319, no. 5870 (2008): 1687–88. For an interesting book on how money can best buy happiness, see Elizabeth Dunn and Michael Norton, *Happy Money: The Science of Smarter Spending* (New York: Simon & Schuster, 2013).

240 Daniel Kahneman and Angus Deaton: Daniel Kahneman and Angus Deaton, "High Income Improves Evaluation of Life but Not Emotional Well-Being," *Proceedings of the National Academy of Sciences* 107, no. 38 (September 2010): 16489–93.

240 Betsey Stevenson and Justin Wolfers: See, for example, Betsey Stevenson and Justin Wolfers, "Subjective Well-Being and Income: Is There Any Evidence of Satiation?" *American Economic Review: Papers and Proceedings* 103, no. 3 (May 2013): 598–604, and Betsey Stevenson and Justin Wolfers, "Economic Growth and Subjective Wellbeing: Reassessing the Easterlin Paradox," *Brookings Papers on Economic Activity,* Spring 2008, 1–102. In a 2013 University of Michigan working paper, "Growth in Income and Subjective Well-Being over Time," Stevenson, Wolfers, and Daniel W. Sacks look at

growth in subjective well-being and income over time. They don't isolate the United States, instead looking at studies across countries over time. Since 1973, they find "a positive relationship between well-being and income, over time, for the mass of countries." The exception is the Gallup World Poll, which covers the period from 2006 to 2011 and finds that world well-being has declined. When they plot average well-being and the prediction from log(GDP), the series has a .66 correlation, "suggesting that much of the growth in well-being over the last 40 years can be explained by growth in income." Wolfers suggests that the "satiation point" for emotional well-being found by Kahneman and Deaton cited above is based on different, less widely used survey data on happiness.

240 the level of self-reported happiness has not changed: Wolfers and Stevenson suggest that the reason may be because average household income in the United States has not increased much since 1972 and that rising inequality has led to more of the pie going to the very wealthy. Some scholars, though, are skeptical of this reasoning.

241 laughter, candy, sex: We were in Mayr's lab as he was walking us through the science, talking about the nucleus accumbens. He told us that evolution had apparently built the pleasure centers to create incentives for beneficial behaviors. But when there's a shortcut to provide that kind of pleasure, such as a lever for a rat or crack cocaine for a human, then things don't turn out so well.

241 an initial foray into brain research: William Harbaugh, Ulrich Mayr, and Dan Burghart, "Neural Responses to Taxation and Voluntary Giving Reveal Motives for Charitable Donations," *Science* 316, no. 5831 (June 2007): 1622–25.

241 people vary significantly. The mere making of a choice—to give or not to give—caused a "warm glow" that generated increased activity in the nucleus accumbens. An international study led by a Brazilian neuroimaging expert, Jorge Moll, used somewhat different techniques but found the same result: the pleasure centers of the brains of research subjects light up when they receive money, and also when they make donations. Jorge Moll et al., "Human Fronto-Mesolimbic Networks Guide Decisions About Charitable Donation," *Proceedings of the National Academy of Sciences* 103, no. 42 (October 2006): 15623–28.

242 "Pride and vanity have built more hospitals": Bernard Mandeville, "An Essay on Charity, and Charity-Schools," in *The Fable of the Bees or Private Vices, Publick Benefits* (London: J. Tonson, 1932), p. 294.

242 A 2006 study: Rachel Piferi and Kathleen A. Lawler, "Social Sup-

port and Ambulatory Blood Pressure: An Examination of Both Receiving and Giving," *International Journal of Psychophysiology* 62, no. 2 (November 2006): 328–36.

242   "Give and you will be healthier": Stephen Post and Jill Neimark, *Why Good Things Happen to Good People: How to Live a Longer, Healthier, Happier Life by the Simple Act of Giving* (New York: Broadway Books, 2007), p. 2.

242   Another study followed nearly 2,000 people: Doug Oman, Carl E. Thoresen, and Kay McMahon, "Volunteerism and Mortality Among the Community-Dwelling Elderly," *Journal of Health Psychology* 4, no. 3 (May 1999): 301–16.

243   What does all this research teach us: For a recent book that examines more of the neuroscience and psychology of altruism, see Elizabeth Svoboda, *What Makes a Hero? The Surprising Science of Selflessness* (New York: Penguin, 2013).

243   "most promising means of altering one's happiness level": Lyubomirsky et al., "Pursuing Happiness," p. 118.

The Most Boring Aid in the World

244   "Iodine deficiency is the most common cause": Michael B. Zimmermann, Pieter L. Jooste, and Chandrakant S. Pandav, "Iodine-Deficiency Disorders," *The Lancet* 372, no. 9645 (October 2008): 1251.

CHAPTER SIXTEEN *When Social Networks Dig a Well*

252   Paul Zak: For more on Paul Zak's work on oxytocin and cortisol, see Paul Zak, *The Moral Molecule: The Source of Love and Prosperity* (New York: Dutton, 2012).

253   Data published by the Rural Water Supply Network: For data on hand pump functionality in Sub-Saharan Africa, see *Handpump Data, Selected Countries in Sub-Saharan Africa* (St. Gallen, Switzerland: Rural Water Supply Network, 2009). This discussion on dysfunctional wells draws also on interviews with hydrologists.

253   In the Menaka region of Mali: See Jamie Skinner, *Where Every Drop Counts: Tackling Rural Africa's Water Crisis*, briefing paper (London: International Institute for Environment and Development, 2009), for more on the 50,000 foreign-funded wells that are no longer working and $300 million in well-drilling investments that have been squandered.

254   A 2004 World Health Organization study: Guy Hutton and Lau-

rence Haller, *Evaluation of the Costs and Benefits of Water and Sanitation Improvements at the Global Level* (Geneva: World Health Organization, 2004).

255 Charity:water had raised $1.2 million: You can read about the campaign at www.charitywater.org/blog/sept-2011-update.

256 In the Central African Republic, for example: Part of this discussion comes from a careful fifty-page unpublished 2012 review by Joachim Boko, "Evaluation Report: Water, Sanitation and Hygiene Program in Central African Republic," prepared for charity:water.

257 Yale University sociologist Nicholas A. Christakis: For more on how cooperative behavior can be contagious, see James H. Fowler and Nicholas Christakis, "Cooperative Behavior Cascades in Human Social Networks," *Proceedings of the National Academy of Sciences* 107, no. 12 (March 2010): 5334–38.

257 Scientists have also found: See Erez Yoeli, Moshe Hoffman, David G. Rand, and Martin A. Nowak, "Powering Up with Indirect Reciprocity in a Large-Scale Field Experiment," *Proceedings of the National Academy of Sciences* 110 (June 2013): 10424–29.

CHAPTER SEVENTEEN *Survival of the Kind*

263 Isn't life a Darwinian struggle: Even Charles Darwin puzzled over generosity and aid. In *The Descent of Man* (New York: American Dome Library Company, 1902), he wrote, "The aid we feel impelled to give to the helpless is mainly an incidental result of the instinct of sympathy, which was originally acquired as part of the social instincts, but subsequently rendered . . . more tender and more widely diffused. Nor could we check our sympathy, even at the urging of hard reason, without deterioration in the noblest part of our nature" (p. 181).

263 Christopher Boehm: For more on the evolution of altruism, see Christopher Boehm, *Moral Origins: The Evolution of Virtue, Altruism, and Shame* (New York: Basic Books, 2012).

264 "competitive altruism": For more on competitive altruism, see Gilbert Rogers, "Competitive Altruism: From Reciprocity to the Handicap Principle," *Proceedings of the Royal Society of London* 265, no. 1394 (March 1998): 427–31. See also Charlie L. Hardy and Mark Van Vugt, "Nice Guys Finish First: The Competitive Altruism Hypothesis," *Personality and Social Psychology Bulletin* 32, no. 10 (October 2006): 1402–13.

265 Saturn has uncovered genetic differences: For one such study, see Aleksandr Kogan et al., "Thin-Slicing Study of the Oxyto-

cin Receptor (OXTR) Gene and the Evaluation and Expression of the Prosocial Disposition," *Proceedings of the National Academy of Sciences* 108, no. 48 (November 2011): 19189–92. However, some scientists have found that, on the contrary, oxytocin receptor genotypes have failed to explain a significant part of human social behavior. See Marian J. Bakermans-Kranenburg and Marinus H. van Ijzendoorn, "A Sociability Gene? Meta-analysis of Oxytocin Receptor Genotype Effects in Humans," *Psychiatric Genetics* 24, no. 2 (August 2013): 45–51.

265 in the degree of altruism: This genetic variation, however, does not determine behavior on its own. For more on how the oxytocin receptor polymorphism interacts with culture, see, for example, Heejung S. Kim et al., "Culture, Distress, and Oxytocin Receptor Polymorphism (OXTR) Interact to Influence Emotional Support Seeking," *Proceedings of the National Academy of Sciences* 107, no. 36 (September 2010): 15717–21. In fact, the oxytocin receptor polymorphism rs53576 can predict opposite behaviors in different cultures. For example, Americans with the AA genotype report more emotional suppression than Americans with the GG genotype, and Koreans show the opposite pattern. Heejung S. Kim et al., "Gene-Culture Interaction: Oxytocin Receptor Polymorphism (OXTR) and Emotion Regulation," *Social Psychological and Personality Science* 2, no. 6 (November 2011): 665–72.

267 "A properly dressed family strolling": Philip Lieberman, *The Unpredictable Species: What Makes Humans Unique* (Princeton, NJ: Princeton University Press, 2013), especially pp. 180–82. Lieberman also notes that Icelandic and Norwegian people were among the world's most bloodthirsty a thousand years ago and now, with the same genes, are among the world's most moral. What has changed, he notes, isn't genes or biology but culture. For more on Lieberman's argument that altruism is more of a culturally transmitted behavior than an innate impulse, see pp. 165–82.

268 "Sneak up on your beloved": Dacher Keltner, *Born to Be Good: The Science of a Meaningful Life* (New York: W. W. Norton, 2009), p. 80.

269 seems to curb the instinct for helpfulness: For more on these experiments with money, see Kathleen D. Vohs, Nicole L. Mead, and Miranda R. Goode, "The Psychological Consequences of Money," *Science* 314 (November 2006): 1154–56, and Kahleen D. Vohs, Nicole L. Mead, and Miranda R. Goode, "Merely Activating the Concept of Money Changes Personal and Interpersonal Behavior," *Current Directions in Psychological Sciences* 17, no. 3 (2008): 208–12.

CHAPTER EIGHTEEN *Healing Through Helping*

279 Volunteering has been associated with lower mortality: In a study of more than a thousand older adults, researchers found that giving social support was associated with lower morbidity, whereas receiving social support was not. The study also looked at improved physical health. See William Michael Brown, Nathan S. Consedine, and Carol Magai, "Altruism Relates to Health in an Ethnically Diverse Sample of Older Adults," *Journals of Gerontology Series B: Psychological Sciences and Social Sciences* 60, no. 3 (May 2005): 143–52.

279 fewer depressive symptoms: See, for example, Yunqing Li and Kenneth F. Ferraro, "Volunteering and Depression in Later Life: Social Benefit or Selection Processes?" *Journal of Health and Social Behavior* 46, no. 1 (March 2005): 68–84.

279 greater life satisfaction: Stephan Meier and Alois Stutzer, "Is Volunteering Rewarding in Itself?" *Economica* 75, no. 297 (February 2008): 39–59.

279 Nancy Morrow-Howell of Washington University: Nancy Morrow-Howell, Jim Hinterlong, Philip A. Rozario, and Fengyan Tan, "Effects of Volunteering on the Well-Being of Older Adults," *Journals of Gerontology Series B: Psychological Sciences and Social Sciences* 58, no. 3 (May 2003): S137–S145.

280 Other research shows: For a good summary of the current research on volunteering and lower mortality, see Nancy Morrow-Howell, "Volunteering in Later Life: Research Frontiers," *Journals of Gerontology Series B: Psychological Sciences and Social Sciences* 65B, no. 4 (July 2010): 461–69.

Encore Careers

285 44 to 51 percent improvement: Michelle C. Carlson et al., "Exploring the Effects of an 'Everyday' Activity Program on Executive Function and Memory in Older Adults: Experience Corps," *Gerontologist* 48, no. 6 (December 2008): 793–801.

285 A second trial: Linda P. Fried et al., "A Social Model for Health Promotion for an Aging Population: Initial Evidence on the Experience Corps Model," *Journal of Urban Health: Bulletin of the New York Academy of Medicine* 81, no. 1 (March 2004): 64–78.

285 Carlson scanned the brains: Michelle C. Carlson et al., "Evidence for Neurocognitive Plasticity in At-Risk Older Adults: The Experience Corps Program," *Journals of Gerontology, Series A: Biological Sciences and Medical Sciences* 64, no. 12 (2009): 1275–82.

CHAPTER NINETEEN *A Hundred Flowers Bloom*

289 manufacturing banana fiber sanitary pads: Sustainable Health Enterprises isn't the only approach to helping impoverished girls stay in school during their menstrual periods. A Columbia University School of Nursing professor, Mary Moran, started an organization called Girls2Women that addresses the problem in Ethiopia. The Girls2Women solution is to make reusable, washable sanitary pads out of cheap Ethiopian cotton. Our take is that there is no single solution to the problem, and any approach has drawbacks. Disposable pads are more expensive and present problems in countries where there is no garbage collection; reusable pads can be embarrassing for families to hang out to dry on a clothesline and can lead to infections or other health problems if not thoroughly washed and dried.

290 One study in Nepal: Emily Oster and Rebecca Thornton, "Menstruation, Sanitary Products and School Attendance: Evidence from a Randomized Evaluation," *American Economic Journal: Applied Economics* 3, no. 1 (January 2011): 91–100.

290 a study in Ghana: Paul Montgomery et al., "Sanitary Pad Interventions for Girls' Education in Ghana: A Pilot Study," *PLoS ONE* 7, no. 10 (October 2012): 1–7.

291 The partnership quickly collapsed: For more on what went wrong with PlayPump, see Ken Stern, *With Charity for All: Why Charities Are Failing and a Better Way to Give* (New York: Anchor Books, 2013).

295 Bridge cites standardized exams: Bridge partnered with a firm to administer Early Grade Reading Assessment (EGRA) and Early Grade Math Assessment (EGMA) to evaluate their students' performance against that of peers at nearby government and private schools. They compare students in bands based on their incoming performance levels, so that students who perform lower at Bridge are compared against students who perform lower at competitive schools, and the same goes for average and higher-performing students.

CHAPTER TWENTY *A Giving Code*

303 What sets him apart from other South Sudanese: Paul Lorem reminds us of Valentino Deng, a "lost boy" from South Sudan who was one of the thousands of orphans separated from their families during the civil war and forced to make terrifying journeys to

refugee camps abroad. Valentino's experiences are the narrative thread of Dave Eggers's outstanding book *What Is the What?* Valentino returned to South Sudan and started a remarkable school in his hometown with a cadre of volunteer teachers from America. The school is supported by donations and by royalties from *What Is the What?* When we visited, we saw students who had traveled by foot, in some cases for hundreds of miles, to register for Valentino's school. Valentino has focused particularly on educating girls, because he sees them as drivers of social change. A $300 contribution to his school, through the Valentino Achak Deng Foundation, supports a girl for a year of high school.

304 "A friend who was working in the Dominican Republic": *Random Acts of Kindness Then and Now: The 20th Anniversary of a Simple Idea that Changes Lives* (San Francisco: Conari Press, 2013), p. 94.

313 "Since I already had most of the things I value": Vanessa Allen, "I Will Give £1m to Charity, Says Oxford Don on £33,000 Salary," *Daily Mail,* November 16, 2009.

314 We're in awe of supergivers like Toby Ord: For more about Toby Ord and his organization, Giving What You Can, see "Would You Give a Third of Your Salary Away to Charity?" *Guardian Money Blog,* November 19, 2009. Also see his organization's website, www .givingwhatwecan.org.

Index

Page numbers in *italics* refer to illustrations.

A NOTE ABOUT THE AUTHORS

Nicholas D. Kristof and Sheryl WuDunn are the first married couple to win a Pulitzer Prize in journalism; they won for their coverage of China as *New York Times* correspondents. Kristof won a second Pulitzer for his op-ed columns in the *Times*. He has also served the newspaper as bureau chief in Hong Kong, Beijing, and Tokyo, and as associate managing editor. At the *Times*, WuDunn worked as a business editor and executive in the strategic planning and circulation marketing departments, and as a foreign correspondent in Tokyo and Beijing. She currently works in finance. They live near New York City.

A NOTE ON THE TYPE

The text of this book was set in a typeface called Times Ten, designed by Stanley Morison (1889–1967) for *The Times* (London) and first introduced by that newspaper in 1932.

Among typographers and designers of the twentieth century, Stanley Morison was a strong forming influence—as a typographical adviser to the Monotype Corporation, as a director of two distinguished publishing houses, and as a writer of sensibility, erudition, and keen practical sense.

Composed by North Market Street Graphics,
Lancaster, Pennsylvania
Printed and bound by Derryville Graphics,
Berryville, Virginia
Designed by Iris Weinstein